The Financial Sector
in the Enlarging European Union

The Financial Sector in the Enlarging European Union

Edited by

Daniel Stavárek & Stanislav Polouček

CAMBRIDGE SCHOLARS PRESS

The Financial Sector in the Enlarging European Union, edited by Daniel Stavárek & Stanislav Polouček

This book first published 2006 by

Cambridge Scholars Press

15 Angerton Gardens, Newcastle, NE5 2JA, UK

British Library Cataloguing in Publication Data
A catalogue record for this book is available from the British Library

ISBN 1-84718-020-5

Printed and bound in Great Britain by
Antony Rowe Ltd, Chippenham, Wiltshire

Table of Contents

LIST OF FIGURES

LIST OF TABLES

ACKNOWLEDGMENTS

There are many people to thank for their input in making the conference and this book possible. We would like to thank everyone who helped to make this conference so successful. We appreciate both the speakers giving their valuable time to share their expertise as well as the discussants and audience participants who actively contributed to very interesting debates. In this context, we should express our gratitude to the invited keynote speakers: Jan Frait, member of the Bank Board of the Czech National Bank; Reint Gropp, deputy head of the Research Division of the European Central Bank; Iikka Korhonen from the Institute for Economies in Transition, Bank of Finland; and Jan Juchelka, head of the Executive Committee, National Property Fund of the Czech Republic. We also would like to thank the members of the International Programme and Organizing Committee and to all reviewers of the papers. A deep sense of gratitude is owed to members and staff of the Department of Finance, School of Business Administration in Karviná.

We offer our deepest appreciation to all the contributors for their enthusiasm about this project and their hard work in completing the chapters to a universally high standard. Secondly, we must thank our colleagues from Bowling Green State University, Ohio, USA who provided language editing of the text. We and all the contributors are much indebted to Cynthia Miglietti, Kay E. Strong, Philip D. Weinsier, Martin S. Anderson, Tracy Goss McGinley and JoEtta Crupi.

We are glad to acknowledge the support provided by the Czech Science Foundation within the project GAČR 402/05/2758 "Integration of the financial sector of the new EU member countries into the EMU" in editing the book and elaborating Chapter Five and Chapter Eight. And a final word of appreciation to Andy Nercessian, Amanda Millar and their colleagues at the publishers, who approved the project and helped to finalize it.

PREFACE

In October 2005, the 10th Annual International Conference on Finance and Banking, *Future of Banking after the Year 2000 in the World and in the Czech Republic,* took place at the Silesian University, School of Business Administration in Karviná, Czech Republic. Every year, the conference focuses on a specific new development in the banking and financial sector. This year, mainly because of the 15th anniversary of the School of Business Administration, and the 10th anniversary of the conference itself, the theme was unspecified and all papers on financial and banking topics were reviewed and considered for presentation. Consequently, the conference hosted 209 participants from 35 countries and 5 continents.

This volume contains eight of the best papers presented at the conference and two invited papers. In spite of the fact that the book is a collection of independent studies it represents a comprehensive and cohesive work. All studies (book chapters) are tied together by common themes. Through original research, the book covers various aspects of financial and banking sectors in the enlarging European Union (EU), giving a comparison of their development in the new and traditional member states. Special attention is paid to prospective integration of the New Member States to the European Economic and Monetary Union and the implications for national economic policies.

The book contains ten chapters arranged in three thematic parts focusing on the structure of financial systems, banking sectors, and equity markets and monetary policy. In the first chapter, *Tamás Isépy* compares the financial superstructure in EU member countries, including the New Member States, and analyses how and to what extent the financial structures have an influence on the economic growth of a national economy or region. Some indices such as size index, activity index or efficiency index of the financial sector are used in the analysis. *Cândida Ferreira* examines a similar issue, the link between financial intermediation and economic growth in the context of European integration, in the second chapter. Panel fixed and random estimates are used to analyse data from 26 EU member and candidate countries. In the third chapter, *Jaan Vainu* presents some historical notes on the development of the Estonian banking system and the capital structure of banks. Several versions of financial ratio analysis are applied to bank performance analysis along with modified DuPont analysis and econometric modelling. The fourth chapter written by *Janek Uiboupin* aims to identify the main effects of the entry of foreign banks on the stability and performance of banks in new EU-members from Central and Eastern Europe. The empirical analysis used is Arellano–Bond dynamic panel estimation. Additionally, the summary of a survey based questionnaire is presented for qualitative analysis. *Daniel Stavárek*, in the fifth chapter, compares commercial banks' efficiency in four groups of homogenous countries with different levels of economic development and involvement in the process of European integration. Employing Data Envelopment Analysis, the hypothesis that the higher degree of European economic integration and economic development goes hand in hand with higher banking efficiency is tested.

In the sixth chapter, *Asma Ben Salem* identifies some countries or characteristics of countries that will affect the trends of foreign direct banking investments via mergers and acquisitions across Europe. A panel data of cross-border banking mergers and acquisitions in the main European countries from 1987 to 2004 are used to reveal the importance of banking market concentration as a determinant of further international growth of European banks. The seventh chapter by *Karel Diviš & Petr Teplý* focuses on testing a weak form of market efficiency in regards to capital markets in some new EU members and developed countries implementing a variance ratio test as a research method. The main conclusion is that the weak form of the efficient market hypothesis could not be rejected for Central European capital markets and that an improvement of market efficiency was observed over time on all markets. *Jan Frait & Luboš* Komárek look at the relationship between monetary policy and asset prices and the recent developments in the New Member States in the eighth chapter. The appropriate reaction of monetary policy to asset price bubbles is discussed, the main pros and cons associated with this reaction are summarized and the risks of asset market bubbles in the New Member States are evaluated. The ninth chapter written by *Luboš Komárek & Martin Melecký* analyses the relevance of the currency substitution phenomenon in the Czech Republic. The authors discuss consequences of euroisation as well as an estimation of a modified Branson and Henderson portfolio model, and application of several cointegration techniques. In the tenth chapter *Jarko Fidrmuc & Roman Horváth* examine the exchange rate dynamics in selected New Member States. To analyse the exchange rate behaviour, they perform the analysis in two steps. First, they estimate the monetary equilibrium exchange rates; and second, they use these exchange rates obtained in the subsequent GARCH estimations.

This book gives a deep insight into the financial sector of the enlarging EU. Additionally, it successfully pulls together theory and actual development of the European financial sectors.

Karviná, May 2006

Daniel Stavárek
Stanislav Polouček

CHAPTER ONE

FINANCIAL STRUCTURE AND ECONOMIC GROWTH

"One of the most important problems in the field of finance, if not the single most important one, almost everyone would agree, is the effect that financial structure and development have on economic growth" (Goldsmith, 1969)

This chapter focuses on the financial structure – economic growth nexus and is divided into three sections. In the first section, we give an overview of the major factors affecting financial structures, and the evolution of the various financial architectures which are characteristic of the individual countries. The second section is the comparative analysis of market-based versus bank-based systems and relationship-based versus arm's length financing systems. In the third section, we take a closer look at the financial structure indexes (size, activity, efficiency) characteristic of certain countries or groups of countries during the period 1997–2003. We concentrate mainly on the Anglo-Saxon countries and the old and new European Union (EU) member states. Using these indexes we aim to examine trends and shifts in the relative importance of banks and financial markets, as well as the effects on economic development and growth.

History of the Financial Structure's Evolution

When examining financial superstructures, we can differentiate between two basic types: bank-based and market-based structures. In a bank-based financial structure, the banks have an intermediary role, collecting deposits and providing loans primarily to the corporate sector. In collecting deposits, banks can rely largely on households, as their willingness to take risks is low, and they mostly prefer bank deposits to the various securities. In contrast, the asset side is dominated by corporate loans. This results from the fact that funds acquired from banks are an almost exclusive, and by all means the primary, source of acquiring external funds. Market financing (equity or bond issues) is only supplementary. The bank-based structure is typical of Germany, France and the majority of the Economic and Monetary Union (EMU) member states (the Netherlands can be mentioned as an exception), as well as Japan. The other group of countries is characterized by the market-based system, where, due to the highly-developed securities market, businesses give preference to corporate bond or equity issues in face of funds acquired from banks. However, this is only possible if households are more willing to make savings and give preference to the more risky market assets over bank deposits that grant a fixed return. A small part of household savings appears on the market directly, whereas the larger part appears through institutional investors. Accordingly, the dominance of these institutions compared to banks is detectable on the market. The market-based structure is typical of the United States and the United Kingdom.

Most publications (see Demirgüc–Kunt and Levine (2002) among others) come to the conclusion that, whereas the degree of development of the financial system has a profound influence on economic results and economic success, the dominance of one or the other financial structure is of lesser importance in this respect. No close connection can be pointed out between the dominance of any type and the success of the economy. The publications suggest that decision-makers should pay attention to the legal and regulatory environment and the reforms that may be necessary in that area, rather than to the prevalence of market-based or bank-based structures. It can be observed, however, that the financial systems of richer countries are much more developed, and therefore the stock exchanges of these countries are far more active and efficient as compared to banks. When examining the legal regulatory environment, a general conclusion can be drawn. The financial systems of countries where shareholders' rights are strongly defended, accounting regulations are well-structured, less emphasis is put on the protection of deposit holders, and the level of corruption is lower, are usually more advanced. On the other hand, countries characterized by weaker protection of shareholders' and loan providers' rights, low-level accounting regulations, high corruption, high inflation and restrictive banking regulations usually have less developed financial systems.

Many economists have studied the connection between financial development (well-functioning financial markets and intermediaries) and growth, leaping to the conclusion that the high level of financial development has a strong positive effect on economic growth. The primary function of financial systems (financial markets and intermediaries) is to forward funds from the savers to the market participants, who have productive investment opportunities. This basic function can be split up into three partial functions: (i) mobilisation of savings, (ii) acquisition of information, and (iii) risk management. By performing these functions, financial systems increase both the quantity and quality of real investment, and thus they also increase general welfare. Financial systems can influence economic growth through three different channels. First, the commissions of financial services motivate the mobilisation of the savings of small market participants. The financial system can achieve capital and productivity increase through better efficiency and can contribute to economic growth by cutting the liquidity risk of corporations. Second, better analysis and monitoring by loan providers lead to the more efficient distribution of funds. Third, the improvement of risk diversification aids the launching of innovative projects through the increase of the saving ratio.

Most researchers draw the conclusion that financial intermediaries and financial markets are complementary to each other in providing financial services. Both market-based and bank-based systems have comparative advantages. Financial markets are better at financing new technologies and projects where there is much disagreement concerning the issue of corporate financing, whereas banks are more efficient in handling the conflicts between lender and debtor (moral hazard).

Relationship Lending Versus Arm's Length Financing

Based on the events of the last 20 years, a clear shift towards market-based structures can be observed (see Polouček, 2004, for a discussion about structures of financial systems). As a result of globalisation, deregulation and technological development, the size of efficient operation has grown significantly. Disintermediation and securitisation have had a negative effect on the profitability of banks, and entailed the necessity to lay off superfluous capacities. Traditional lines of business proved insufficient to maintain profitability; therefore it became necessary to provide supplementary banking services. Since the 1980s, the investment products division has gained increasing importance as part of the banks' core activities, and contributed to their increasing efficiency. Most banks recognized that it is more worthwhile to keep their clients by making investment products available than to lose their clients' deposits. They considered it more important for the disintermediation process to slow down greatly if banks are able to meet the financial service demands of their clients. In the mid 1990s, numerous studies showed that client retention depends directly on the number of products and services offered by the bank. See Gackle and Andelman (1994) for more about this issue privatisation.

The market-based and bank-based intermediary systems are difficult to mark off for several reasons. In countries where the structure is traditionally bank-based, like Germany and Japan, there is a stable and long-term relationship between bank and corporation. This is called relationship-based financing. In German banks, the investment division has acquired an important role alongside traditional banking, and now we can speak about the system of powerful universal banks. Through their investment banking activities, the banks can monitor the way by which the corporations enter the capital market. Beyond the creditor's position, the regulatory environment also makes it possible for banks to hold stakes in corporations. Japanese banks own 20 per cent of corporate shares, whereas German banks have a package of approximately 10 per cent. The same ratio is around 2 per cent in the United States (Ujiie, 2002)

Table 1-1 Indicators of financial development in 1980 and 2000 (ratio to nominal GDP)

Country	Bank loan to private sector		Stock market capitalisation	
	1980	2000	1980	2000
Austria	0.742	1.040	0.030	0.156
Belgium	0.272	0.792	0.090	0.783
Denmark	0.244	NA	0.090	0.686
Finland	0.462	0.464	NA	2.383
France	0.731	0.636	0.090	1.087
Germany	0.864	0.925	0.090	0.668
Greece	0.520	0.566	0.085	0.942
Ireland	0.315	0.793	NA	0.843
Italy	0.555	0.514	0.070	0.703
Luxembourg	1.210	3.367	0.001	1.771
Netherlands	0.632	0.963	0.190	1.070
Portugal	0.855	0.997	0.006	0.567
Spain	NA	0.816	0.087	0.882
Sweden	0.415	0.391	0.110	1.476
Average continental Europe	**0.601**	**0.930**	**0.078**	**1.046**
United Kingdom	0.276	1.069	0.380	1.840
United States	0.354	0.379	0.460	1.549
Average Anglo-American	**0.315**	**0.724**	**0.420**	**1.694**

Source: Rajan and Zingales (2003, p. 126)

In relationship-based financing, the financier (who can be an owner, a sole or primary creditor, a supplier or a customer) makes an attempt to ensure the return on the investment by establishing a certain degree of monopoly at the financed company. The lack of regulation and system transparency means that other players have only limited access to the market, and the cost of entering the market is significant. In "arm's-length" financing, however, the financier is protected mainly or exclusively by an explicit contract. In the relationship-based system, the bank has a close relationship with the financed company either because of its past contacts or because of its role as a stakeholder. Therefore, beyond the loan applicant's current liquidity, the bank also inspects its long-term solvency, as well as numerous other factors not mentioned in the contract that help the bank enforce repayment. The current interest rate is negotiable and is not necessarily in line with the extent of the project's actual risk. In the case of arm's-length financing, the loan applicant can choose from a wide range of creditors, thanks to the accessibility of relevant financial information. The loan contract is arranged for a specified period, the interest rate is competitive, and in line with the risk factor and period of the loan. As the relationship-based system is characterized by the lack of competition, transparency and publicity, the decision-making involves no realistic price signals. As opposed to the arm's-length financing, where the creditors are in competition with each other, and make independent assessments of the project cost, the cost of the loan in the relationship-based system depends on the negotiations between the creditor and the borrower.

There is no doubt about some overlap between bank-based / market-based and relationship-based / arm's length approaches when it comes to the classification of structures / systems of financing. The bank-based structure is primarily, but not exclusively, characterized by the relationship-based system of financing. Venture capital financing is typically relationship-based, despite the fact that it is not a typical banking activity, and can be seen mostly in market-based countries. Similarly, the client's diverse banking relations lead to loss of strength for the individual banks, and point to the formation of a system that shares quite a few features of the arm's-length system. (Rajan and Zingales, 2003)

Cross-country Financial Structure Index Comparison

For the cross-country comparison of financial structures we used the indexes as in Demirgüc–Kunt and Levine (2002). The authors performed a comparative analysis involving 130 countries using the 1997 data. Consequently, they classified the countries by the relative development of markets and banks (size, activity and efficiency) as market-based, bank-based and undeveloped financial structures (the latter term means that both banks and markets are developed below the average level of the examined countries).

Because of a lack of the data, the above mentioned study did not include the new EU member states figures. The current database of the characteristics of the individual countries' financial structures already contains the relevant country data for the period 1997–2003, which consequently allow us to carry out the empirical analysis. All data were extracted from the Financial structure and economic development database provided by the World Bank. At the comparative analysis of the financial structure indexes of the different groups of countries, we were interested in whether the financial structure of the new member states (whose average GDP growth rate is higher than that of the EU15) had become similar to that of the old member states, and whether it shifted towards the market-based structure during the seven-year period.

We examined the relative size of banks and the stock market with the financial structure size index (*FSS*), which is defined as follows:

$$FSS = \frac{SMC}{GDP} \div \frac{DAB}{GDP}, \tag{1.1}$$

where *SMC* is stock market capitalisation, *DAB* denotes domestic assets of deposit money banks and *GDP* is nominal GDP. The growth of the resulting indicator shows the relative increase of market capitalisation as compared to the size of banks. The examined groups of countries were the following: old EU member states (EU15), new member states (NMS), Anglo-Saxon countries (United Kingdom and United States), and "continental Europe", i.e. the old member states without the United Kingdom.

Figure 1-1 shows the average index values of the different groups of countries in the given period. Up to 1999, or up to 2000 for the NMS, a clear shift towards the growth of the market at the expense of banks is detectable, fitting into a 20-year trend (from 1980 to 2000 presented in Table 1-1). This was caused by the general trend of increasing equity prices and wave of the initial public offerings and going public. In the periods 1999–2003 and 2000–03, however, the trend clearly turned, and the relative size of banks grew at the expense of markets. The reasons can be found in the bearish sentiment in the stock markets, shrinking role of the new markets and process of integration in the banking sector.

Fig. 1-1 Financial structure size index

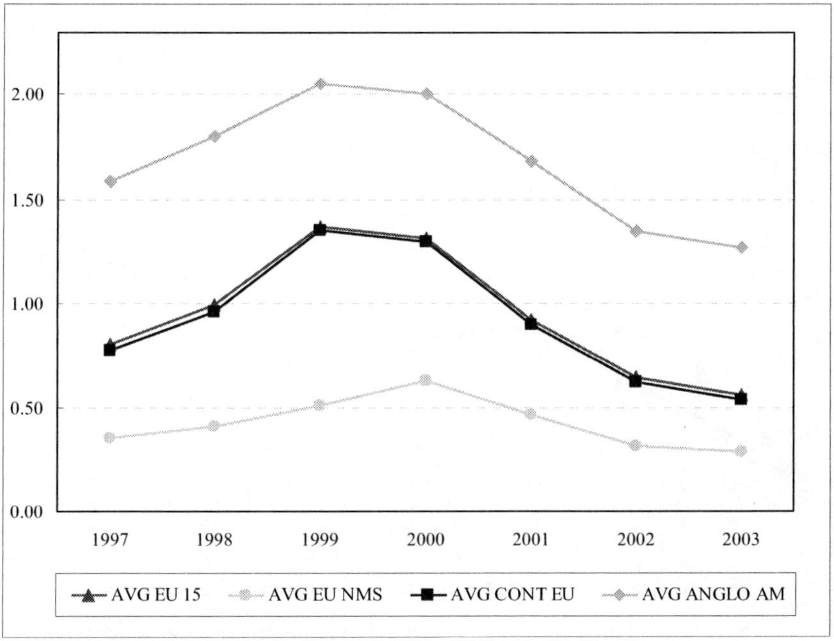

Source: Author's calculations

We interpreted the relative activity of stock markets and banks as the financial structure activity index *(FSA)* defined by the following formula:

$$FSA = \frac{TVD}{GDP} \div \frac{CBP}{GDP}, \tag{1.2}$$

where *TVD* is total value traded in the stock market and *CBP* denotes claims of deposit money banks on private sector. The rise of the resulting indicator shows the increasing activity of the stock market as compared to the banks.

Figure 1-2 depicts that this phenomenon can be observed until 2000 in Anglo-Saxon countries. In the old EU member states and countries with fundamentally bank-based financial structures it lasted until 1999. The *FSA* indicator started to fall after 1999 in the above-mentioned groups of countries, whereas in the NMS it was on the fall almost throughout the examined period. The falling *FSA* index in EU countries after 1999 can be explained by the increasing role of bank mergers and acquisitions, the introduction of the Euro and the start of the EMU.

Fig. 1-2 Financial structure activity index

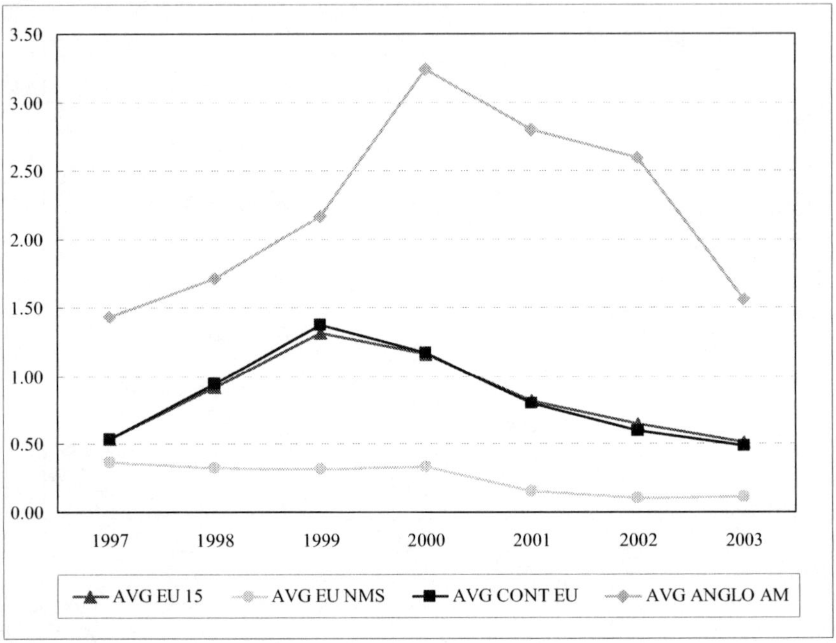

Source: Author's calculations

The last indicator used and calculated is the financial structure efficiency index *(FSE)* constructed as follows:

$$FSE = \frac{TVD}{GDP} \cdot \frac{NIM}{TBA}, \tag{1.3}$$

where *NIM* is net interest margin of banks and *TBA* denotes total banking assets. The rise of the resulting indicator shows the increasing relative weight (efficiency) of the market-based structure, as the increase of net interest margin is indicative of the decreasing efficiency of banks, and thus implicitly indicative of the growing relative efficiency of markets.

When examining the chart of the average indexes of the different groups of countries as a function of time (Figure 1-3), a clear growth in the relative efficiency of markets can be observed until 2000. After that, a decreasing trend can be seen in both old and new EU member states. This same trend is strongly characteristic of Anglo-Saxon countries only after 2002. This development in the NMS and old EU members is primarily due to bank integration and higher competition among banking institutions leading to a lower net interest margin.

Fig. 1-3 Financial structure efficiency index

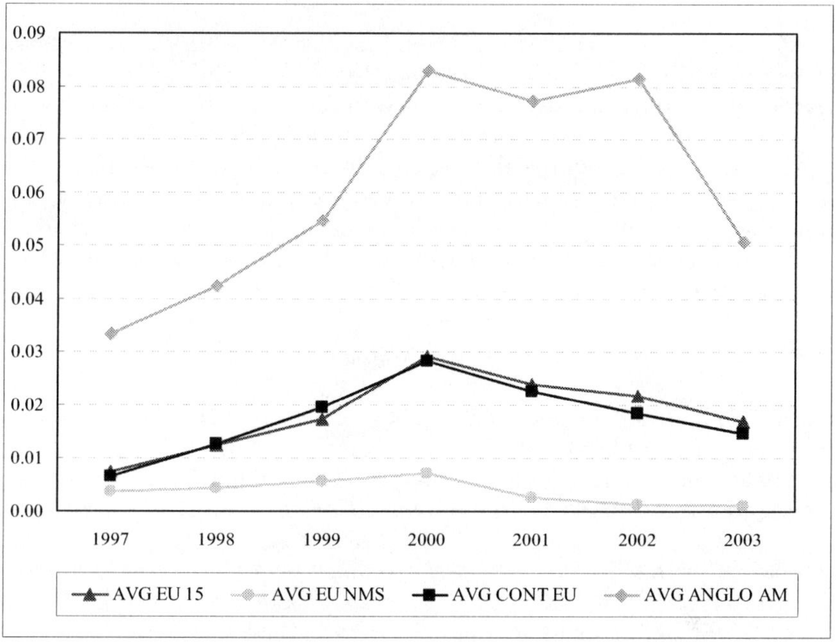

Source: Author's calculations

Numerous factors must be taken into consideration for the assessment of these indexes. Naturally, the fall of equity prices must have had a great influence on relative size, activity and efficiency. Earlier studies have pointed out that in higher income countries, the activity and efficiency of domestic stock markets had grown in comparison with the activity and efficiency of domestic banks. The higher average GDP growth rate of new EU member states as compared to the old member states did not result in a category rise in the World Bank's classification (low income, lower middle income, upper middle income, high income countries) Based on the financial structure indexes, the rise of the activity and efficiency of domestic stock markets, as compared to the activity and efficiency of domestic banks, is not detectable during the whole period. Until 2000 relative activity almost stagnated and efficiency was on the increase, whereas after 2000 the values of both indicators fell. However, considering the relative activity and efficiency index of the former and the new member states, there is a clear phenomenon of convergence. The financial structure of the new member states has become similar to that of the old member states.

Conclusion

The comparative analysis of bank-based and market-based financial structures can be performed from numerous aspects. The indexes used for describing the financial structures of the different groups of countries are suitable for analyzing the relative size, activity and efficiency of markets and banks. Based on the trend of the last 20 years, which shows a shift towards market-based financial structures, it can be observed that the relative weight of markets was falling in comparison to banks in the years after 2000. However, considering the old and the new EU member states there is a convergence of relative activity and efficiency of markets versus banks.

References

Allen, Franklin and Douglas Gale. 2001. *Comparing Financial Systems.* Cambridge, MA: MIT Press.

Demirgüç–Kunt, Asli and Ross Levine. 2004. *Financial Structure and Economic Growth: A Cross-Country Comparison of Banks, Markets, and Development.* Cambridge, MA: MIT Press.

European Central Bank. 2003. *The Transformation of the European Financial System Second ECB Central Banking Conference October 2002.* Frankfurt am Main: European Central Bank.

Gackle, Merlin and Bob Andelman. 1994. *Bankers as Brokers: The Complete Guide to Selling Mutual Funds, Annuities and Other Fee-Based Investment Products (A Bankline Publication).* Chicago, IL: Probus Professional Pub.

Goldsmith, Raymond W. 1969. *Financial Structure and Development.* New Haven, CT: Yale University Press.

Karmann, Alexander. 2000. *Financial Structure and Stability.* New York: Physica-Verlag Heidelberg.

Magyar Nemzeti Bank. 2002. *Tanulmányok a bankszektor középtávú fejlődési irányairól MNB Műhelytanulmány.* Budapest: Magyar Nemzeti Bank.

Monnet, Cyril and Erwan Quintin. 2005. *Why do financial system differ? History matters.* ECB Working paper series No. 442. Frankfurt am Main: European Central Bank.

Polouček, Stanislav. 2004. *Reforming the Financial Sector in Central European Countries.* Houndmills, Basingstoke, Hampshire: Palgrave Macmillan.

Rajan, Raghuram and Luigi Zingales. 2003. *Banks and Markets: The Changing Character of European Finance.* Paper presented at the Second ECB Central Banking Conference in Frankfurt am Main, October 24–25, 2002.

Ujiie, Junichi. 2002. *Nomura Holdings Inc.: Shift to a Market-Focused Financial Structure.* Paper presented at *Nihon* Keizai Shimbun symposium 2002.

CHAPTER TWO

BANK SECTOR PERFORMANCES, ECONOMIC GROWTH AND EUROPEAN INTEGRATION

Well-developed financial systems are usually considered as an important and necessary foundation on which credit sectors can play their particular role in processes of economic development. More efficient credit sectors may represent a necessary condition for the transmission mechanism of monetary policy, but they should also contribute to the economic benefits of the other sectors and agents which use financial services.

The introduction of the single currency accelerated the process of consolidation and financial integration not only in the Economic and Monetary Union (EMU), but in the European Union (EU) as a whole. The new 10 Member States (NMS) of the EU also have a voice, in spite of the heterogeneous nature of their specific financial systems.

The process of financial integration is, on one hand, a necessary pre-requisite for the adoption of the single currency and the implementation of the single monetary policy, with the predominance of the banking intermediation in the context of the EU. On the other hand, this process raises the potential to incite liquidity crises, which could become contagious and affect the increasingly integrated European financial system.

This chapter expands the general analysis provided in Chapter One and examines the link between financial intermediation and economic growth in the context of the EU and particularly in the context of the integration of NMS and their specific financial systems.

This chapter is developed following two main vectors. The first vector considers the role that financial systems play in economic growth, taking into account not only some historically important theoretical contributions to this subject and, more significantly, recent empirical studies. These studies–using different financial variables, different estimation techniques and different sets of countries–confirm the linkage between financial systems and economic growth. The second vector analyses how financial integration may affect financial structure. In the context of the EU, the focus is on the present role of financial sectors, in particular the credit sector, under the conditions of the EMU. The analysis particularly proceeds from the view of the recent and future enlargements embracing countries with specific financial systems, some of which still present many limitations in financial-sector intermediation

Our principal contribution is an empirical data analysis of the influence of the financial systems in the economic growth of the EU countries using IMF and Eurostat quarterly data. More precisely, we explain the growth of per-capita GDP by the growth of domestic credit, foreign liabilities, interest rate on the demand deposits, and two ratios: the ratio of the liabilities of the deposit money banks to GDP and the ratio of domestic credit to GDP.

In the estimations, we consider two sub-sets of EU countries: (i) 11 "old" EU member-countries (excluding Luxembourg, Denmark, Ireland and Sweden) for the period between Q2 1980 and Q4 1998; (ii) 26 EU countries (excluding only Luxembourg and including the future EU members, Bulgaria and Romania) for the period between Q2 1999 and Q4 2002. The results obtained allow us to draw conclusions not only on the importance of banking-sector performance to economic growth, but also on some differences in the level of integration in the two sub-sets being considered.

The remainder of the chapter is organized as follows: The next section presents relevant literature on the link between financial systems and growth. Further, we underline some specific questions arising from financial integration within the EU and present our estimations. Finally, we make our concluding remarks in the last section.

Financial Systems and Economic Growth

The link between economic growth and the quality of financial systems dates back at least as far as Schumpeter (1911), who maintained that the services provided by financial intermediaries are essential for economic innovation, productive investment and economic growth.

During the Great Depression, there was a collapse of the financial systems along with other economic sectors. Fisher (1933) analysed the possible connection between the performance of the financial markets and the 1929 crisis and subsequent depression that ravaged the real economic activity, both of which can be linked to the slowdown of the redistribution of wealth from debtors to creditors. Other authors like Hicks (1937) and Modigliani (1944) underlined the role of the credit markets and the real interest rate in the context of the Keynesian liquidity theory.

Later, Mishkin (1978) used data from the Great Depression to study the interaction between output, consumer balance sheets and consumer spending. The conclusion was that during the crisis the increase in consumer real indebtedness, resulting mainly from the decline in incomes, induced consumers to lower spending, particularly on durable goods and housing investment, which further contributed to a lowering of output.

The connection between real economic output and the characteristics and quality of the financial structure, in particular in the process of financial intermediation, was also emphasised by Gurley and Shaw (1955). In addition, they focused on the differentiation of the financial systems of the more developed and less developed countries.

More recently, and particularly during the last decade, the link between economic growth and the quality of financial systems has been investigated. According to most of these studies, financial development may be an important condition to economic growth, since well-functioning markets and financial institutions may decrease the transaction costs and asymmetric information problems. At the same time, financial institutions play an increasingly important role in identifying investment opportunities, selecting the most profitable projects, mobilising savings, facilitating trading and diversification of risk, as well as improving corporate governance mechanisms.

Other authors, for example, Stiglitz (1985), Bhide (1993), Bencivenga *et al.* (1995), stress that there may exist some costs associated with the role of financial intermediaries and that sometimes these intermediaries may be subject to adverse selection and moral hazard problems. Such problems may constrain real economic growth-enhancing resource allocation, exaggerate the increase in interest rates, or contribute to the decrease in the saving rates.

During the last decade, and particularly since the renowned King and Levine (1993) paper, there has been an increase of empirical studies at the aggregate level which explain output variables with financial ratios and variables such as liquid liabilities, bank loans to the private-sector, or stock market capitalisation. Any of these may be representative of the performance of the financial systems and institutions.

In one such study, Levine and Zervos (1998) use data for 49 countries for the period 1976–90 and conclude that there is a strong correlation between the rates of real per-capita output growth and stock market liquidity.

The influence of financial variables (particularly the liquid liabilities and the private credit from deposit banks in relation to GDP) in real per-capita output growth is also demonstrated by Leahy *et al.* (2001), using data for 19 OECD countries for the years between 1970 and 1997. Similar variables (more precisely, liquid liabilities, private credit from deposit banks and stock market capitalisation, all in relation to GDP) are used by Bassanini *et al.* (2001), who use data for 24 OECD countries (1997–98), obtaining better results for stock markets than for bank variables.

Examining nine OECD countries and available series with different starts between 1960 and 1986 and ending in 1998, Shan *et al.* (2001) explain real per-capita GDP by bank credit to GDP and conclude that the causality varies among countries.

Demirgüç–Kunt and Levine (1999), with data for 150 countries during the 1990s, conclude that the rich countries have more developed financial systems, characterising this development by the size and efficiency of the financial sector (measured by the assets, liabilities, overhead costs and interest margins). See Chapter One for the application of this approach on more recent data.

Comparing financial systems of different countries and regions, Allen and Gale (2000) conclude that there is inherent inefficiency within the monopolistic power of banks. This inefficiency, then, may cause banks to adopt an excessively conservative approach while the competitive nature of markets tends to encourage innovation and growth-enhancing activities.

Recently, Beck *et al.* (2004) used the ratio of the value of the credit by financial intermediaries to the private sector divided by GDP as a proxy to capture the depth and breath of the financial intermediation in a panel of 52 countries during the period from 1960 to 1999. They conclude that financial development is not only clearly pro-growth but also pro-poor. That is, in countries with better-developed financial intermediation, income inequality declines more rapidly.

Summarising these studies, we must agree with Khan and Senhadji (2000). These authors, in providing a review of the literature and empirical evidence of the relationship between financial development and economic growth, conclude that the results indicate that the general effects of financial development on the outputs are positive. On the other hand, the size of these effects varies with the different variables considered, with indicators of financial development and with the estimation method, data frequency or the defined functional form of the relationship.

Financial Integration in the EU

The relation between financial integration and economic growth is currently emphasised by authors like Obstfeld and Taylor (2003) and is of particular relevance in the context of the enlarged EU. Following the historically remarkable enlargement, which brought the simultaneous entry of 10 NMS in 2004, the EU is still adapting to the conditions of the EMU and to this new universe of 25 members, while preparing to receive the next Member States (Bulgaria and Romania are due to join in the near future). Moreover, it is recognised that some of these NMS have particular characteristics in terms of their financial systems.[1]

Financial institutions play a unique role in the context of the Single Market Program and the EMU, although the EU banking sector has been considered as one of the sectors least affected by the Single Market Programme (Monti, 1996, Gardener *et al.*, 2002). The introduction of the

EMU reduces some of the competitive advantages of local and national banks (advantages which were based on factors like currency risk, lack of price transparency and greater knowledge of national monetary policy), but it also increases competition in all financial-product market segments.

The structural changes due to the adoption of the single currency and a common monetary policy are exerting a profound impact on the Euro area finance sector and intensifying competition for banking services. Some common trends may be identified in the context of the pressures of globalisation, specifically, a process of disintermediation, new technologies and increased competition (Belaisch *et al.*, 2001). Such trends affect the Euro area with particular intensity.

Despite all the changes and disintermediation, the bank asset structure of the EU reflects the rapid increase of lending since the advent of the EMU. It is a process which started before the implementation of the single currency and reflects the growing demand for credit provoked by the downward path of interest rate levels.

At the present time, it remains true that the EMU's financial and credit systems continue to be bank-based; the ECB (more precisely, the European System of Central Banks and its Banking Supervision Committee) is obliged to monitor and supervise closely the banking activity and structural developments in the EU banking sector.

The inadequacy of the present extent of financial regulation in the context of the EMU is emphasised by authors such as Vives (2001). He defends a reform to establish clear procedures for confronting hypothetical crises in lending and, furthermore, to prepare the implementation of more centralised supervisory arrangements in the whole financial system, with specific regard to the banking sector. Measures are required in order to increase the competition and to prevent and limit the national power of the "too-big-to-fail" institutions.

The "Structural Analysis of the EU Banking Sector", published by the ECB in November 2002, identifies three sets of trends which contribute to the present resilience of the European banking systems, namely:

- the need of banks to increase income and control costs – in order to increase income, banks must diversify their credit lines (looking for new business and geographical areas);
- the financial innovation to face the changes in risk and risk management – to develop more sophisticated approaches to risk management, like the use of credit derivatives and securitisation;
- the growing importance of consumer issues – with financial innovation, commercial banks have moved into specific areas, such as investment banking and asset management, and are now more

exposed to the performance of the other markets and global economical conditions.

Generally speaking, in the last few years, and in spite of all the remaining limitations in the supervision process, structural changes due to the implementation of the single currency and the common monetary policy, and the recent political shocks, EU banks have demonstrated a remarkable robustness. They have diversified their activities and financial innovations against a background of increasing competition, under continuing pressure not only to increase their income and profits, but also to guarantee most of the transmission mechanisms of the monetary policy and to maintain the financial stability of the whole system.

Particular attention must be paid to the sector after the last enlargement to 10 NMS, particularly those under the former Soviet Union sphere of influence. Until the collapse of the Warsaw Pact, central banks and the state-owned commercial banks were mere instruments in the hands of the respective governments, passively executing the payment orders to the public employees and monitoring the payment flows between the enterprises, which were also state-owned. Under these conditions, there was no need for financial systems to allocate savings to investment as this was carried out in accordance with the Plan, without compensation or any assigning of value.

According to the characteristics of the recent transition processes in these countries, and in spite of their specificities (Holscher, 2000; Dimitrova, 2004), it is possible to define some groups according to their similarities in the financial sector transition. Winkler (2002) divided the countries into four groups: the "advanced reformers" (Poland and Hungary), the "reluctant modernisers" (Czech Republic and Slovenia), those "struggling with a double legacy" (Slovakia and Croatia), or the "desperate reformers" (Romania and Bulgaria).

However, three essential pillars are in place to assist the financial-sector development of the NMS and to assure the conditions propitious to an increasing integration in the EU (and possibly also in the EMU) financial systems. According to Winkler (2002), the pillars are:

- internal and external government structures;
- domestic and international competition
- prudential regulation supervision

All three points could also be accepted as strong and necessary pillars for the development of the financial systems, particularly the banking sectors, of the older EU Member States and above all, of the EMU members.

Empirical Estimation

The methods used in the different aggregate estimations which look for empirical evidence of the relationship between financial development and economic growth are mainly: cointegration analysis, correlations, cross-country regressions and panel regressions.

One of the most common problems of these estimations is the difficulty in harmonising and making compatible the available data. In spite of all the efforts of the ECB, Eurostat, IMF and other international institutions, the study of financial structures and financial developments in the context of the EU remains a difficult task. This is not only due to the lack of data, but also to the inherent complexity of the financial structures, to the constant changes and to the specificities of the financial structures in the different EU countries.

Using quarterly data of the Eurostat and IMF statistics, we contribute to the existing empirical evidence of the influence of financial systems and EU integration on economic growth in two ways. First, the use of panel-fixed and random-effects estimates to explain the nominal per-capita GDP growth, admitting five variables to represent the conditions and the role of the financial systems. Second, two balanced panels with two sub-sets of EU countries were used to analyse the degree of integration in each of these sub-sets and establish some possible comparisons.

With regard to the use of panel (fixed-effects and random-effects) estimates, the five selected representative variables are:

- domestic credit – since available credit is one of the important guarantees for the financing of the economic activity, especially for productive investment and GDP per-capita growth;
- foreign liabilities – introducing also the influence of the other countries, more precisely the liabilities to these countries, which imply the payment of the debts and consequently less resources to be applied in the domestic activities;
- deposit interest rate – representing the market conditions and the incentives to the savings and deposits which are still a necessary condition for the available credit to finance the economic activities;
- the ratio liabilities of the deposit money banks/nominal GDP – as a proxy to represent the contribution of the bank conditions to GDP;
- the ratio of domestic credit/nominal GDP – as a measure of the effectiveness of the domestic credit. A high ratio will indicate that the credits are allocated less effectively, and more credits are necessary to one unit of GDP.

In order to analyse the degree of integration of the EU countries, we compare the results obtained for two sub-sets:

- balanced panel with 825 observations, with data for the period between Q2 1980 and Q4 1998 for 11 "old" countries (excluding Luxembourg, Denmark, Ireland and Sweden);
- balanced panel for 26 EU countries (excluding only Luxembourg, but including Bulgaria and Romania) for the period between Q2 1999 and Q4 2002, with 390 observations.

Panel Estimation

Following Wooldridge (2002, 2003) we use in our estimations a panel data approach which provides more observations for estimations and reduces the possibility of multicolinearity among the different variables. In order to control for individual country-specific effects, we specify a linear model and estimate panel regressions with fixed and random effects:

$$GDP_{it} = a_i + b_i CR_{it} + b_2 FL_{it} + b_3 IR_{it} + b_4 LGDP_{it} + b_5 CGDP_{it} + u_{it}, \quad (2.1)$$

where GDP_{it} is the nominal per-capita GDP growth, CR_{it} is domestic credit, FL_{it} represents foreign liabilities, IR_{it} is deposit interest rate, $LGDP_{it}$ stands for the ratio of the deposit money banks' liabilities to GDP, $CGDP_{it}$ is the ratio of domestic credit to GDP. Further, a_i is the intercept, u_{it} is the error term, i defines the particular country, and t denotes time. With the fixed-effects (within) estimates, we assume that slopes (b_1 … b_5) are common to all the countries, whilst intercepts a_i vary across the countries. The random-effects (variance components) estimates are similar to the fixed-effects estimates, but require that the individual intercepts are drawn from a common distribution and that they are not correlated with the independent variables.

To conclude, for the possible differences in the intercepts and for the existence of common slopes we present the F test of $A_i,B = A_i,B_i$ and also the F test $A,B = Ai, B$.[2] We also present the "*Vwith*", which is the variance of the basic error terms U_{it} and the "*Vbet*", which is the variance of the individual specific terms A_i. To compare the results obtained with random effects and with the fixed-effects estimates, we compute and present the Hausman test. All results estimated are summarised in Table 2-1.

Table 2-1 Panel estimates for 11 EU countries (Q2 1980–Q4 1998, N=825)

	Coefficient	Std. error	t-statistics	P-value
Fixed effects (within estimates)				
log CR	0.576955	0.045742	12.6133	0.000
log FL	-0.319793	0.031831	-10.0467	0.000
IR	0.337229	0.023651	14.2585	0.000
LGDP	-0.409737E-06	0.156636E-06	-2.61585	0.009
CGDP	-0.142574E-04	0.750584E-06	-18.9950	0.000
Adjusted R^2 = 0.634				
F test: $A_i,B = A_i,B_i$ F (50,759) = 2.6175		P-value = 0.000 Critical F-value = 7.6248		
F test: $A,B = A_i,B$ F (10,809) = 39.670		P-value = 0.000 Critical F-value = 6.8606		
Random effects (variance components estimates)				
Vwith (Variance of U_{it}) = 8.4170				
Vbet (Variance of A_i) = 6.8606				
log CR	0.589798	0.045568	12.9432	0.000
log FL	-0.319609	0.031827	-10.0420	0.000
IR	0.329147	0.023537	13.9844	0.000
LGDP	-0.394619E-06	0.156563E-06	-2.52052	0.012
CGDP	-0.142972E-04	0.750320E-06	-19.0548	0.000
intercept	-5.51422	1.54027	-3.58004	0.000
Adjusted R^2 = 0.404				
Hausman test H0: random-effects vs. fixed-effects: CHISQ (5) = 13.283		P-value = 0.0209		

Source: Author's calculations

The results confirm the influence of the conditions and role of the financial institutions on the real per-capita GDP growth. As was expected, we observe evidence of the positive influence of the credit growth and the negative influence of the foreign liabilities. The incentive to save and create the conditions for investment (here, the incentive is represented by the deposit interest rate) shows its positive influence on the per-capita GDP growth. Although less significant, the ratio of the deposit money banks to GDP has a negative influence. At the same time, and as expected, there is clear evidence that the ratio of domestic credit to GDP has a strong negative influence on the per-capita GDP growth, as a high ratio is synonymous with less productive results of the allocation of domestic credit.

Looking at the values obtained for the Hausman test, we can conclude that the fixed-effects estimates are acceptable. Moreover, since we are not using a large panel (N = 825), we may conclude that the system responds well to the within (fixed-effects) estimations, which are more adequate and, in all situations, demonstrate consistency.

At the same time, the "*Vwith*" variances of the basic error terms U_{it}, are higher than the "*Vbet*" variances of the individual specific terms A_i indicating that the variation of time evolution in each country is more important than the cross-differences among the countries in the same periods of time. Simultaneously, by the values obtained with the F-tests, we can confirm that there are common slopes, meaning that within the "old" European Union, there are clear signs of integration, since the growth of the real per-capita GDP presents similar reactions to the considered explaining variables.

Table 2-2 Panel estimates for 26 EU countries (Q2 1999–Q4 2002, N=390)

	Coefficient	**Std. error**	**t-statistics**	**P-value**
Fixed effects (within estimates)				
log CR	0.428570	0.044455	9.64047	0.000
log FL	-0.246805	0.068911	-3.58150	0.000
IR	0.176064	0.044596	3.94801	0.000
LGDP	0.315935E-06	0.819831E-07	3.85366	0.000
CGDP	-0.280220E-06	0.407679E-07	-6.87355	0.000
Adjusted R^2 = 0.291				
F test: $A_i,B = A_i,B_i$ F (125,234) = 1.2393		P-value = 0.081 Critical F-value = 10.798		
F test: $A,B = A_i,B$ F (25,359) = 0.311		P-value = 0.999 Critical F-value = 6.6898		
Random effects (variance components estimates)				
Vwith (Variance of U_{it}) = 25.821				
Vbet (Variance of A_i) = -1.1585				
log CR	0.437721	0.042145	10.3860	0.000
log FL	-0.261481	0.065218	-4.00936	0.000
IR	0.184449	0.041871	4.40512	0.000
LGDP	0.311725E-06	0.778020E-07	4.00664	0.000
CGDP	-0.277853E-06	0.387067E-07	-7.17840	0.000
intercept	3.24132	1.62799	1.99099	0.046
Adjusted R^2 = 0.323				
Hausman test H0: random-effects vs. fixed-effects: CHISQ (5) = 0.93245		P-value = 0.9678		

Source: Author's calculations

Not surprisingly, the results obtained for the second panel (Table 2-2) are relevant but less consistent than those for the first panel. The second panel comprises fewer observations (N = 390) and a shorter time-span (Q2 1999 –

Q4 2002). Moreover, we analyse the influence of the considered variables on the per-capita GDP growth in 26 EU countries: the 14 "old" (without Luxembourg), the 10 NMS and the two future members (Bulgaria and Romania). The adjusted R-squared value is lower than for the first sub-set of countries (although we must remember that for panel estimates the R-squared is sometimes very low), the F tests and the t-statistics in particular, which are much lower.

Nevertheless, there is still clear evidence of the influence of the considered explaining variables in the per-capita GDP growth. The obtained signs of the coefficients confirm the expected effects, except for the ratio liabilities of the deposit money banks to GDP, which now present a positive influence on GDP. It can be due to some changes in the bank liabilities and the general and continuous decrease of the interest rates during the considered period of time.

As in the first panel, the "*Vwith*" variances of the basic error terms U_{it} are higher (indeed, now much higher) than the "*Vbet*" variances of the individual specific terms A_i meaning that in the second panel, the dynamic changes in each country are much more relevant than the individual differences among the 26 countries included in this panel.

According to the values of the Hausman test, we can conclude that the random-effects (variance components) estimates are preferable to the fixed-effect estimates, but this is valid only if we consider that the panel used is a sample from a larger set. However, in this case, it would be appropriate to consider randomly-distributed, country-specific intercepts, which is not easily acceptable for our panel. In reality, our second panel is still smaller (N=390) than the first; thus, it seems quite appropriate to accept the fixed-effects (within) estimates.

Furthermore the obtained results for the intercept (obtained only by the random-effects estimates) are not so relevant. Therefore, it is not difficult to accept that the countries of this second panel still have different intercepts, meaning that there are country-specific initial conditions. This is consistent both with the historically-known conditions and the fact that the financial institutions of these 26 countries have sometimes had to follow a specific course, facing different individual consequences, while adapting to the new conditions of the EU integration process.

At the same time, and in all situations, there is clear evidence of the existence of common slopes as a result of the process of financial integration. Under the conditions of increasing competition, the bank institutions, which are all active in the same market, must develop homogenous performances and contribute in a similar way to the per-capita GDP growth of the different countries.

Conclusion

This paper confirms the influence of financial systems, particularly of the banking institutions' conditions and performance, on the output growth as well as their efforts to adapt to the new conditions of the EU and EMU market, in spite of all the differences among EU Member States.

We contribute to the existing empirical evidence by introducing five variables to explain the real per-capita GDP growth: domestic credit growth, foreign liabilities growth, the deposit rate, the ratio of liabilities of the deposit money banks to GDP and the ratio of domestic credit to GDP. The results obtained confirm the importance of these variables to the per-capita GDP growth.

In our estimations, we use panel fixed-effects and random-effects estimates considering two panels of EU countries: one with data from 11 "old" countries, from the beginning of the 1980s until the implementation of the EMU, and the other with data from that time until the end of 2002 for 26 EU countries, excluding Luxembourg and including Bulgaria and Romania.

Our estimates show relatively more homogenous results for the first panel of 11 EU countries, with common slopes. Even before the EMU, the integration process had already brought about a similar response of their output growth to the behaviour of the banking institutions. Nevertheless, in this panel there are still different intercepts, which is evidence of the specific initial conditions of these "old" and relatively more homogenous countries.

The results obtained for the second panel are also consistent. They confirm the increasing competition among the banking institutions, which, in spite of some differences in their historical evolution and initial conditions, have had to adapt rapidly to the new EU market conditions.

References

Allen, Franklin and Douglas Gale. 2001. *Comparing Financial Systems.* Cambridge, MA: MIT Press

Bassanini, Andrea, Stefano Scarpetta and Philip Hemings. 2001. *Economic Growth: The role of Policies and Institution. Panel Data Evidence from OECE Countries.* OECE Economics Department Working Paper No. 283. Paris: OECD.

Beck, Thorsten, Asli Demirgüç–Kunt and Ross Levine. 2004. *Finance, Inequality and Poverty: Cross-Country Evidence.* World Bank Policy Research Working Paper No. 3338. [online]. Access from: < http://ideas.repec.org/p/wbk/wbrwps/3338.html

Belaisch, Agnes, Laura Kodres, Joaquim Levy and Angel Ubide. 2001. *Euro-Area Banking at the Crossroads*, IMF Working Paper No. 01/28 Washington, D.C.: International Monetary Fund.

Bencivenga, V., B. Smith and R. Starr. 1995. Transaction Costs, Technological Choice and Endogenous Growth. *Journal of Economic Theory* 67(1):53–117.

Bhide, A. 1993. The Hidden Costs of Stock Market Liquidity. *Journal of Financial Economics* 34(1):31–51.

Bokros, Lajos. 2002. Finacial Sector Development in Central and Eastern Europe. In *Banking and Monetary Policy in Eastern Europe*, ed. Adalbert Winkler, 11–41. New York: Palgrave Publishers.

Buch, Claudia. 2002. Governance and Restructuring of Commercial Banks. In *Banking and Monetary Policy in Eastern Europe*, ed. Adalbert Winkler, 43–71. New York: Palgrave Publishers.

Claessens, Stijn. 1996. *Banking reform in transition countries*. Policy Research Working Paper Series 1642. Washington, D.C.: World Bank. [online]. Access from: < http://www.wds.worldbank.org/servlet/WDSContentServer/WDSP/IB/1996/08/01/000009265_3961019225429/Rendered/PDF/multi_page.pdf >

Demirgüç–Kunt, Asli and Ross Levine. 1999. *Bank-Based and Market-Based Financial Systems: Cross Country Comparisons*. World Bank Policy Research Working Paper No. 2143. Washington, D.C.: World Bank.

Dimitrova, Antoaneta, ed. 2004. *Driven to Change: The European Union's Enlargement views from the East*. Manchetser: Manchester University Press.

European Central Bank. 2002. *Structural Analysis of EU Banking Sector – Year 2001*. Frankfurt am Main: European Central Bank.

Fisher, I. 1933. The Debt-Deflation Theory of Great Depression. *Econometrica* 1(4):337–57.

Fries, Steven, Damien Neven and Paul Seabright. 2002. *Bank Performance in Transition Economies*. William Davidson Institute Working Papers Series 505. Ann Arbor: University of Michigan. [online]. Access from: < www.bus.umich.edu/KresgeLibrary/Collections/Workingpapers/wdi/wp505.pdf >

Frowen, Stephen. 2000. Financial Markets in Transition Economies. In *Financial Turbulence and Capital Markets in Transition Countries*, ed. Jens Holscher, 179–85. Hampshire: Macmillan Press.

Gardener, Eduard, Philip Molyneux and Barry Moore, ed. 2002. *Banking in the New Europe – The Impact of the Single Market Program and EMU on the European Banking Sector*. Houndmills Hampshire Basingstoke: Palgrave Macmillan.

Gurley, J. and E. Shaw. 1955. Financial Aspects of Economic Development. *American Economic Review* 45(4):391–414.

Haas, Ralph and Ilko Naaborg. 2005. *Foreign Banks in Transition Economies: Small Business Lending and Internal Capital Markets*. Economics Working Paper Archive EconWPA. [online]. Access from: < http://econwpa.wustl.edu:80/eps/if/papers/0504/0504004.pdf >.

Hainz, Christa and Monika Schnitzer. 2002. The Development of the Banking Sector in Eastern Europe. In *Banking and Monetary Policy in Eastern Europe*, ed. Adalbert Winkler, 205–16. New York: Palgrave Publishers.

Hicks, J. 1937. Mr. Keynes and the Classics: A Suggested Interpretation. *Econometrica* 5(2):147–59.

Holscher, Jens, ed. 2000. *Financial Turbulence and Capital Markets in Transition Countries*. Hampshire: Macmillan Press.

Khan, Mohsin S. and Abdelhak Senhadji. 2000. *Financial Development and Economic Growth: An Overview.* IMF Working Paper No 209 Washington, D.C.: International Monetary Fund.

King, R. and R. Levine. 1993. Finance and Growth: Schumpeter might be right. *Quarterly Journal of Economics* 108:717–37.

Leahy, Michael, Sebastian Schich, Gert Wehinger, Florian Pelgrin and Thorsteinn Thorgeirsson. 2001. *Contribution of Financial Systems to Growth in OECD Countries.* OECD Economics Department Working Papers, No 280. Paris: OECD.

Levine, R. and S. Zervos. 1998. Stock Markets, Banks and Economic Growth. *American Economic Review* 88(3):537–58.

Matoušek, Roman and Anita Taci, 2000. The Assessment of the Costs and Benefits of the Small and Medium Commercial Banks within the Czech Banking Sector. In *Financial Turbulence and Capital Markets in Transition Countries*, ed. Jens Holscher, 118–38. Hampshire: Macmillan Press.

Mishkin, F. 1978. The Household Balance Sheet and the Great Depression. *Journal of Economic History* 38(4):918–37.

Modigliani, F. 1944. Liquidity Preference and the Theory of Interest and Money. *Econometrica* 12(1):45–88

Monti, Mario. 1996. *The Single Market and Tomorrow's Europe: A Progress Report from the European Commission.* Brussels: European Commission.

Obstfeld, Maurice and Alan Taylor. 2003. *Global Capital Markets: Integration, Crises and Growth.* Cambridge: Cambridge University Press.

Polanski, Zbigniew, 2000. Poland and International Financial Turbulences of the Second Half of the 1990s in Transition Economies. In *Financial Turbulence in and Capital Markets Transition Countries*, ed. Jens Holscher, 53–75. Hampshire: Macmillan Press.

———. 2002. Promoting Financial Development: Lessons from Poland. In *Banking and Monetary Policy in Eastern Europe*, ed. Adalbert Winkler, 104–24. New York: Palgrave Publishers.

Shan, J., A. Morris and F. Sun. 2001. Financial Development and Economic growth: an Egg and Chicken Problem? *Review of International Economics* 9(3):443–54.

Schumpeter, Joseph A. 1911. *The Theory of Economic Development: An Inquiry into Profits, Capital, Credit Interest and Business Cycle.* Harvard: Harvard University Press.

Stavárek, D. 2004. Banking Efficiency in Visegrad Countries Before Joining the European Union. *European Review of Economics and Finance* 3(3):129–67.

Stavárek, Daniel and Stanislav Polouček. 2004. Efficiency and Profitability in the Banking Sector. In *Reforming the Financial Sector in Central European Countries*, ed Stanislav Polouček, 75–135. Houndmills, Basingstoke, Hampshire: Palgrave Macmillan.

Stiglitz, J. 1985. Credit markets and the Control of Capital. *Journal of Money, Credit and Banking* 17(1):133–52.

Tomann, Horst. 2000. The Return of the Habsburgs – Reflections on the Role of Institutions in Transition Economies. In *Financial Turbulence in and Capital Markets Transition Countries*, ed. Jens Holscher, 3–12. Hampshire: Macmillan Press.

Török, Adam, 2000. Turbulences and Emergency Landings in Leased Planes: Macroeconomic Stabilization and Financial Sector Reform in Hungary in the 1990s. In *Financial Turbulence in and Capital Markets Transition Countries*, ed. Jens Holscher, 141–62. Hampshire: Macmillan Press.

Turnovec, František. 2000. Privatization and Transparency: Evidence from the Czech Republic. In *Financial Turbulence and Capital Markets in Transition Countries*, ed. Jens Holscher, 83–101. Hampshire: Macmillan Press.

Vives, X. 2001. Restructuring Financial Regulation in the European Monetary Union. *Journal of Financial Services Research* 19(1):57–82.

Winkler, Adalbert, ed. 2002. *Banking and Monetary Policy in the Eastern Europe: The First Ten Years*. Houndmills Hampshire Basingstoke: Palgrave Editions.

Wooldridge, Jeffrey. 2002. *Econometric Analysis of Cross Section and Panel Data*. London: The MIT Press.

———. 2003. *Introductory Econometrics – A Modern Approach*. Ohio: Thomson South-Western.

Notes

[1] For more about this issue see see Bokros (2002), Buch (2002), Claessens (1996), Stavárek (2004), Stavárek and Polouček (2004), Fries *et al.* (2002), Frowen (2000), Haas and Naaborg (2005), Hainz and Schnitzer (2002), Matoušek and Taci (2000), Polanski (2000), Polanski (2002), Tomann (2000), Török (2000) or Turnovec (2000).

[2] Following TSP commands and the F-test used in the panel estimates, A = common intercept; Ai = different, individual intercepts; B = common slope; Bi = different, individual slopes of the estimated equations.

Appendix 2-A

Univariate statistics of panel estimates for 11 EU countries (Q2 1980 – Q4 1998, N=825)

	Mean	Std Dev	Minimum	Maximum
log CR	10.61949	4.79528	0.009950	17.86032
log FL	33.05318	2.58599	18.16061	38.37608
IR	17.30423	3.39878	10.59663	23.36232
LGDP	9.009980	5.31875	1.500000	28.00000
CGDP	91977.81	658420.3	0.001270	9440000
log CR	53136.42	148161.6	0.049200	620000.0
	Sum	**Variance**	**Skewness**	**Kurtosis**
log CR	8761.07637	22.99471	-0.64011	-0.85131
log FL	27268.8718	6.687330	-1.16582	7.226080
IR	14275.9860	11.55170	-0.05891	-1.02744
LGDP	7433.23000	28.28906	0.94225	0.536050
CGDP	7.58817D+07	4.33517D+11	11.9439	151.1892
log CR	4.38375D+07	2.19519D+10	2.71814	5.734520

Source: Author's calculations

Correlation matrix of panel estimates for 11 EU countries (Q2 1980 – Q4 1998, N=825)

	log GDP	log CR	log FL	IR	LGDP	CGDP
log GDP	1.0000					
log CR	0.4150	1.0000				
log FL	0.0129	0.2752	1.0000			
IR	0.3372	0.1104	0.1573	1.0000		
LGDP	0.0322	-0.0247	-0.0898	0.0224	1.0000	
CGDP	-0.4646	0.0428	-0.1663	-0.3573	-0.0477	1.0000

Source: Author's calculations

Appendix 2-B

Univariate statistics of panel estimates for 26 EU countries (Q2 1999 – Q4 1999, N=390)

	Mean	Std Dev	Minimum	Maximum
log CR	12.72364	6.03636	3.79549	28.88378
log FL	32.05316	6.26965	20.2769	40.25909
IR	19.80299	4.01747	8.90653	27.30391
LGDP	5.71810	6.13733	1.46000	35.00000
CGDP	626149.1	5621915	1.35000D-06	7.97000D+07
log CR	2230689	1.14557D+07	3.61000D-06	1.35000D+07
	Sum	**Variance**	**Skewness**	**Kurtosis**
log CR	4962.21899	36.43758	0.47357	-0.20954
log FL	12500.7342	39.30851	-0.55433	-1.12042
IR	7723.16702	16.14003	-0.28791	-0.47235
LGDP	2230.06000	37.66680	3.75956	14.70480
CGDP	2.44198D+08	3.16059D+13	12.8973	173.3345
log CR	8.69969D+08	1.31234D+14	8.31479	84.59690

Source: Author's calculations

Correlation matrix of panel estimates for 26 EU countries (Q2 1999 – Q4 1999, N=390)

	log GDP	log CR	log FL	IR	LGDP	CGDP
log GDP	1.0000					
log CR	0.3802	1.0000				
log FL	-0.0694	0.2579	1.0000			
IR	0.2731	0.1744	0.1533	1.0000		
LGDP	-0.1335	0.1031	0.1705	-0.0419	1.0000	
CGDP	-0.2516	0.1799	0.1689	-0.0808	0.8207	1.0000

Source: Author's calculations

CHAPTER THREE

DEVELOPMENT OF THE ESTONIAN BANKING SYSTEM, 1995–2004

During the recent years, issues concerning the soundness of banking and financial systems have become more important in all countries. The financial sector (especially the banking system) is vulnerable to systemic crises, which has led to the creation of costly safety nets as depositor insurance schemes with the well-known moral hazard problem. It is argued there is increasing evidence that banks are "black boxes" due to the weak transparency and banks' unwillingness to disclose information (Hyytinen and Takalo, 2003). Measurement of banks' creditworthiness and risk exposures are complicated issues and it is not easy to interpret banks' accounting data. Kaminsky and Reinhart (1999, p. 476) argued that "Indicators of business failures and non-performing loans are also usually available only at low frequencies, if at all; the latter are also made less informative by banks' desires to hide their problems for as long as possible." This means that it is necessary to use all available financial information from the official financial statements of banks as fully and comprehensively as possible for making financial analysis of a bank's performance.

For the performance analysis, various measures of rates of return are mainly used. We fully agree with the opinion that "Relying too heavily on just a few indicators of bank profitability can be misleading. While the Return on Assets (ROA), Return on Equity (ROE), and interest margin (and non-interest expenses) to gross income remain the key measures, they should ideally be supplemented by the analysis of other operating ratios" (Sundararajan *et al.*, p. 20). In this chapter, we use one of the possible approaches to the financial analysis of banks – a modified version of the DuPont analysis. For more about the DuPont analysis see Dietrich (1997) or Vensel (2001). We have selected the following years for the empirical analysis of the Estonian banking system performance:

- 1995: the first year of macroeconomic stabilisation after resolution of the first banking crisis in Estonia;
- 1997: an extraordinarily optimistic year, the first unsuccessful attempts of Estonian banks to expand into Russian and Baltic

countries' markets, "stock-price bubble" on the Tallinn Stock Exchange;
- 2000: the second phase of macroeconomic stabilisation and resolution of the second banking crisis in Estonia;
- 2002–03: the last years before joining the European Union.

This chapter is structured as follows. In the next section, a theoretical background and literature overview is provided. Further, we discuss the most important recent developments in the Estonian banking system. The following section presents a modified version of the DuPont analysis applied and the empirical results of the Estonian banking system performance. The chapter ends with some concluding remarks.

Theoretical Background and Review of the Related Literature

The contemporary banking crises can be classified mostly as "growth crises", which are characterized by economic deregulation and liberalisation, removal of cross-border restrictions on capital flows, and increased competition in the financial sector. Based on a newly constructed cross-country database of financial liberalisation, Abiad and Mody (2003) examined the experience of 35 countries, over the period 1973–96, to analyze the underlying causes of financial sector reforms. They found that liberalisation is a combination of discrete changes in response to economic and political "shocks", reinforced by self-sustaining dynamics (they called it "learning"). They draw five specific conclusions about what produces change (reform):

- Countries whose financial sectors are fully repressed (unliberalised) are the ones with the strongest tendency to maintain their policy stance and hence remain closed and highly regulated, with initial reforms causing changes that make further reforms necessary.
- Regional diffusion effects appear to be important – the further a country's stage of liberalisation is from that of the regional leader, the greater is the pressure to liberalize.
- Shocks to the economic environment (a new government, decline in the U.S. interest rates) play an important role in weakening the status quo and making reforms possible.
- Crises do trigger action, but not always in the direction of reform – balance of payments crises raise the likelihood of reform; banking crises have the opposite effect.
- Among variables representing ideology and structure, only trade openness appears related to the pace of reform; presidential or

parliamentary regimes, right-wing or left-wing governments, and the legal system prove not to be influential as well.

It is evident that to study results of financial sector reform and restructuring, a profound performance analysis is needed. The traditional financial ratio analysis is mainly used for bank performance analysis. We can find different versions of this approach from various textbooks about banking and financial institutions. Different versions of DuPont's financial ratio analysis seem to be more promising for banks' and other financial institutions' performance analyses (see Dietrich, 1997, among others). The focus of financial analysis for the management of any bank (or the banking sector as a whole) should be on the efficiency of performance of the bank measured from the viewpoint of investors'/owners' income maximisation. More widely, all stakeholders have to be interested in the performance of the bank.

The concept of a "stakeholder monitor" is useful in designing performance analysis of any bank. This concept was developed by Llewellyn (2002) and Llewellyn and Mayes (2003). We agree with the suggestion that "Stakeholders, as the name implies, have something in stake in the relative success or failure of the firm. Those who participate in the process of observing the behaviour of the firm and forming judgments in light of it can be described as "monitors". Such monitors may have access to both market and private information. Combining these ideas, "Stakeholder monitors" are all those agents who have an interest in the outcome of the monitoring process" (Llewellyn and Mayes, 2003, p. 11). The incomplete list of "stakeholder monitors" includes: supervisory agencies, rating agencies, market traders, shareholders, board of directors, debt-holders, depositors, managers, borrowers, and employees.

In carrying out bank performance analysis, it is important to emphasize that banks differ in their corporate governance from firms in other less regulated industries. These differences, in turn, present their own challenges for all stakeholders. "Bank managers live in a more complex environment than their peers in industry due to bank regulations. In addition to the demands placed on them by shareholders, regulators have strong incentives to influence managerial action, and this may be in conflict with shareholder demands" (Harm, 2002, p. 5). Governance is a set of mechanisms with which the providers of capital and other stakeholders are defending their interests against the firm. The firm is run by managers, and this is the point where conflicts of interests begin. Harm (2002) also presents an excellent survey of recent literature (both theoretical and empirical).

Macey and O'Hara (2003) argue that bank officers and directors should be held to a broader (if not higher) set of standards than their counterparts in less regulated non-financial firms, and banks pose special corporate governance problems. Kose and Qian (2003) consider another important theme in the corporate governance of banks – the effect of the incentive features built into the compensation schemes of bank managers. Adams and Mehran (2003) also focus on the differences between the corporate governance of banks and manufacturing firms and support the theory that governance structures are industry-specific. In general, the components of a firm's governance structure are determined by various factors, all of which will also influence performance analysis aims and techniques: the nature and structure of a firm's assets and liabilities (leverage, share of financial assets, business risk, cash flow patterns), firm size, industry, regulations, etc.

Development of the Estonian Banking System

The first commercial bank (Tartu Commercial Bank) on the territory of the former Soviet Union was established in Estonia in 1988. This bank went bankrupt and was liquidated in 1992–93. As there was a great demand for banking services by the emerging private sector, the maximum number of commercial banks operating simultaneously in the small Estonian banking market was 42 in 1992. Some of them were liquidated during the banking crises and some of them were merged into larger commercial banks.

Estonia has experienced two serious banking crises during its roughly 12-year period of its banking sector development and restructuring, the first crisis in 1992–94 and the second in 1998–99. The first banking crisis occurred during the difficult period when drastic economic restructuring was started and when production output was reducing dramatically and the country underwent a period of hyperinflation. The characteristic feature of the first banking crisis in Estonia was that it was caused by internal reasons and it was overcome with Estonia's own resources and management skills. The main causes of this banking crisis were severe problems in the whole economy, poor bank management, lack of professional skills, and weak supervision from the side of the central bank and owners. The depositors' losses in the banking crisis were large, the money supply decreased, many loans were depreciated, and the trustworthiness of the banking system fell significantly. During the first banking crisis, Estonia had to resolve the problems by itself. Then, during the second banking crisis, foreign banks also provided help and support to get over the crises.

In 1998, a wave of mergers and restructuring took place in the Estonian banking sector. After the completion of these mergers, Scandinavian banks started to show greater interest in the Estonian banking market. As a result, Swedbank acquired 56 per cent of Hansapank, and Skandinaviska Enskilda Banken acquired 32 per cent of the Union Bank of Estonia. We may conclude that the Estonian banking sector became healthier when Swedish banks and other Nordic investors joined the circle of bank owners, improving the future outlook of the banking system.

Looking back, we are now able to establish some signs of the banking crisis in 1998–99.

- Estonian banks took extraordinarily high financial risks through investment companies and their subsidiary companies to get large profits via speculating in stock markets. The rapid fall of prices in the stock market during the autumn of 1997 until the end of the year significantly reduced banks' profits. At the end of 1997 and in 1998 almost all banks operated at losses.
- Banks held a very high negative level of gap (interest rate sensitive liabilities exceeded significantly rate-sensitive assets) for earning excessive profits in the environment where interest rates steadily decreased during the previous years. They were not able to adjust to a changed environment with increasing interest rates from the second half of 1997.
- Commercial banks absorbed heavily into non-banking business. For example, the later bankrupted Land Bank of Estonia owned seven subordinate establishments and related companies which dealt with leasing, investing, and anything else except banking (hotels, processing agricultural products, broadcasting, etc.). Similarly, other banks were absorbed in risky non-banking businesses.
- The decision to expand to the Eastern market (Russia and other Baltic States), where the interest rates and possible profitability seemed to be higher, was also too risky and premature, especially in the framework of the Russian crisis in 1998.
- There were various disputes and conflicts of interests between the owners and management which led to wrong (mismanagement) decisions. The cases in point were Land Bank of Estonia and Estonian Investment Bank. For example, the shareholders of the Investment Bank intended to sell the bank to the German Schleswig-Holstein Bank in autumn 1997, but the top executives threatened to hand in a collective resignation; therefore, the bank was sold to them.
- Sometimes there were inadvisable relations between the bank management and political powers, along with corresponding political pressure. A typical "political" bank was the Land Bank of Estonia where almost all financial risks were ignored. Later the government lost its deposits in the bank amounting to more than EEK 800 million (more than EUR 50 million).

The authors are of the opinion that the currency board arrangement helped to resolve the banking crises rapidly; most effectively without excessive rehabilitation costs in Estonia. The main instruments for anticipating banking crises were to tighten the prudential requirements and strengthen the banking supervision. Recent changes in the operational framework for monetary policy and banks' prudential ratios in Estonia were aimed at enhancing financial stability and increasing the liquidity buffers of the financial system. In short-term, the priority focused on restoring foreign investors' confidence in Estonian economic viability.

We may argue that the currency board arrangement barely helped banks that were in trouble because its resources were intended for guaranteeing the local currency and the central bank was not acting as the lender of the last resort. The currency board was not able to avoid banking crises and could not guarantee a "soft landing" and rehabilitation of banks in trouble. At the same time, the currency board arrangement supported and strengthened the discipline and responsibility of the main actors – banks, the central bank, depositors, and the government. A stable currency and presence of a respective financial safety net compensated for the absence of classical lender-of-last resort facility and ensured the development of a generally reliable banking sector.

The structure of the Estonian banking sector has changed fundamentally during the last years. Today, the banking system is highly concentrated and two Swedish-owned banks dominate in the market. The consolidation process continued throughout the second banking crisis in 1998–99 and resulted in fundamental bank reorganisations. We can also notice all three worldwide trends in the financial consolidation process in the Estonian market: domestic consolidation, foreign entry and cross-border consolidation, and the formation of financial conglomerates and bank assurances. The dependence of the Estonian banking system on the developments in international financial markets and on foreign investors' preferences has deepened from year to year. In the course of the restructuring process, foreign banks increased their share in equity capital from 10.3 per cent in 1996 to 79 per cent at the end of 2002. The total share of non-resident owners had risen to 86.7 per cent by the end of 2002.

DuPont Financial Ratio Analysis

The starting point of bank performance analysis is to calculate the book rate of return on equity, *ROE*.

$$ROE = \frac{\text{Earnings After Taxes, } EAT}{\text{Book Value of Equity, } BVE}, \tag{3.1}$$

which consists of three components:

(i) pull-through, *U*

$$U = \frac{\text{Earnings After Taxes, } EAT}{\text{Earnings Before Taxes, } EBT}, \tag{3.2}$$

(ii) financial leverage, *LEV*

$$LEV = \frac{\text{Total Assets, } TA}{\text{Book Value of Equity, } BVE}, \tag{3.3}$$

(iii) return on total assets, *ROA*

$$ROA = \frac{\text{Earnings Before Taxes, } EBT}{\text{Total Assets, } TA}. \tag{3.4}$$

These financial ratios form the multiple factor system:

$$ROE = \frac{EAT}{EBT} \cdot \frac{TA}{BVE} \cdot \frac{EBT}{TA} = \frac{EAT}{BVE}. \tag{3.5}$$

Changes in *ROA* are usually the cause of the most important changes in banks' performances and need a more detailed analysis. The other components of *ROE*, pull-through (*U*) and financial leverage (*LEV*), reflect tax treatment and capitalisation rate, and they usually change less. *ROA* may be divided into the following components:

(i) bank burden, *B*

$$B = \frac{\text{Net Non - Interest Revenue, } NNIR}{\text{Total Assets, } TA} = \frac{NIR - NIE}{TA}, \tag{3.6}$$

where *NIR* is the non-interest revenues and *NIE* is the non-interest expenses.

(ii) earning assets ratio, *EAR*

$$EAR = \frac{\text{Earning Assets, } EA}{\text{Total Assets, } TA}, \tag{3.7}$$

(iii) net interest margin, *NIM*

$$NIM = \frac{\text{Net Interest Revenue, } NIR}{\text{Earning Assets, } EA} = \frac{IR - IE}{EA}, \qquad (3.8)$$

where *IR* is the interest revenues and *IE* is the interest expenses. Financial ratios (3.6) – (3.8) form the following factor system:

$$ROA = \frac{NNIR}{TA} + \frac{EA}{TA} \cdot \frac{NIR}{EA} = \frac{NNIR + NIR}{TA} = \frac{EBT}{TA}. \qquad (3.9)$$

For a more detailed analysis, *NIM* may be divided into the following three components:

(i) return on earning assets, *REA*

$$REA = \frac{\text{Interest Revenue, } IR}{\text{Earning Assets, } EA}, \qquad (3.10)$$

(ii) cost of liabilities, *COL*

$$COL = \frac{\text{Interest Expense, } IE}{\text{Liabilities, } L}, \qquad (3.11)$$

(iii) liabilities to earning assets ratio, *LEA*

$$LEA = \frac{\text{Liabilities, } L}{\text{Earning Assets, } EA}, \qquad (3.12)$$

which form the factor system:

$$NIM = \frac{IR}{EA} - \frac{IE}{L} \cdot \frac{L}{EA} = \frac{IR - IE}{EA} = \frac{NIR}{EA}. \qquad (3.13)$$

Initial financial information for Estonian banking sector performance analysis (1997–2003) is presented in Table 3-1 on the basis of aggregated consolidated financial statements published by the Bank of Estonia.

Table 3-1 Simplified consolidated financial statements of the Estonian banking system (1997–2003, in EEK bln, ratios in units)

	1997	2000	2001	2002	2003	ratio 03/97	ratio 03/02
Income statement data							
Interest revenues	2658.5	3744.2	4308.1	4253.5	3868.7	1.455	0.910
Interest expenses	1217.5	1811.9	2125.7	1883.0	1708.2	1.403	0.907
Net interest revenue	1444.1	1932.3	2182.4	2370.5	2160.5	1.496	0.911
Non-interest revenues	3272.0	2065.6	2895.1	2613.4	2716.2	0.830	1.039
Non-interest expenses	3644.4	3384.8	3373.7	3769.1	2547.5	0.699	0.676
Net non-interest revenue	-372.4	-1319.2	-478.6	-1155.7	-168.7	0.453	0.146
Earnings before taxes	1068.9	613.1	1703.8	1214.8	2717.5	2.542	2.237
Earnings after taxes	963.1	613.1	1683.4	1153.2	2562.5	2.661	2.222
Balance sheet data							
Cash and reserves	3203.8	6578.0	6212.3	5166.2	5100.3	1.592	0.987
Earning assets	25817.0	42019.6	53544.0	66827.5	78098.7	3.025	1.169
Fixed and other assets	2743.1	3847.3	3358.7	3054.9	2604.4	0.949	0.853
Total assets	31763.9	52444.9	63115.0	75048.6	85803.4	2.701	1.143
Liabilities	28562.7	45164.2	54936.0	65549.2	72504.9	2.538	1.106
Book value of equity	3201.2	7280.7	8179.0	9499.4	13298.5	4.154	1.400

Source: The Bank of Estonia annual reports

We used the initial data from Table 3-1 (the balance sheet data are averaged), to carry out the DuPont financial ratio analysis. The results obtained are presented in Table 3-2.

Table 3-2 DuPont financial ratio analysis of Estonian commercial banks (1997–2003, in %, ratios in units)

	1997	2000	2001	2002	2003	ratio 03/97	ratio 03/02
ROE = EAT/BE	30.09	8.59	20.58	12.14	19.26	0.640	1,586
U = EAT/EBT	90.10	100.0	98.80	94.93	94.30	1.047	0.993
LEV = TA/BE	9.92	7.203	7.717	7.90	6.43	0.648	0.814
ROTA = EBT/TA	3.365	1.192	2.700	1.619	3.167	0.941	1.956
Components of ROTA							
B = NNIR/TA	-1.172	-2.493	-0.755	-1.540	-0.197	0.168	0.128
EAR = EA/TA	81.28	80.12	84.84	89.05	91.02	1.120	1.022
NIM = NIR/EA	5.594	4.599	4.076	3.547	2.766	0.494	0.780
Components of NIM							
REA = IR/EA	10.30	8.921	8.046	6.365	4.954	0.481	0.778
COL = IE/L	4.263	4.012	3.869	2.873	2.356	0.553	0.820
LEA = L/EA	1.106	1.075	1.026	0.981	0.928	0.839	0.946

Source: Author's calculations

Econometric Modelling

As far as we know, nobody has previously used the existing information about banks to construct production function type econometric models treating banking as a separate sector of a country (Aarma and Vainu, 2003). One can ask: What is the production or product of a bank? In our opinion, the product of the bank is the amount of the services, the volume of which can be measured by the total income of the bank. We selected the total income of banks (y) as the output variable (dependent variable) and used profit earning assets (x_1), equity (x_2), liabilities (x_3) and fixed assets (x_4) as factors (explanatory variables). The time series were treated as consisting of three components:

$$y(t) = f(t) + h(t) + e_t \,, \tag{3.14}$$

where $y(t)$ is the actual time series, $f(t)$ denotes the linear trend in the time series, $h(t)$ is the harmonious component in the time series, and e_t defines residuals.

The harmonious component is determined as Fourier's series:

$$h(t) = a_0 + \sum_{j=1}^{k} (a_j \cos\alpha + b_j \sin\alpha), \qquad \alpha = j\frac{t2\pi}{T}, \tag{3.15}$$

where a,b are unknown coefficients, $\pi = 3.14$, j is the number of harmonious component, t denotes the time, and T is the number of observations. We chose the power function as the type of the model.

$$y = ax^{\alpha}z^{\beta}, \qquad \alpha + \beta = 1. \tag{3.16}$$

To estimate the parameters a, α, and β (a is intercept, α and β are elasticity coefficients) with the method of least squares it was first necessary to find logarithms of the primary data. Then, according to the rules of analyzing time series, we checked the existence of trend and harmonious component in the time series of the logarithms of the selected parameters and calculated the following results.

Trendlines:

$$\ln y = 6.2067 + 0.0398t \tag{3.17}$$
$$\ln x_1 = 9.2500 + 0.0612t \tag{3.18}$$
$$\ln x_2 = 7.0659 + 0.0738t \tag{3.19}$$
$$\ln x_3 = 9.4373 + 0.0542t \tag{3.20}$$
$$\ln x_4 = 7.0913 + 0.3206 \ln t \tag{3.21}$$

Harmonious components:

$$u \ln y = \ln y - f(t) = -0.1006 \cos \alpha - 0.0134 \sin \alpha - 0.0421 \cos 2\alpha + 0.0994 \sin 2\alpha - 0.0787 \cos 3\alpha - 0.0696 \sin 3\alpha, \tag{3.22}$$

$$u \ln x_1 = -0,1749 \cos \alpha + 0.0583 \sin \alpha - 0.0850 \cos 2\alpha - - 0.0992 \sin 2\alpha, \tag{3.23}$$

$$u \ln x_2 = -0.3193 \cos \alpha + 0.0691 \sin \alpha + 0.0326 \cos 2\alpha - - 0.1142 \sin 2\alpha, \tag{3.24}$$

$$u \ln x_3 = -0.1743 \cos \alpha + 0.0514 \sin \alpha - 0.0749 \cos 2\alpha - - 0.0861 \sin 2\alpha, \tag{3.25}$$

$$u \ln x_4 = -0.2073 \cos \alpha + 0.0453 \sin \alpha. \tag{3.26}$$

We treated all possible combinations of the factors and obtained only one model that proved to be statistically significant:

$$\ln y = -2.2884 + 0.0074t - 0.1288 \ln t + 0.087 \cos \alpha - 0.0092 \sin \alpha + 0.0027 \cos 2\alpha + 0.1009 \sin 2\alpha - 0.0787 \cos 3\alpha - 0.0696 \sin 3\alpha + 0.5984 \ln x_3 + 0.4016 \ln x_4, \tag{3.27}$$

which provides for the final result:

$$y = 0.1014 x_3^{0.5984} x_4^{0.4016} t^{-0.1288} \cdot \exp\begin{bmatrix} 0.0074t + 0.087\cos\alpha - 0.0092\sin\alpha + \\ + 0.0027\cos 2\alpha + 0.1009\sin 2\alpha - \\ - 0.0787\cos 3\alpha - 0.0696\sin 3\alpha \end{bmatrix} \tag{3.28}$$

Conclusion

The development of the Estonian banking sector is described by a quite rapid nominal growth of total assets, loan portfolios, net income and other quantitative financial indicators. The capitalisation of Estonian banks improved and the share of non-residents in the capital increased significantly.

Some of the most important empirical results of the use of the DuPont financial ratio analysis for the Estonian commercial banking system (1997–2003) are as follows:

- The book rate of return on equity (*ROE*) decreased during the analyzed period from 31.73 per cent in 1997 to 19.26 per cent in 2003. We can also mention a very high volatility of profitability ratios (both *ROE* and *ROA*) during the analyzed period. Banks' financial leverage ratios (*LEV*) decreased substantially due to the central bank's new equity requirements, which forced banks to either raise equity or to merge.
- The average return on earning assets (*REA*) has fallen substantially over the recent years due to the overall falling of interest rates in the Estonian banking market. *REA* has fallen much faster than the average cost of liabilities (*COL*), which means that the interest spread decreased considerably over the analyzed period. This change reflects the sharpened competition between banks themselves and with other financial institutions such as insurance companies and investment funds.
- It is possible to treat and analyse a bank as an enterprise. Model (3.14) shows that liabilities (loan resources) and fixed assets have been the most important factors in the development of the Estonian banking system.

References

Abiad, Abdul and Ashoka Mody. 2003. *Financial Reform: What Shakes It? What Shapes It?* IMF Working Paper No. 03/70. Washington, D.C.: International Monetary Fund.

Adams, R. and H. Mehran. 2003. Is Corporate Governance Different for Bank Holding Companies? *Federal Reserve Bank of New York Economic Policy Review* 9(1):123–42.

Dietrich, Kimbell J. 1997. *Financial Services and Financial Institutions.* New York: Prentice Hall.

Harm, Christian. 2002. *Bank Management between Shareholders and Regulators.* SUERF Studies No. 21. Vienna: SUERF.

Hyytinen, Ari and Tuomas Takalo. 2003. *Preventing Systemic Crises through Bank Transparency.* Bank of Finland Discussion Papers No. 25/2003. Helsinki: Bank of Finland.

Kaminsky, G.L. and C.M. Reinhart. 1999. The Twin Crises: The Causes of Banking and Balance-of-Payments Problems. *American Economic Review* 89(2):473–500.

Kose, J. and Y. Qian. 2003. Incentive Features in CEO Compensation in the Banking Industry. *Federal Reserve Bank of New York Economic Policy Review* 9(1):107–21.

Llevellyn, David T. 2002. Comment. In *Prompt Corrective Actions: Ten Years Later*, ed Gerhardt G. Kaufmann, 321–33. Amsterdam: JAI.

Llevellyn, David T. and David G. Mayes. 2003. *The Role of Market Discipline in Handling Problem Banks.* Bank of Finland Discussion Papers 21/2003. Helsinki: Bank of Finland.

Macay, J.R. and M. O'Hara. 2003. The Corporate Governance of Banks. *Federal Reserve Bank of New York Economic Policy Review* 9(1): 91–107.

Sundararajan, Vasudevan, Charles Enoh, Armida San Jose, Paul Hilbers, Russell Krueger, Marina Moretti and Graham Slack. 2002. *Financial Soundness Indicators: Analytical Aspects and Country Practices.* IMF Occasional Paper No. 212. Washington, D.C.: International Monetary Fund.

Vensel, Vello 2001. Estonian Banking System Performance, 1994–2000. In *Estonia on the Threshold of the European Union: Financial Sector and Enterprise Restructuring in the Changing Economic Environment*, ed Vello Vensel and Clas Wihlborg, 23–43. Tallinn: Tallinn Technical University Press.

CHAPTER FOUR

THE IMPACT OF FOREIGN BANK ENTRY ON THE STABILITY AND PERFORMANCE OF BANKS: EVIDENCE FROM THE CEE COUNTRIES

The internationalisation process of firms has been intensively studied since the 1960s. Due to the increase in international capital flows, foreign direct investments and international trade at that time, active development of international banking also began. In the transition countries, international banks have operated only since the beginning of the 1990s, after a significant liberalisation of the financial market and elimination of entry barriers. At present, foreign banks already have more than 60 per cent of the market in the Central and Eastern European (CEE) countries.

Growing foreign ownership in the banking sector raises several interesting questions about the entry process of foreign banks into transition economies. There are no generally accepted theory to explain the internationalisation process of banks in the transition economies and its implications. The main reason for this gap in the literature is that foreign bank entry into emerging markets has occurred only with the "third wave" of international banks activities during the second half of the 1990s (Herrero and Simón, 2003).

The aim of the chapter is to identify the effect of foreign banks entry on bank performance and stability in the CEE countries. In the second section, the recent foreign bank entry literature is discussed and the effect of foreign banks entry on the performance of banks is discussed in section three. The volatility of credit supply and the effect of foreign banks entry on the quality of loan portfolio of local banks is analyzed in section four. In section five, the results of a questionnaire-based survey are presented. Conclusions of the paper are summarized in section six.

Theoretical Aspects of Foreign Bank Entry Effects

The main reason that greater international financial competition should improve the credit supply is based on the financial liberalisation framework. McKinnon (1973) and Shaw (1973) proposed that there is an excess of credit demanded in less developed countries and elimination of entry restriction would make it possible for multinational banks to satisfy the excess of credit demand.

Theorists who discuss the impact of FDI underscore the importance of inter-industry and intra-industry spill-over effects. The extent of intra-industry spill-over effects of FDI on technology transfer depends on a particular local firm's own ability to innovate and imitate (Glass and Saggi, 1998; Petit and Sanna–Randaccio 2000). Technology diffusion with FDI is rather a complicated topic. Teece (1977) pointed out several channels for technology diffusion, namely labour flow from foreign to domestic firms, imitation and liberalisation (removal of entry barriers to foreign firms).

It is also suggested that spill-over effects of foreign entry depend on how much the domestic and foreign banking market differ in their levels of development. This phenomenon is known as the "technology gap hypothesis" which suggests that the spill-over effects from FDI to domestic firms will occur only if the technology gap is not overly large and if the country has a minimum required level of human capital (Borensztein *et al.* 1998; Kokko 1994; Konings, 1999). An overly large technology gap between the foreign enterprise and domestic firm will lead to the dominance of competition effects. Aitken and Harrison (1999) showed that the productivity of domestic firms was negatively affected by FDI in Venezuela, where the competition effect dominated slightly. The reason was that foreign firms were "market stealers" who forced the domestic firms to produce less, which lead to an increase in the average cost.

Besides the quantity of knowledge transfer, it is important to consider the level of quality of the knowledge transfer. Glass and Saggi (1998) found in their general equilibrium model that host countries with a higher technology gap receive lower technological quality with FDI. The capability to imitate and accept technology transfer is known as "absorptive capacity". Countries that are able to imitate well and have a more intensive level of local research and development (R&D) receive more high-quality technological FDI. Therefore, their conclusion about policy is that host countries should enhance the imitation by supporting local R&D to receive high-quality FDI. Glass and Saggi (1998) found, for example, using the oligopoly model, that if a host firm (country) has a lower technological level than the source firm (country), then there are at least two rationales for attracting FDI: higher profits of the host firm or a wage premium benefiting workers.

The application of FDI literature on the banking sector would mean that the transfer of knowledge from parent bank to a subsidiary has both competition and spill-over effects on the host banking sector (see Figure 4-1). There could also be spill-over effects – domestic banks can learn from foreign banks. Thus the competition effect can work in two ways: either domestic banks have high absorptive capacity and become more effective (catch-up effect), or if the technology gap is too high then domestic banks are unable to compete with foreign banks and foreign banks will just easily increase their market shares (market-stealing effect). The technology transfer and local firms' reaction to foreign banks entry therefore depends on the development of the financial sector.

Fig. 4-1 Effect of technology transfer on the local banking sector

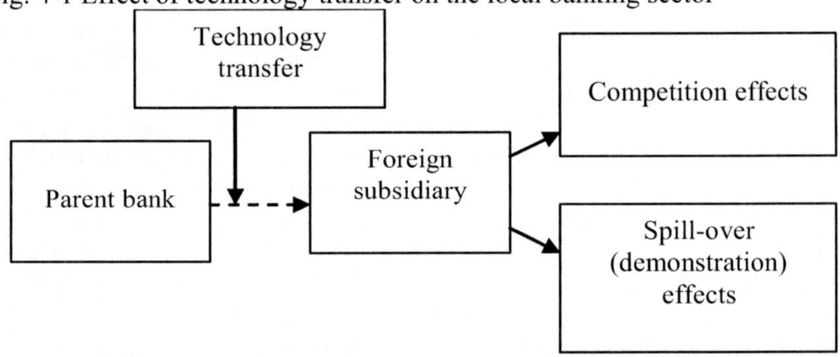

The most comprehensive empirical survey about foreign banks entry was carried out by Claessens *et al.* (2001) who investigated the relationship between foreign banks entry and the performance of the domestic banking sector in 80 countries. They used panel estimations with 7,900 bank observations from 1988–95. The main result of the study was that foreign banks tend to have higher profits than domestic banks in the developing countries, while in developed countries foreign banks are less profitable than domestic banks. Their results also indicated that a higher foreign bank presence is related to the lower profitability, costs and margins of domestic banks.

Hermes and Lensink (2003) further developed the model used by Claessens *et al.* (2001). They used bank-level accounting data from 990 banks in 48 countries for the period 1990–96. Threshold estimations were used to study how foreign banks entry effects are related, in the short term, to the economic development of the countries involved. The results indicated that at a lower level of economic development, foreign banks entry was associated with higher costs and margins for domestic banks. At a higher level of economic development, on the other hand, foreign banks entry had a less significant effect on domestic banks profitability. This result adds some support to the technology gap hypothesis.

Zajc (2004) analysed foreign banks entry effects on domestic banks in the Czech Republic, Estonia, Hungary, Poland, Slovakia and Slovenia for the period 1995–2000. His results are somewhat different from those presented by Claessens *et al.* (2001). He found that foreign bank entry was associated with lower non-interest income but increased overhead expenses.

Mathieson and Roldos (2001) pointed out two related issues: whether the presence of foreign banks makes systemic banking crises more or less likely to occur, and whether there is a tendency for foreign banks to "cut and run" during the crises periods. In general, it has been suggested that foreign banks can provide a more stable source of credit because branches and subsidiaries of large international banks can draw on their parent (which typically hold more diversified portfolios) for additional funding. Large international banks are likely to have better access to global financial markets and the entry of foreign banks can improve the overall stability of the host country's banking system (stronger prudential supervision; better disclosure, accounting and reporting practice, etc.).

Bonin and Ábel (2000) stated that foreign bank entry is a double-edged sword. It is welfare enhancing for the host country's banking sector as a whole but often threatens the market position of already weak domestic banks because foreign banks usually take away good clients from them. Cárdenas *et al.* (2002) suggest that along with better services and management techniques, there can also be some adverse effects of foreign control. Foreign subsidiaries are often centrally controlled and are supposed to focus only on local market, not on international activities. This can be harmful for subsidiary's stability if there is a shock in the local market as their asset portfolio is concentrated in the local market.

One of the important issues of foreign bank entry is a possible reduction of credit in the host country. For example Weller (2000) found that foreign bank entry led to a reduction of the credit supply by Polish domestic banks. Clarke *et al.* (2005) concluded that the privatisation and foreign bank entry were not negatively associated with the credit supply in Argentina, at least not in the long term.

The Effect of Foreign Bank Entry on Bank Performance in the CEE Countries

In this chapter, we use both bank-level and macro-level data to investigate the relationship between foreign bank entry and their performance. A foreign bank is defined as foreign if it is at least 50 per cent foreign owned, that is, more than 50 per cent of its share capital is owned by foreign residents. The study covers the 1995–2001 data of 10 countries: Bulgaria, Croatia, the Czech Republic, Estonia, Hungary Latvia, Lithuania, Poland, Slovakia and Slovenia. The annual data is used in the following subgroups: bank-level accounting data, foreign banks entry data, the country's specific variables and the banking market development data. A detailed description of all variables used in the analysis is given in Appendix 4-A.

Bank-level accounting data was obtained from the BankScope database; panel data for 319 banks during 1995–2001 was used. An important difference between the current and previous studies is that both foreign and domestic banks are included in the sample. Several balance sheet variables and profit statement variables are used. First, we use two variables measuring the income of banks: net interest margin (*NIM*) and non-interest income to total assets (*OOITA*). Second, a bank's profitability is characterised by the ratio of its before-tax profits to total assets (*PTPTA*). Third, a bank's costs are measured by two variables: overhead costs to total assets (*OHTA*) and loan loss provisions to total assets (*LLPTA*). These variables are calculated on the basis of the bank's income statement and balance sheet. The following internationally comparable accounting identity is used:

$$PTPTA = NIM + OOITA - OHTA - LLPTA. \tag{4.1}$$

The bank-specific exogenous variables are as follows: short-term and long-term deposits and other funding to total assets (*CSTFTA*), equity ratio to total assets (*ETA*), and non-earning assets to total assets (*NEATA*).

We use two different foreign entry variables: the share of foreign bank assets in the total banking market assets (*FSA*), and the ratio of foreign banks to the total number of banks (*FBSN*). Since BankScope covers about 90 per cent of the banks on the market and the precise ownership structure of a bank is described only in the last reporting period, it is not possible to calculate foreign ownership by aggregating the data of the reporting banks, because of the danger to either overestimate or underestimate the proportion of foreign ownership on the market. The possibility to overestimate foreign ownership comes from the fact that foreign banks are more active internationally and also provide data more actively to BankScope. The possibility to underestimate foreign ownership in some countries is also quite high because BankScope does not cover branches of foreign banks. Therefore, the countries where the main foreign bank entry mode has been branches will tend to significantly underestimate foreign ownership on the market. The problem of data is more relevant for small countries like Estonia, Latvia and Lithuania, where the number of banks is small, and the absence of even two or three banks from the database may significantly affect foreign ownership data. To overcome these problems, different sources of data were used. Foreign banks' share in the total assets (*FSA*) data was drawn from BankScope and national central banks, while foreign banks' share in the total number of banks (*FBSN*) was obtained from the EBRD Transition Report 2003.

The development of the banking sector is characterised by the ratio of domestic private credit to the GDP (*DCGDP*). This is a widely used measure of banking sector development, as stated by Hermes and Lensink (2003). Another banking-market-specific variable used is the concentration index, calculated as the ratio of three biggest bank's assets to total banking market assets in the given country (*CONC*). Market concentration data is obtained from the database provided by the website of A. Demirgüç–Kunt from World Bank. The *DCGDP* data is extracted from the EBRD Transition report 2002.

Three country-specific variables are included. Similarly to Claessens *et al.* (2001), Hermes and Lensink (2003), and Zajc (2004) the real GDP growth (*GDPG*), GDP per capita (*INCOME*, in logarithm) and inflation rate (*CPI*) are included as indicators of macroeconomic development. All country variables were obtained from the EBRD Transition Report 2002. The sample is unbalanced because of the lack of data for some banks in some periods. The number of observations varies between 884 and 1041.

Next the short-term relationship between foreign banks entry and bank performance is tested empirically. The analysis starts with the empirical model which is similar to that used by Claessens *et al.* (2001):

$$\Delta I_{ijt} = \alpha_0 + \beta_j \Delta FS_{jt} + \delta_{ij} \Delta B_{ijt} + \gamma_j \Delta X_{jt} + \varepsilon_{ijt}, \qquad (4.2)$$

where I_{ijt} is a vector of dependent variables for bank i in country j at time t, FS_{jt} is a measure of foreign bank penetration in country j at time t, B_{ijt} is a set of bank-specific variables for bank i in country j at time t. B_{ijt} is included in the equation as a set of control variables. X_{jt} is a vector of country variables in country j at time t.

Then the initial empirical model characterised by equation (4.2) is developed further, adding banking market development variables and an interactive term of foreign banks entry and banking market development; the same methodology was also used by Hermes and Lensink (2003). The model involving banking sector development and interactive term is as follows:

$$\begin{aligned}\Delta I_{ijt} &= \alpha_0 + \beta_j \Delta FS_{jt} + \gamma_j \Delta FS_{jt} \cdot DCGDP_{jt} + \delta_{ij} \Delta B_{ijt} + \\ &+ \varphi_j BMD_{jt} + \varepsilon_j \Delta X_{jt} + \varepsilon_{ijt},\end{aligned} \qquad (4.3)$$

where $DC{\cdot}GDP_{jt}$ is a proxy for banking market development in country j at time t, *FS*DCGDP* is a variable that has been created by interacting the foreign banks entry variable with the banking market development variable.

The interactive term is included to test whether foreign banks entry effects in a particular country depend on the level of development of that country's banking market. One can expect that foreign banks entry has a more relevant impact in the early stage of internationalisation and to be lower when the banking market in the target country is well-developed. It may even be the case that the sign of the coefficient of *FS* changes from negative to positive and vice versa. The banking market development variables are expected to have a negative effect on the cost and income of a bank.

Finally, the interactive term of foreign banks entry and bank market share are included in the equation. Banks with different market shares may not react similarly to the foreign banks entry. We suggest that smaller banks react more actively, because they are more flexible to changes in market conditions and have to adjust themselves more readily in order to be competitive. The model is defined as follows:

$$\begin{aligned} \Delta I_{ijt} = \alpha_0 + \beta_j \Delta FS_{jt} + \gamma_j \Delta FS_{jt} \cdot MSHARE_{jt} + \delta_{ij} \Delta B_{ijt} + \\ + \varphi_j BMD_{jt} + \varepsilon_j \Delta X_{jt} + \varepsilon_{ijt}, \end{aligned} \tag{4.4}$$

where *FS·MSHARE* is a variable that has been created by interacting the foreign banks entry variable with the banking market development variable. Two variables are used to measure foreign banks presence: the number of foreign banks as the share of the total number of banks (*FBSN*) and foreign banks share in the total assets of the banking market (*FSA*). The interactive terms with private credit to the GDP (*DCGDP*) and the bank market share (*MSHARE*) are also included. Five bank performance measures (*ALINT* (interest income on interest earning assets), *PTPTA*, *OOITA*, *OHTA* and *LLPTA*) are the main dependent variables. The software package Stata SE 8 was used for estimations.

Compared with Claessens *et al.* (2001), who used a fixed effects model, the methodology for estimating regression coefficients is somewhat different. The Arellano–Bond linear dynamic panel data estimation technique is implemented which enables one to use a lagged term of dependent variable as exogenous variable. Moreover, the instrumental variables (Arellano and Bond, 1991) are applied to reduce the endogeneity problem and get more consistent estimates. To reduce the heteroskedasticity which often affects data in micro-level panels, robust standard errors are reported (Stata, 2003). Robust standard errors are higher and therefore relationships are statistically less significant.

It is a general assumption that foreign banks entry at time *t* is exogenous. It means that *FBSN* or *FSA* does not depend on bank-specific variables at time *t* (Zajc, 2004). In practice, foreign banks entry may be associated with timing, thus a bank enters the market in year *t* because of the market conditions in period *t*. It may be the case that foreign banks are entering by acquisition at time *t* because of the crisis period of a single bank or the entire banking market in order to acquire banks at a low price. It can be argued that this makes foreign banks entry partly endogenous. The endogenity problem here is not very strong, because all variables are in first differences. Nevertheless, some endogeneity may remain because occasionally foreign banks consider the average performance of the entire market in period *t* when making entry decisions.

To reduce possible endogeneity problems in estimations, it is suggested that levels of lag operators can be used (Stata, 2003). Levels of lag operators of foreign banks entry variables (one period lag of *FBSN* and *FSA*) are included as instrument variables.

An important difference between this study and previous works is that we analyse foreign banks entry effects on both foreign and domestic banks' performance. The first differences of variables ensure that the observations of a foreign bank entering the market at time *t* are not included. Yearly time dummies (1996–2001) are included into the estimations, while regression coefficients of time dummies are not reported. Arellano–Bond estimations also include tests of autocorrelations AR(1) and AR(2) that are not reported. Autocorrelation was not significantly present in the regressions except for *ALINT*. The estimation results with *FBSN* as the foreign banks entry variable are given in Table 4-1.

Foreign banks entry variable *FBSN* has a statistically significant and negative effect on the bank's average interest rate on earning assets and loan loss provisions (*LLPTA*). The author tested the foreign banks entry effect also on the bank's net interest margin, but found no statistically significant relation. Therefore *ALINT* was used to analyse the effect on interest revenues. It seems that foreign banks entry has a significant effect only on interest income of interest earning assets and not on interest expense. Hermes and Lensink (2003) found a positive and significant effect of *FBSN* on non-interest income, whereas Zajc (2004) found results similar to our findings. A negative relationship with profitability measures indicates that foreign banks entry enhances the level of competition in the banking sector.

A negative relationship between *FBSN* and *LLPTA* shows that foreign banks entry leads to more strict lending policies of the local banks. *FBSN* is not statistically associated with profits, overhead costs and non-interest income of banks. The banking market concentration index was excluded from the regression equations because of no significant effect on any dependent variables.

Table 4-1 Foreign banks entry (FBSN) effect on banks performance

Variable	D(ALINT)	D(PTPTA)	D(OOITA)	D(OHTA)	D(LLPTA)
LD(DEP)	0.0185 (0.0238)	0.1898 (0.1304)	0.0217 (0.0961)	0.3240 (0.2795)	0.2061* (0.1096)
D(FBSN)	-0.128*** (0.0387)	-0.0252 (0.0408)	-0.0583 (0.0713)	-0.0024 (0.0503)	-0.0700* (0.0409)
D(NEATA)	0.1109* (0.0603)	0.0355 (0.0414)	0.4998* (0.2979)	0.4282 (0.3328)	-0.0251 (0.0773)
D(ETA)	-0.1535 (0.1027)	0.3968*** (0.1310)	-0.0244 (0.3568)	-0.2211 (0.3459)	0.0100 (0.0964)
D(CSTFTA)	-0.0242 (0.0345)	0.0543 (0.0369)	0.1437 (0.0886)	0.0100 (0.0767)	0.0498 (0.0416)
D(MSHARE)	0.1722 (0.1698)	0.2006* (0.1089)	-0.6116** (0.3001)	-0.6354* (0.3334)	-0.1750* (0.1032)
FD	0.0119 (0.0147)	-0.0347 (0.0295)	0.0086 (0.0579)	0.0347 (0.0677)	0.0249 (0.0226)
D(DCGDP)	-0.0247** (0.0295)	0.0574 (0.0505)	0.5085*** (0.1736)	0.5294* (0.3165)	0.1648*** (0.0610)
D(GGDP)	-0.470*** (0.1669)	-0.0125 (0.1186)	-0.3006** (0.1462)	-0.4822* (0.2508)	-0.0464 (0.1218)
D(LNIN-COME)	0.0039 (0.0440)	-0.0072 (0.0488)	-0.2695** (0.1293)	-0.2694* (0.1454)	-0.0651 (0.0519)
D(CPI)	-0.0036 (0.0033)	0.0051 (0.0043)	0.0344 (0.0266)	0.0103 (0.0259)	0.0026 (0.0018)
D(MMR)	0.0322 (0.0480)	NA	NA	NA	NA
No. observat.	1036	1041	1035	2021	895
F-Statistic	4.13	2.91	2.08	1.29	2.60

Note: LD(DEP): one lag first difference of the dependent variable;
*, **, *** denote significance at 10 per cent, 5 per cent, 1 per cent level respectively;
standard errors in parentheses.

Source: Author's calculations

FSA has a somewhat different effect on banks performance. The estimation results in Table 4-2 show that FSA has a negative effect on the average loan interest rate and a positive effect on loan loss provisions. *FSA* reflects the relative size of foreign banks compared to domestic banks.

The estimation results indicate that if entering foreign banks are comparatively larger than the local banks, then due to the increasing competition on the loan market, the banks offer better loan conditions to firms, which could result in increasing loan losses. From other explanatory variables, *MSHARE* is negatively associated with overhead costs and non-interest income and positively associated with profits. The results indicate that larger banks are able to achieve some economies of scale.

Table 4-2 Foreign banks entry (FSA) effect on banks performance

Variable	D(ALINT)	D(PTPTA)	D(OOITA)	D(OHTA)	D(LLPTA)
LD(DEP)	0.0167 (0.0223)	0.1809 (0.1274)	0.0537 (0.1099)	0.3541 (0.2848)	0.2162** (0.1112)
D(FSA)	-0.0417** (0.0168)	-0.0203 (0.0145)	0.0512 (0.0340)	0.0617 (0.0478)	0.0251** (0.0117)
D(NEATA)	0.1116* (0.0594)	0.0379 (0.0425)	0.5076* (0.3065)	0.4375 (0.3451)	-0.0253 (0.0791)
D(ETA)	-0.1648 (0.1036)	0.3966*** (0.1315)	-0.0321 (0.3647)	-0.2304 80.3555)	0.0101 (0.0957)
D(CSTFTA)	-0.0285 (0.0316)	0.0495 (0.0370)	0.1345 (0.0889)	-0.0029 80.0796)	0.0469 (0.0403)
D(MSHARE)	0.2048 (0.1695)	0.2166 (0.1135)	-0.6168** (0.3141)	-0.6512* (0.3422)	-0.1766* (0.0963)
FD	0.0125 (0.0193)	-0.0284 (0.0308)	-0.0067 (0.0539)	0.0227 (0.0648)	0.0140 (0.0187)
D(DCGDP)	0.0088 (0.0340)	0.0598 (0.0472)	0.5347*** (0.1814)	0.5350 (0.3362)	0.1897*** (0.0641)
D(GGDP)	-0.475*** (0.1681)	-0.0120 (0.1133)	-0.3154** (0.1453)	-0.4654** (0.2470)	-0.0700 (0.1092)
D(LNIN-COME)	0.0280 (0.0447)	0.0018 (0.0503)	-0.2905** (0.1367)	-0.2909** (0.1591)	-0.0675 (0.0523)
D(CPI)	-0.0028 (0.0031)	0.0054 (0.0043)	0.0347 (0.0261)	0.0104 (0.0264)	0.0037* (0.0020)
D(MMR)	0.0703 (0.0463)	NA	NA	NA	NA
No. observat.	1023	1028	1022	1009	884
F-Statistic	3.63	3.57	1.75	1.26	2.88

Note: LD(DEP): one lag first difference of the dependent variable;
*, **, *** denote significance at 10 per cent, 5 per cent, 1 per cent level respectively;
standard errors in parentheses.

Source: Author's calculations

The estimation results with interactive term with foreign ownership (*FBSN*) and banking sector development are presented in Table 4-3. The results indicate that the development of the banking sector has some impact on the short-term foreign banks entry effects. As indicated previously, foreign banks entry is generally associated with decreasing interest income. Estimations with interactive term *FBSN·DCGDP* show that in more developed banking markets this fall in interest revenue is lower, because interest rates are already more converged with developed markets.

Table 4-3 Foreign banks entry (FBSN) effects: role of the banking market development

Variable	D(ALINT)	D(PTPTA)	D(OOITA)	D(OHTA)	D(LLPTA)
LD(DEP)	0.0165 (0.0220)	0.1916 (0.1302)	0.0450 (0.1183)	0.3229 (0.2899)	0.2013* (0.1095)
D(FBSN)	-0.229*** (0.0820)	0.0617 (0.0790)	0.3104 (0.2312)	0.3382* (0.2036)	-0.0388 (0.0845)
D(FBSN· DCGDP)	0.3620** (0.1768)	-0.2922* (0.1644)	-1.2258** (0.5979)	-1.1266* (0.6814)	-0.1072 (0.1862)
D(NEATA)	0.1008* (0.0609)	0.0408 (0.0413)	0.5233* (0.3022)	0.4417 (0.3260)	-0.0251 (0.0786)
D(ETA)	-0.1497 (0.1008)	0.3929*** (0.1316)	-0.0455 (0.3722)	-0.2406 (0.3540)	0.0091 (0.0972)
D(CSTFTA)	-0.0233 (0.0341)	0.0535 (0.0371)	0.1394 (0.0892)	0.0075 (0.0757)	0.0491 (0.0414)
D(MSHARE)	0.1581 (0.1731)	0.2099** (0.1043)	-0.5791** (0.2922)	-0.6052* (0.3291)	-0.1727* (0.1021)
FD	0.0083 (0.0146)	-0.0345 (0.0291)	0.0094 (0.0609)	0.0362 (0.0699)	0.0253 (0.0225)
D(DCGDP)	-0.1552** (0.0751)	0.1395 (0.0858)	0.8693*** (0.3375)	0.8543* (0.5093)	0.1952* (0.0925)
D(GGDP)	-0.425*** (0.1514)	-0.0146 (0.1196)	-0.3061** (0.1466)	-0.4932** (0.2479)	-0.0561 (0.1268)
D(LNIN- COME)	0.0191 (0.0463)	-0.0013 (0.0468)	-0.2621** (0.1269)	-0.2606* (0.1431)	-0.0610 (0.0518)
D(CPI)	-0.0063 (0.0041)	0.0067 (0.0042)	0.0404 (0.0287)	0.0164 (0.0277)	0.0033* (0.0018)
D(MMR)	0.0702* (0.0402)	NA	NA	NA	NA
No. observat.	1036	1041	1035	1021	895
F-Statistic	4.02	2.97	1.85	1.2	2.63

Note: LD(DEP): one lag first difference of the dependent variable;
*, **, *** denote significance at 10 per cent, 5 per cent, 1 per cent level respectively;
standard errors in parentheses.

Source: Author's calculations

The *FSA·DCGDP* variable has a significant effect on average loan interest rates, pre-tax profits and non-interest income. Foreign banks entry reduces the profitability of the local banks, but in more developed markets this decline is lower because the entering bank does not have such a high competitive advantage as in less developed countries (Table 4-4).

Table 4-4 Foreign banks entry (FSA) effects: role of the banking market development

Variable	D(ALINT)	D(PTPTA)	D(OOITA)	D(OHTA)	D(LLPTA)
LD(DEP)	0.0160 (0.0220)	0.1805 (0.1264)	0.1391 (0.1446)	0.4027 (0.3073)	0.2184** (0.1117)
D(FSA)	0.0651* (0.0347)	-0.137*** (0.0387)	-0.3075** (0.1248)	-0.2444 (0.1864)	-0.0235 (0.0409)
D(FSA·DCGDP)	-0.337*** (0.1066)	0.3512*** (0.1135)	1.0882** (0.4342)	0.9311 (0.6640)	0.1476 (0.1287)
D(NEATA)	0.1103* (0.0588)	0.0382 (0.0414)	0.5074 (0.3104)	0.4342 (0.3474)	-0.0266 (0.0779)
D(ETA)	-0.1665 (0.1036)	0.3948*** (0.1309)	-0.0314 (0.3819)	-0.2306 (0.3653)	0.0114 (0.0960)
D(CSTFTA)	-0.0282 (0.0314)	0.0492 (0.0368)	0.1318 (0.0914)	-0.0064 (0.0820)	0.0469 (0.0402)
D(MSHARE)	0.2130 (0.1696)	0.2043* (0.1106)	-0.6698** (0.3350)	-0.6962* (0.3746)	-0.1838* (0.0989)
FD	0.0109 (0.0167)	-0.0286 (0.0376)	0.0019 (0.0389)	0.0301 (0.0564)	0.0144 (0.0166)
D(DCGDP)	0.1894*** (0.0738)	-0.169*** (0.0569)	-0.1452** (0.1361)	-0.0507 (0.1324)	0.0989 (0.0539)
D(GGDP)	-0.415*** (0.1570)	-0.0095 (0.1121)	-0.3574 (0.1718)	-0.4927** (0.2740)	-0.0690 (0.1094)
D(LNIN-COME)	-0.0017 (0.0450)	0.0530 (0.0491)	-0.1173 (0.0771)	-0.1498* (0.0752)	-0.0476 (0.0459)
D(CPI)	-0.0057* (0.0034)	0.0071* (0.0043)	0.0376 (0.0280)	0.0136 (0.0288)	0.0044** (0.0022)
D(MMR)	0.1173*** (0.0433)	NA	NA	NA	NA
No. observat.	1023	1028	1022	1009	884
F-Statistic	4.53	3.93	1.32	1.36	3.00

Note: LD(DEP): one lag first difference of the dependent variable;
*, **, *** denote significance at 10 per cent, 5 per cent, 1 per cent level respectively;
standard errors in parentheses.

Source: Author's calculations

The development of the banking market has also some effect on banks overhead costs. The results indicate that in countries with a lower level of financial sector development, foreign banks entry is more related with higher overhead costs. Nevertheless, for countries with a higher level of financial sector development, foreign banks entry causes less and less extra costs for banks because the banking system is already developed and fewer additional investments are needed to upgrade the banking equipment.

The results show that foreign banks entry reduces non-interest income of the local banks, but the coefficient may turn positive in more developed markets, where competition is more intense. One reason for the limited role of the banking sector development on the foreign banks entry effects can be found in the homogenous sample of countries. Generally, lags of difference of the dependent variables do not have statistically significant coefficients. Considering other explanatory variables, the ratio of bank equity to total assets is positively correlated with bank profits.

Next, the interactive term with foreign banks entry variable and a bank's market share is introduced. It can be expected that small banks react to foreign banks entry somewhat differently from large banks. Obviously, banks having a higher market share react less to foreign banks entry. This is so because they are too big to react so quickly and banks with high market share may care less about foreign entry since it affects them less than small banks.

The estimation results in Table 4-5 show that the role of the bank's market share in the foreign banks entry effects is very limited. The interactive term *FBSN·MSHARE* has a statistically significant negative effect on non-interest income and loan loss provisions. Bigger banks tend to have lower loss provisions, indicating that they have comparably more creditworthy clients and/or a better credit risk policy. Since no significant coefficient for *FSA·MSHARE* was found, those results are not reported.

The results are consistent with earlier studies. However, some differences do exist. It can be generalized that foreign banks entry is negatively correlated with the income variables (*ALINT*, *PTPTA*, and *OOITA*) and foreign banks entry is also negatively associated with loan loss provisions. Overhead costs are positively correlated with *FBSN*, but the increase is less important for countries with higher *DCGDP*. Therefore, the results support the technology gap hypothesis. Hermes and Lensink (2003) and Zajc (2004) also found positive and significant effects of foreign banks entry on overhead costs. In most studies, foreign banks entry is negatively correlated with non-interest income. However, Hermes and Lensink (2003) found positive and significant correlation between these two variables.

Table 4-5 Foreign banks entry (FBSN) and bank performance: role of a bank's market share

Variable	D(ALINT)	D(PTPTA)	D(OOITA)	D(OHTA)	D(LLPTA)
LD(DEP)	0.0184 (0.0238)	0.1876 (0.1299)	0.0307 (0.0989)	0.3429 (0.2916)	0.2015* (0.1079)
D(FBSN)	-0.117*** (0.0415)	-0.0103 (0.0419)	-0.1275** (0.0642)	-0.0816 (0.0822)	-0.1008** (0.0426)
D(FBSN· MSHARE)	-0.1664 (0.2358)	-0.2505 (0.1551)	1.1796* (0.6216)	1.3582 (0.9280)	0.4665*** (0.1414)
D(NEATA)	0.1103* (0.0601)	0.0348 (0.0413)	0.5029* (0.2977)	0.4302 (0.3335)	-0.0236 (0.0760)
D(ETA)	-0.1542 (0.1026)	0.3968*** (0.1310)	-0.0243 (0.3582)	-0.2209 (0.3504)	0.0103 (0.0961)
D(CSTFTA)	-0.0253 (0.0346)	0.0534 (0.0371)	0.1482* (0.0885)	0.0148 (0.0760)	0.0517 (0.0413)
D(MSHARE)	0.2071 (0.2053)	0.2526** (0.1083)	-0.8549** (0.4245)	-0.9185* (0.5143)	-0.2989** (0.1204)
FD	0.0162 (0.0110)	-0.0246 (0.0262)	-0.0401 (0.0380)	-0.0245 (0.0315)	0.0084 (0.0134)
D(DCGDP)	-0.0259 (0.0290)	0.0561 (0.0506)	0.5178*** (0.1736)	0.5461* (0.3270)	0.1717*** (0.0606)
D(GGDP)	-0.465*** (0.1693)	-0.0080 (0.1194)	-0.3201** (0.1529)	-0.5040* (0.2648)	-0.0542 (0.1203)
D(LNIN-COME)	0.0051 (0.0447)	-0.0054 (0.0488)	-0.2790** (0.1318)	-0.2819* (0.1527)	-0.0721 (0.0521)
D(CPI)	-0.0036 (0.0033)	0.0052 (0.0043)	0.0339 (0.0265)	0.0096 (0.0258)	0.0024 (0.0018)
D(MMR)	0.0335 (0.0484)	NA	NA	NA	NA
No. observat.	1036	1041	1035	1021	895
F-Statistic	4.27	3.87	2.1	1.24	2.59

Note: LD(DEP): one lag first difference of the dependent variable;
*, **, *** denote significance at 10 per cent, 5 per cent, 1 per cent level respectively;
standard errors in parentheses.

Source: Author's calculations

The Effect of Foreign Bank Entry on Stability of Banks in the CEE Countries

One of the main issues of the banking market development in transition countries is the level of financial intermediation and the volume of credit disbursed to the private sector. Despite the rapid growth of banking markets in transition countries, the level of financial intermediation remains relatively low, compared with the EMU, where the average ratio of bank credit to private sector to GDP is about 150 per cent (Thimann, 2002). The credit supply growth and loan loss provisions are analyzed as indicators of banking market stability.

To analyse whether foreign banks have more stable credit supply growth in the CEE countries, the mean values and standard deviations of the credit growth in each country were calculated. The credit growth is calculated based on bank level data from the BankScope database. Bank market shares are used as weights to calculate the average credit supply growth. The standard deviation of credit growth of foreign and domestic banks in 1995 to 2003 is reported in Figure 4-2. The volatility of credit growth among foreign and domestic banks was quite equal. The average standard deviation of the credit supply growth in the CEE countries for domestic banks is 0.15 and 0.14 for foreign banks respectively. Nevertheless, Figure 4-2 shows that in majority of the CEE countries the volatility of credit supply of foreign banks is lower than the volatility of domestic banks.

Fig. 4-2 Standard deviation of credit growth in the CEE countries

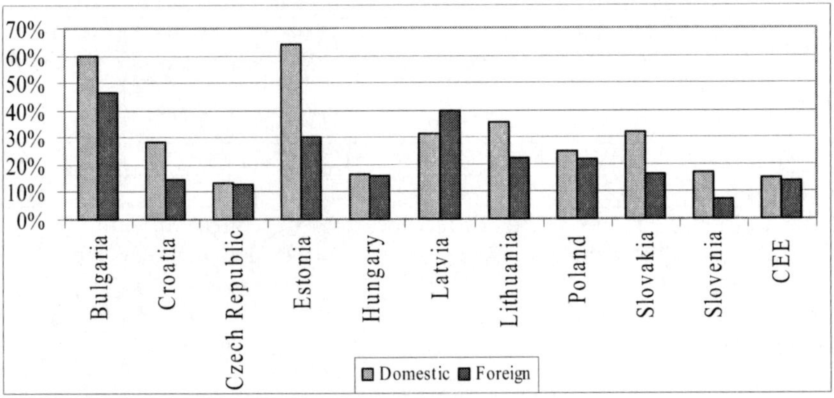

Source: BankScope 2005, author's calculations

The following conclusion can be drawn. Foreign banks contributed to the stability of the credit supply in the CEE countries during crises, although the differences of credit supply volatility are rather marginal. Further studies are required to get deeper understanding of the effects of foreign banks entry on credit market stability.

As the regression analysis presented above shows, a more detailed analysis of foreign banks entry effect on loan losses of local banks is required since current results are mixed. Therefore, all the regressions were recalculated. In the final version of regressions, the only significant bank level independent variable is the bank market share *D(MSHARE)*. The accounting variables do not have a statistically significant effect on the dependent variable *D(LLPTA)*. This result indicates that accounting variables do not reflect the credit risk of a bank.

The estimation results in Table 4-6 and column A suggest that foreign banks entry in terms of number of foreign banks on the market has negative effect on banks loan loss provisions to total assets. This result is similar to Weller (2000), who showed that in the presence of foreign banks entry, local banks may reduce credit supply by applying more strict credit conditions to firms because of their comparatively weak financial situation and fear of bankruptcy. The negative relationship between foreign bank entry and banks loan loss provisions can be also interpreted as a positive effect of foreign bank entry on banking market stability.

In column B, the regression results with combination of foreign entry and bank market share *D(FBSN·MSHARE)* is introduced. The regression estimation shows that banks with higher market share have less loan loss provisions to total assets and react less intensively on foreign bank entry. This can be concluded from column B, where the regression coefficient for *D(FBSN·MSHARE)* is positive but the regression coefficients for *D(FBSN)* and for *D(MSHARE)* are negative.

The foreign bank entry variable *D(FSA)* does not have statistically a significant effect on banks loan loss provisions in the regressions. The results are reported in column C. The results in column D show that domestic banks react similarly to the foreign banks entry as does the entire sample. The most significant difference is that the regression coefficient of *MSHARE* in column D is -0.449, while it is -0.11 in the regression presented in column A. This result indicates that market share (as well as size) is an important determinant of loan losses for the domestic banks. Larger domestic banks have lower loan loss provisions, that is, their loan portfolio quality is higher.

Table 4-6 Effects of foreign banks entry on loan loss provisions of banks

Variable	D(LLPTA) A	D(LLPTA) B	D(LLPTA) C	D(LLPTA) D
LD(DEP)	0.159*** (5.59)	0.156*** (5.47)	0.171*** (5.93)	0.1578*** (4.18)
D(FBSN)	-0.076*** (-3.53)	-0.095*** (-4.15)	NA	-0.150*** (-4.00)
D(FSA)	NA	NA	0.018 (1.33)	NA
D(FBSN·MSHARE)	NA	0.305** (2.11)	NA	NA
D(MSHARE)	-0.111* (-1.68)	-0.188** (-2.38)	-0.107 (1.60)	-0.449*** (-2.54)
D(DCGDP)	0.184*** (4.30)	0.184*** (4.32)	0.213*** (5.08)	0.2470*** (2.99)
D(CONC)	0.057* (1.80)	0.052* (1.63)	0.039 (1.16)	0.06652 (1.28)
C	0.005 (1.52)	0.003 (1.55)	(-0.003)*** (-2.85)	0.0059* (1.86)
No. observat.	897	897	886	469
F-Statistic	15.9	14.4	14.69	9.90
Wald Chi^2	95.47	100.45	88.13	59.43

Note: LD(DEP): one lag first difference of the dependent variable;
*, **, *** denote significance at 10 per cent, 5 per cent, 1 per cent level respectively;
standard errors in parentheses.

Source: Author's calculations

The regression coefficient for *D(DCGDP)* is positive in all regressions, indicating that higher private sector credit is associated with higher loan loss provisions to total assets. The interpretation of this result can be twofold. If we take *DCGDP* as the indicator of banking market development, like in Hermes and Lensink (2003), the higher average loan loss provisions to total assets of banks would be associated with a higher stage of the banking market development. The second possible interpretation is that in transition countries with higher private sector debt to GDP, there are higher average loan loss provisions to total assets of banks.

The results show that banking market concentration *D(CONC)* is positively associated with banks loan loss provisions to total assets. An interpretation of that result for transition countries where major banks are foreign owned could be that the large foreign banks focus on creditworthy and less risky firms and leave more risky credit projects to smaller domestic banks.

The general conclusion of this section is that foreign banks entry tends to be negatively associated with banks loan loss provisions. It indicates that the foreign banks entry is contributing to banking market stability in the transition countries.

Results of the Survey

In order to analyze the effect of foreign banks entry into the CEE countries from another point of view, a survey has been carried out. A special questionnaire has been designed to study various aspects of bank internationalisation in the CEE countries using the experience and lessons of previous analogous studies (see Konopielko, 1999; Kraft and Galac, 2000; Pomerleano and Vojta, 2001). A survey of foreign and domestic banks was carried out in 2001–02 in Estonia (ES), Lithuania (LI), Poland (PO), and Romania (RO). Some comparative data was also available from the analogous Croatian (CR) study (Kraft and Galac, 2000).

The transfer of various types of know-how from foreign banks has been important, especially for the management of domestic-owned banks (see Figure 4-3). The transfer of know-how about interest rates, solvency and credit risks management techniques was evaluated by respondents as being the highest (over 4.0 points by Estonian foreign bank respondents). Liquidity risk management techniques, information systems, credit policy and personnel policy transfer from foreign banks were also evaluated as being quite high by Estonian domestic banks. On the other hand, the average grades given by the responding Polish domestic banks were somewhat different. The transfer of information systems and banking services/products mix policy from foreign banks was considered to be of greatest importance (4.3 and 4.2 points, respectively). This difference between Estonia and Poland can be explained by the technology gap argument. Electronic banking and up-to-date computer technology are considered to be at a much higher level in Estonia than in other CEE countries. Therefore, the additional know-how transfer from the parent bank has not been as relevant. It is even frequently argued that the Estonian e-banking system is more advanced than the corresponding systems in many older, developed EU member countries.

Fig. 4-3 Evaluations of the parent bank policies and systems adoption

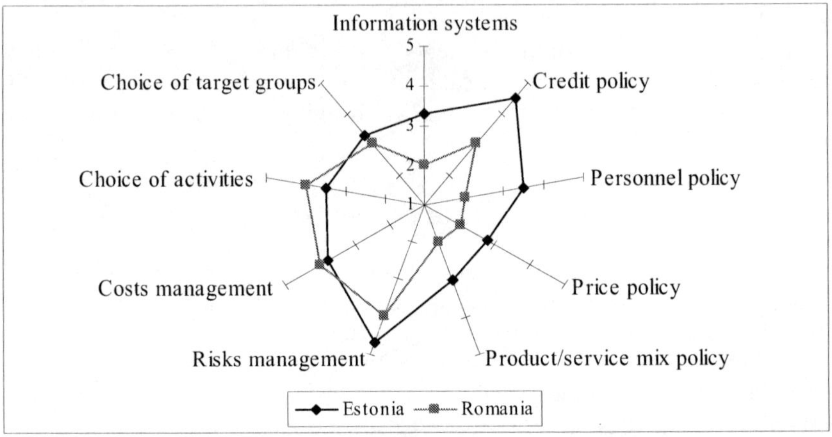

Source: Uiboupin (2005)

The impact of foreign banks entry into the observed CEE banking markets (as evaluated by the responding domestic banks) is presented in Figure 4-4. The results show that foreign banks entry significantly intensified the overall competition in the banking market (average grade 4.0 points in Estonia and Romania, 4.5 in Poland), reducing the domestic bank's profitability and efficiency of operation. All other impacts were evaluated by Estonian respondents as unimportant, among them, surprisingly, even corporate governance of private firms (average grade only 1.7 points).

Fig. 4-4 Impact of foreign banks entry into the host country's market

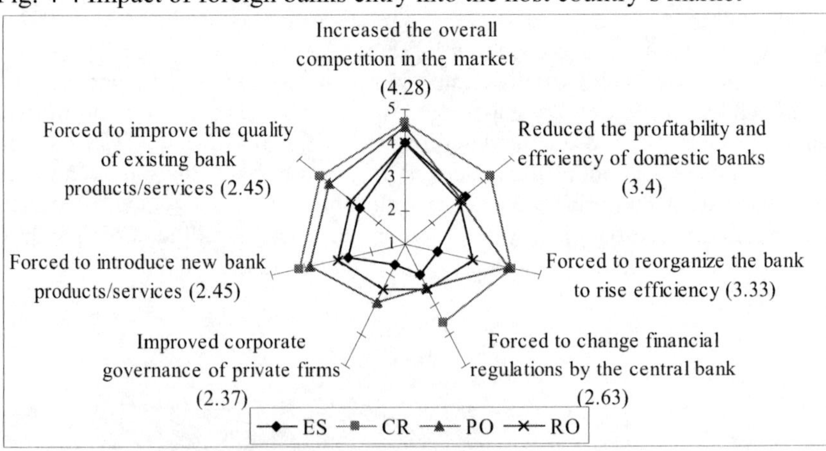

Source: Uiboupin (2005)

Polish respondents were of the opinion that foreign banks entry significantly forced banks to reorganize their internal structure in order to raise efficiency (4.1 points) as well as to introduce new banking products and services and improve the quality of the existing banking products (both 3.9 points). It is quite interesting that the Croatian respondents evaluated the impact of foreign banks entry into the Croatian banking market more highly than the respondents from other countries.

It is interesting to note that the average effect of foreign banks entry was clearly different in individual countries. It can be seen in Figure 4-4 that the general importance of the foreign banks entry impact is as follows (in descending order): Croatia, Poland, Romania, and Estonia. Seemingly, the general effect of foreign banks entry depends on market-specific factors. The Estonian banking market is comparatively more developed and so the overall effect of foreign banks has been evaluated as lower. Therefore, the technology gap hypothesis seems to hold.

Fig. 4-5 Degree of competitive pressure from foreign banks

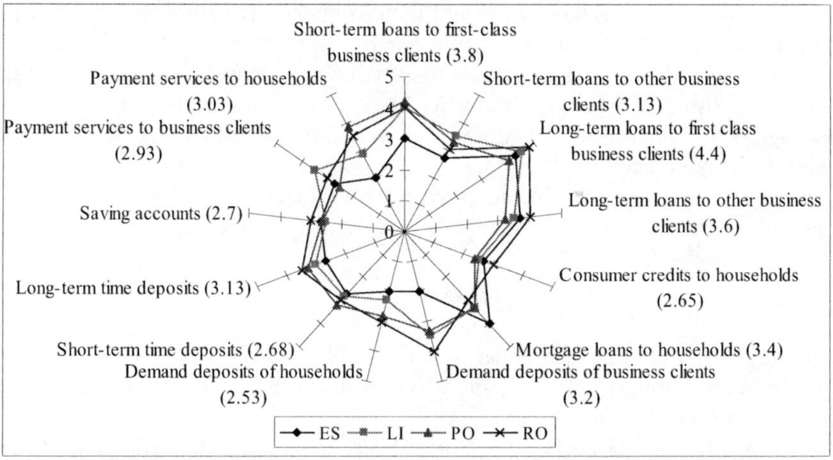

Source: Uiboupin (2005)

The responding domestic banks evaluations about the degree of competitive pressure resulting from foreign banks entry are given in Figure 4-5. Quite clearly, the long-term loans to first-class business clients (average grade 4.4 points) dominated among the other market segments. Mortgage loans to households (average grade 4.0 points) were mentioned as the most important market segments on the Estonian banking market that were influenced by the pressure from foreign banks. The Lithuanian, Polish and Romanian respondents' evaluations were somewhat different. The short-term loans to the first-class business clients were mentioned as the most important competitive market segment (average grades 4.0, 4.2, and 4.0 points respectively). Additionally, the Romanian respondents ranked highly the long-term loans to other business clients and demand deposits of business clients.

Conclusion

This chapter tries to shed light on some aspects of foreign banks entry in the CEE countries. We suggest that foreign banks entry can have both a competition and spill-over effect on the domestic banking sector in the CEE countries.

The negative competition effects of foreign banks entry were weaker in the countries whose banking market is more advanced. This finding indicates that the technology gap hypothesis holds in the CEE banking markets. The entry of foreign banks was positively correlated with the quality of loan portfolios of local banks. This result also supports the existence of the positive competition effect of foreign banks entry on the stability of domestic banks. Additionally, there were some positive spill-over effects of know-how transfer to local banks. The survey results indicate that the main technology spill-over from foreign to domestic banks has been in the field of risk management. Therefore, there is also a positive spill-over effect on the stability of domestic banks. The general conclusion of this study is that foreign banks entry is likely to have positive effects on transition banking markets by increasing the competition and stability of the banking sector.

References

Aitken, B.J. and A.E. Harrison. 1999. Do Domestic Firms Benefit from Direct Foreign Investment? Evidence from Venezuela. *American Economic Review* 89(3):605–18.

Arellano, M. and S. Bond. 1991. Some Tests of Specification for Panel Data: Monte-Carlo Evidence and an Application to Employment Equations. *The Review of Economic Studies* 58(2):277–97.

BankScope. January 2005. Fitch-IBCA & Bureau van Dijk.

Bonin, P. John, and Istvan Ábel. 2000. *Retail Banking in Hungary: A Foreign Affair?* Hungarian National Bank Working Paper 356. Budapest: Hungarian National Bank.

Borensztein, E., J. De Gregorio and J.W. Lee. 1998. How Does Foreign Direct Investment Affect Economic Growth? *Journal of International Economics*. 45(1):115–35.

Cárdenas, Juan, Juan P. Graf and Pascual O'Dogherty. 2003. *Foreign banks entry in emerging market economies: a host country perspective.* [online] Access from: http://www.bis.org/publ/cgfs22mexico.pdf (accessed October 15, 2005).

Claessens, S., A. Demirgüç–Kunt and H. Huizinga. 2001. How Does Foreign Entry Affect Domestic Banking Markets? *Journal of Banking and Finance* 25(5):891–911.

Clarke, G., J.M. Crivelly and R. Cull. 2005. The direct and indirect impact of bank privatization and foreign entry on access to credit in Argentina's provinces. *Journal of Banking and Finance* 29(1):5–29.

Demirgüç–Kunt, Asli, Ross Levine and Hong–Ghi Min. 1998. Opening to Foreign Banks. Issues of Stability, Efficiency, and Growth. In *The Implications of Globalization of World Financial Markets*, ed Seongtae Lee. Seoul: Bank of Korea.

Demirgüç–Kunt, Asli. 2004. *Financial Structure and Economic Development Database.* [online] Access from: http://www.worldbank.org/research/projects/Finstructure/database.htm (accessed December 12, 2004).

European Bank for Reconstruction and Development. 2003. *Transition Report 2002: Agriculture and rural development.* London: European Bank for Reconstruction and Development.

European Bank for Reconstruction and Development. 2004. *Transition Report 2003: Integration and regional cooperation.* London: European Bank for Reconstruction and Development.

Glass, A.J. and K. Saggi. 1998. International technology transfer and the technology gap. *Journal of Development Economics* 55(2):369–98.

Hermes, Niels and Robert Lensink. 2003. *Foreign bank presence, domestic bank performance and financial development.* Paper presented at the SUERF colloquium 2003.

Herrero, Alicia G. and Daniel N. Simón. 2003. *Determinants and impact of financial sector FDI to emerging economies: A home country's perspective.* [online] Access from: http://www.bis.org/publ/cgfs22bde2.pdf (accessed November 3, 2005)

International Monetary Fund. *International Financial Statistics Yearbook 2002.*

International Monetary Fund. *International Financial Statistics Yearbook 2003.*

Kokko, A. 1994. Technology, Market Characteristics and Spillovers. *Journal of Development Economics* 43(2):279–93.

Konings, Jozef. 1999. *The Effect of Direct Foreign Investment on Domestic Firms: Evidence from Firm Level Panel Data in Emerging Economies.* CEPR Discussion Paper 2586. mimeo.

Konopielko, L. 1999. Foreign Banks' Entry into Central and East European Markets: Motives and Activities. *Post-Communist Economies* 11(4): 463–85.

Kraft, Evan and Tomislav Galac. 2000. *The Impact of Foreign Banks on the Croatian Banking Market.* Paper presented at the 6th European Association of Comparative Economic Systems Conference in Barcelona, 7–9 September 2000.

Mathieson, Donald J. and Jorge Roldos. 2001. *The Role of Foreign Banks in Emerging Markets.* Paper presented at the World Bank, IMF, and Brookings Institution 3rd Annual Financial Markets and Development Conference in New York, 19–21 April 2001.

McKinnon, Ronald I. 1973. *Money and Capital in Economic Development.* Washington, D.C.: The Brookings Institution.

Petit, M.L. and F. Sanna–Randaccio. 2000. Endogenous R&D and foreign direct investment in international oligopolies. *International Journal of Industrial Organization* 18(2):339–67.

Pomerleano, Michael and George J. Vojta. 2001. *What Do Foreign Banks Do in Emerging Markets? An Institutional Study.* Paper presented at the World Bank, IMF, and Brookings Institution 3rd Annual Financial Markets and Development Conference in New York, 19–21 April 2001.

Shaw, Edward 1973. *Financial Deepening in Economic Development.* New York: Oxford University Press.

Stata Cross-Sectional Time-Series. 2003. Reference Manual, Release 8. Oregon: Stata Press.

Teece, J. D. 1977. Technology Transfer by Multinational Firms: The Resource Cost of Transferring Technological Know-How. *Economic Journal* 87(346):242–61.

Thimann, Christian ed. 2002. *Financial Sectors in EU Accession Countries.* Frankfurt am Main: European Central Bank.

Uiboupin, Janek. 2005. *Foreign Banks in Central and Eastern European Markets: Their Entry and Influence on the Banking Sector*. Doctoral dissertation. Tartu: Tartu University Press.

Weller, C. E. 2000. Financial Liberalization, Multinational Banks and Credit Supply: The Case of Poland. *International Review of Applied Economics* 14(2):193–211.

Zajc, Peter 2004. The effect of foreign bank entry on domestic banks in Central and Eastern Europe. In *Financial markets in Central and Eastern Europe*, ed. Moretn Balling, Frank Lierman and Andy Mullineux, 189–206. London: Routlege.

Appendix 4-A

List of variables used in the analysis

Variable	Source	Description
FBSN	Central banks, EBRD	Number of foreign banks as percentage of all banks in a given country and year
FSA	BankScope	Share of foreign banks assets in total banking market assets in a given country and year
FD	BankScope, bank web sites	Dummy variable with value 1 if bank is foreign-owned and 0 for domestic bank
NIM	BankScope	Net interest income (interest income minus interest expense) over total assets
ALINT	BankScope	Interest income to interest earning assets
PTPTA	BankScope	Before tax profit over total assets
OOITA	BankScope	Non-interest income over total assets
OHTA	BankScope	Total operating expenses (all but interest expense) over total assets
LLPTA	BankScope	Loan loss provisions over total assets
ETA	BankScope	Equity over total assets
NEATA	BankScope	Non-interest earning assets over total assets
CSTFTA	BankScope	Short-term and long-term deposits, and other non-deposit short-term funding over total assets
MSHARE	BankScope	Bank assets to total banking market assets in a given year
GGDP	EBRD	Real GDP annual growth rate
INCOME	EBRD	GDP per capita in U.S. dollars
CPI	EBRD	Annual CPI change
MMR	IFS	End of year money market interest rate
DCGDP	IFS	Private credit to the GDP in a given country and year

Note: all variables are in per cent except for GDP per capita (USD th, 1995 prices).

CHAPTER FIVE

ARE THE MORE INTEGRATED ALSO MORE EFFICIENT? INVESTIGATION ON SELECTED EU BANKING SECTORS[1]

The enlargement of the European Union (EU) that took place in May 2004 along with the proposed joining of Balkan countries in near future and gradual implementation of Euro in ten new EU-member countries are the principal economic and political phenomena in the European continent. Europe is consequently divided into several groups of countries that differ in the stages of integration and levels of economic development. One tail of the integration path is occupied by countries which belong to the prestigious group of the most developed economies that have also achieved the final stage of the integration process – membership in the European Economic and Monetary Union (EMU). This group consists of countries such as Germany, France and Italy. On the other side, there are countries standing at the very beginning of their integration to the European structures since the only step made is a declaration of interest to become members of the EU. This group is represented mainly by poor post-Soviet countries such as Ukraine or Moldavia. However, many differently numerous groups of countries with similar economic progress and stage of integration process are positioned somewhere between these two extremes of the development path. Thus, the majority of Europe resembles a pursuit competition where each group aims to catch up as fast as possible with the group ahead.

Since the financial sector is a backbone of every market economy and banks play an important and in some countries even a dominant role[2], the aim of this paper is to estimate and compare efficiency of banking intermediation in 11 countries representing four relatively homogenous groups at different stages of the European integration and different economic levels during the period 2001–04. The analysis aims to verify or reject the hypothesis that the advanced phase of integration and higher economic levels are associated with the higher efficiency of banking intermediation. Thus, this chapter should answer the question whether the banking sector fulfils its intermediation function sufficiently to catch-up with the forerunners or the low efficiency of intermediation could be an obstacle in the convergence process.

The first group in this study is Portugal and Greece, countries that are not only long-time members of the EU and countries adopting the Euro as the common currency, but also countries with the lowest GDP per capita in the traditional part of the EU (EU15). The second group is represented by the Czech Republic, Hungary, Poland and Slovakia, Central European countries that became members of the EU in May 2004 and are on the way to adopt the Euro at the beginning of the next decade (V4 hereafter). Their economic level is below the EU15 average; however the figures of Greece and Portugal are most easily attainable by this group. The third group comprises Estonia, Latvia and Lithuania, Baltic countries that are members of the EU since May 2004 and countries with the best prospects to fulfil the Maastricht criteria and adopt the Euro as the first of the new EU-members (B3 hereafter). Although the overall path of reform and banking sector development has been quite similar in all three countries, Estonia took the lead fairly early in all aspects. The fourth group includes Bulgaria and Romania, countries with a clear perspective to join the EU in 2007 or 2008 with GDP per capita far below the EU (C2 hereafter). Selection of such countries is backed up by the fact that each group is a moving target for the next group's efforts in the integration and convergence process.

In order for this chapter to attain its objectives, we will proceed as follows: The first section will give a brief comparison of the banking sectors of these countries. The second section discusses methodology and its strengths and provides a review of the recent relevant literature evaluating banking efficiency. The third section describes the data and deals with the variable selection. The fourth section presents findings and discussions and the final section provides conclusions.

Comparison of Banking Sectors

Greek and Portuguese banking sectors substantially resemble each other in global figures and differ mainly in the degree of financial intermediation, since Portugal posts almost twice as high a level as Greece. Both countries also witnessed a similar development of some indicators during 2001–04. The share of banks with foreign ownership and the banking sector concentration were stable in the period analyzed. Whereas the Greek figures are below the EU average (15.2 per cent) as well as the EMU average (13.5 percent), the share of foreign-owned banks in Portugal exceeded both averages. The shares of the top five banks surpassing two thirds of the entire market are considerably higher than the EU average of 59 per cent and the EMU average of 52.9 per cent. The number of banks did not change significantly and the profitability decreased as the improvement in 2003 did not compensate for the substantial slump in 2002 and was followed by a decrease in 2004. The development of the "total banking assets / national GDP" ratio followed a different trend. Whereas the share dropped by seven percentage points in Greece, it increased by 5.3 points in Portugal. Such a contradictory development may be addressed to the different stages of the business cycle. While Greece has emerged as one of the strongest growing economies in the EMU, Portugal's economy is gradually recovering from the recession that started in 2002 and continued throughout 2003.[3] However, the GDP growth is still rather limited, being one of the lowest in the EU. The other indicators of the banking sector's shape exhibited in Tables 5-1 and 5-2 correspond with the usual values in the EU15 and the EMU including the interest rate spreads that followed in Greece and Portugal a general downward trend coming through the whole Euro area.

Table 5-1 Selected indicators of banking sector in Greece (2001–2004)

	2001	**2002**	**2003**	**2004**
Number of banks	61	61	59	62
Share of foreign-owned banks in banking sector assets in %	9.6	8.9	9.3	10.0
Share of five largest banks in banking sector assets in %	67.0	67.4	66.9	65.0
Total assets in % of GDP	146.6	140.3	137.4	139.5
Capital adequacy in %	13.6	12.5	12.9	12.9
NPL in % of total loans	4.7	4.1	3.8	3.4
ROE (tier 1 capital) in %	16.5	8.4	13.0	10.8
Interest spread in %	5.5	5.0	4.6	4.1

Source: ECB (2005a, 2005b), Bank of Greece

Table 5-2 Selected indicators of banking sector in Portugal (2001–2004)

	2001	**2002**	**2003**	**2004**
Number of banks	57	60	62	62
Share of foreign-owned banks in banking sector assets in %	19.7	21.2	19.3	23.5
Share of five largest banks in banking sector assets in %	59.8	60.5	62.7	66.5
Total assets in % of GDP	262.1	264.2	266.7	267.4
Capital adequacy in %	9.5	9.8	10.0	10.4
NPL in % of total loans	2.8	2.7	2.5	2.2
ROE (tier 1 capital) in %	14.9	11.7	13.9	12.8
Interest spread in %	5.0	4.8	4.2	3.8

Source: ECB (2005a, 2005b), Banco de Portugal

Restructuring and transformation of the banking systems in the V4 and B3 countries have been completed for the very most part. Overriding some minor issues, one may accept this statement also for Bulgaria and Romania. However, the way towards a functioning banking sector has not been easy and all the countries have had to face serious changes and challenges. Since the banking sectors have not been able to absorb such fundamental shifts smoothly, most of the countries in the region suffered banking crises in the course of the 1990s affecting their economies and societies more or less painfully. The crises were caused in the majority of cases by a combination of the entire economic system transformation, a wild and non-regulated increase in the number of small banks funded by domestic capital, a lack of banking expertise and a high share of non-performing loans partly inherited from the Communist past and partly originating recently. The phase of consolidation that took place afterwards comprised state participation in cleaning banking portfolios from bad loans and raising the capital of state-owned banks, collapses of small and medium-sized banks, mergers and acquisitions, improvement of legal and regulatory framework, and privatisation. Although the speed of consolidation and selection of measures applied have varied among countries, banking sectors in all of them can nowadays be characterized as consolidated, universally-based, and under dominant control of strategic foreign investors.[4]

Table 5-3 Selected indicators of banking sector in the Czech Republic (2001–2004)

	2001	**2002**	**2003**	**2004**
Number of banks	38	37	35	35
Share of foreign-owned banks in banking sector assets in %	93.3	94.2	95.0	94.8
Share of five largest banks in banking sector assets in %	58.2	66.9	68.0	69.6
Total assets in % of GDP	118.3	106.8	100.9	97.1
Capital adequacy in %	15.4	14.3	14.5	12.7
NPL in % of total loans	20.8	15.8	11.2	10.8
ROE (tier 1 capital) in %	16.6	27.4	23.8	23.3
Interest spread in %	2.4	2.1	2.1	2.2

Source: Demel *et al.* (2005), Czech National Bank

Despite the success achieved in recent years, banking sectors in V4, B3 and C2 countries (CEE-9) are quite modest compared to that in the EU15 or the Euro area. In 2004, the banking sectors in the CEE-9 countries consisted of 264 banks and total assets were about EUR 385 billion.[5] This is equivalent to roughly 1.75 per cent of the consolidated balance sheet of all banks in the

Euro area. The depth of banking intermediation measured as a share of total banking assets on GDP was at 68.7 per cent in CEE-9 countries in 2004, which means considerably lower than 283 per cent in the EMU. The low degree of intermediation is pronounced also in Bruckbauer *et al.* (2004, p. 5) using total loans as a percentage of GDP. While the indicator's value was 120 per cent in the EU15 in 2003, the same share did not exceed 25 per cent in CEE-9 countries. Such a situation demonstrates that even now, 15 years after the beginning of their transition, the CEE-9 banking markets still exhibit vast potential.

Table 5-4 Selected indicators of banking sector in Hungary (2001–2004)

	2001	2002	2003	2004
Number of banks	38	37	38	35
Share of foreign-owned banks in banking sector assets in %	63.0	78.3	81.9	80.4
Share of five largest banks in banking sector assets in %	61.2	59.3	56.9	56.2
Total assets in % of GDP	68.4	69.3	78.2	83.0
Capital adequacy in %	15.6	12.2	11.9	11.8
NPL in % of total loans	2.8	3.6	3.2	1.9
ROE (tier 1 capital) in %	18.6	19.6	21.1	26.5
Interest spread in %	3.1	2.8	2.5	3.7

Source: Demel *et al.* (2005), Hungarian Financial Supervisory Authority

Table 5-5 Selected indicators of banking sector in Poland (2001–2004)

	2001	2002	2003	2004
Number of banks	71	62	60	57
Share of foreign-owned banks in banking sector assets in %	72.0	70.9	71.6	67.6
Share of five largest banks in banking sector assets in %	54.7	53.4	49.3	47.0
Total assets in % of GDP	66.5	65.2	64.7	65.3
Capital adequacy in %	15.1	13.8	13.6	15.6
NPL in % of total loans	18.6	22.0	22.2	15.5
ROE (tier 1 capital) in %	12.8	5.2	5.4	17.6
Interest spread in %	8.3	8.5	7.6	6.6

Source: Demel *et al.* (2005), National Bank of Poland

Regarding the number of banks, no dramatic fluctuations can be seen and such development can be considered as a sign of the banking sectors' stability. Due to large scale privatisation of the state-owned banks, all CEE-9 banking sectors are to a great extent controlled by foreign credit institutions originating mainly from the EMU member countries. Increase of the foreign capital importance in the CEE-9 banking sectors has also been facilitated by the fact that there have been few local institutional investors and the desire to import banking know-how via privatisation and foreign strategic investors. Thus the share of banks with majority foreign ownership is noticeably higher in this region than in Greece, Portugal or the Euro area as a whole. Concentration of the CEE-9 banking markets is relatively higher owing to the unique market position of traditional banks persisting from the Communist era. However, thanks to the successful effort of medium-sized banks (mainly subsidiaries of foreign banks such as Citibank, Raiffeisenbank, HVB, Volksbank or ING) in winning larger market shares, the level of concentration has been stagnating or decreasing in the past several years.

Table 5-6 Selected indicators of banking sector in Slovakia (2001–2004)

	2001	2002	2003	2004
Number of banks	21	21	22	22
Share of foreign-owned banks in banking sector assets in %	90.5	95.6	98.3	96.7
Share of five largest banks in banking sector assets in %	66.2	66.9	67.5	66.9
Total assets in % of GDP	92.0	92.3	82.0	87.4
Capital adequacy in %	19.8	21.3	21.7	19.0
NPL in % of total loans	20.9	9.2	6.4	4.6
ROE (tier 1 capital) in %	22.7	29.4	27.2	29.4
Interest spread in %	5.0	5.3	4.8	5.3

Source: Demel *et al.* (2005), National Bank of Slovakia

Table 5-7 Selected indicators of banking sector in Estonia (2001–2004)

	2001	2002	2003	2004
Number of banks	7	7	7	6
Share of foreign-owned banks in banking sector assets in %	97.9	98.2	98.1	98.6
Share of five largest banks in banking sector assets in %	98.9	98.4	98.3	98.5
Total assets in % of GDP	69.9	75.6	85.8	96.1
Capital adequacy in %	14.4	15.3	14.5	13.2
NPL in % of total loans	1.2	0.8	0.6	0.4
ROE (tier 1 capital) in %	18.8	12.2	12.9	23.0
Interest spread in %	7.1	2.8	3.2	3.1

Source: Bruckbauer *et al.* (2004), ECB (2005a, 2005b), Bank of Estonia

Table 5-8 Selected indicators of banking sector in Latvia (2001–2004)

	2001	2002	2003	2004
Number of banks	23	23	23	23
Share of foreign-owned banks in banking sector assets in %	57.8	54.4	53.9	55.3
Share of five largest banks in banking sector assets in %	67.8	66.7	64.3	62.5
Total assets in % of GDP	70.5	83.6	96.1	107.1
Capital adequacy in %	14.2	13.1	11.7	11.8
NPL in % of total loans	3.1	2.0	1.4	1.2
ROE (tier 1 capital) in %	19.0	16.4	16.7	21.4
Interest spread in %	4.2	2.2	2.4	2.5

Source: Bruckbauer *et al.* (2004), ECB (2005a, 2005b), Bank of Latvia

Table 5-9 Selected indicators of banking sector in Lithuania (2001–2004)

	2001	2002	2003	2004
Number of banks	13	14	14	12
Share of foreign-owned banks in banking sector assets in %	81.1	88.1	88.7	90.5
Share of five largest banks in banking sector assets in %	89.5	85.4	82.6	79.4
Total assets in % of GDP	32.1	33.5	39.9	46.9
Capital adequacy in %	15.7	14.8	13.6	13.9
NPL in % of total loans	7.4	5.8	3.5	3.4
ROE (tier 1 capital) in %	-1.1	8.5	13.4	13.0
Interest spread in %	7.3	6.3	5.6	5.5

Source: Bruckbauer *et al.* (2004), ECB (2005a, 2005b), Bank of Lithuania

Table 5-10 Selected indicators of banking sector in Bulgaria (2001–2004)

	2001	2002	2003	2004
Number of banks	35	35	35	35
Share of foreign-owned banks in banking sector assets in %	70.6	72.4	82.2	74.6
Share of five largest banks in banking sector assets in %	56.5	55.2	54.6	52.2
Total assets in % of GDP	41.1	45.0	50.3	65.1
Capital adequacy in %	31.1	25.2	22.2	16.6
NPL in % of total loans	7.0	5.5	8.0	7.1
ROE (tier 1 capital) in %	20.5	15.6	18.7	20.0
Interest spread in %	8.6	7.1	6.4	6.2

Source: Demel *et al.* (2005), Bulgarian National Bank

Table 5-11 Selected indicators of banking sector in Romania (2001–2004)

	2001	2002	2003	2004
Number of banks	41	39	38	39
Share of foreign-owned banks in banking sector assets in %	55.2	56.4	58.2	62.1
Share of five largest banks in banking sector assets in %	66.1	62.8	63.0	58.9
Total assets in % of GDP	30.2	31.6	32.4	38.3
Capital adequacy in %	28.8	25.0	18.2	18.8
NPL in % of total loans	3.9	2.8	33.1	32.5
ROE (tier 1 capital) in %	21.8	18.3	15.6	17.0
Interest spread in %	18.7	16.5	14.6	14.1

Source: Demel *et al.* (2005), Bank of Romania

Problems associated with non-performing loans have already been solved in all CEE-9 countries, though the shares in Romania and to lesser extend in Poland are still quite non-standard. Large bulks of non-performing loans have been shifted from banks' portfolios to special consolidation institutions significantly harming the government budgets and public finance.[6] In some countries such as Bulgaria, Romania or Poland, high inflation in the early and middle phase of transformation also helped to alleviate the bad loans problems. Consequently, the capital adequacy in the region increased and actual figures of the ratio are in some cases more than twice as high as required. Similarly, the level of capital adequacy in the CEE-9 countries exceeds the EU average of 12.3 per cent evidencing the substantially higher levels of own funds with respect to the extent of active banking operations.

With the improving quality of the credit portfolio, the need for loan loss provisions has been steadily declining and profitability of the banking sectors is being boosted. The last values of ROE ratios recorded in the CEE-9 are notably higher than the average of 12.2 per cent return on equity in the EU and 10.5 per cent in the EMU. The interest rate spreads vary among the CEE-9 banking sectors due to different level of inflation and interest rates. However, the common trend of stabilisation and narrowing the difference between lending and deposit rates can be revealed in the whole region. The nominal convergence and strong competition on the credit market are the main reasons for this.

Methodology and Review of Relevant Literature

Meaning and Measuring of Efficiency

Farrell (1957) in his pioneer paper distinguishes two components of the efficiency of a firm: technical efficiency, which reflects the ability of a firm to obtain maximum output from a given set of inputs; and allocative efficiency, which indicates the ability of a firm to use the inputs in optimal proportions, given their respective prices and production technology. These two measures can be combined to provide a measure of total economic efficiency, or, when cost instead of production is considered, cost efficiency. The optimal or most efficient production, depending on various circumstances such as the scale of the firm in particular, is called efficient frontier. Errors, lags between the choice of the production plan and its implementation, human inertia, distorted communications and uncertainty cause deviations from the efficient frontier, called X-inefficiency (Leibenstein, 1966). Measuring X-inefficiency in financial intermediation in eight banking industries is the main subject of this chapter.[7]

The two approaches used to assess X-efficiency of an entity, parametric (econometric) and non-parametric (mathematical programming), employ different techniques to envelop a dataset with different assumptions for random noise and for the structure of the production technology. In this study we use Data Envelopment Analysis (DEA) representing non-parametric methods. DEA is a mathematical programming approach for the construction of production frontiers and the measurement of efficiency relative to the frontiers constructed. DEA is based on a concept of efficiency very similar to the microeconomic one; the main difference is that the DEA production frontier is not determined by some specific functional form, but it is generated from the actual data for the firms evaluated. In other words, the DEA frontier is formed as the piecewise linear combination that connects the set of "best-practice observations" in the dataset under analysis. As a consequence, the DEA efficiency score for a specific decision making unit (DMU) is not defined by an absolute standard, but it is defined relative to the other DMUs in the specific dataset under consideration (Stavárek, 2004).

A great number of DEA models, specifications and versions can be found in literature. However, the two most frequently applied models are: the CCR model – after Charnes, Cooper and Rhodes (1978) and the BCC model – after Banker, Charnes and Cooper (1984). The basic difference between these two models is the treatment of returns to scale. While the latter takes into account the effect of variable returns to scale (VRS), the former restricts DMUs to operate with constant returns to scale (CRS).

Under restriction that each DMU's efficiency is judged against its individual criteria (individual weighting system), efficiency of a target DMU_0 can be obtained as a solution to the following problem.

$$\max_{u,v} h_0(u,v) = \frac{\sum_{r=1}^{s} u_r y_{r_0}}{\sum_{i=1}^{m} v_i x_{i_0}}, \tag{5.1}$$

subject to

$$\frac{\sum_{r=1}^{s} u_r y_{r_j}}{\sum_{i=1}^{m} v_i x_{i_j}} \leq 1, j = 1,2,\ldots, j_0,\ldots, n, \tag{5.2}$$

$$u_r \geq 0, \quad r = 1,2,\ldots,s, \tag{5.3}$$

$$v_i \geq 0, \quad i = 1,2,\ldots,m, \tag{5.4}$$

where h_0 is the technical efficiency of DMU_0 to be estimated, u_r and v_i are weights to be optimized, y_{rj} is the observed amount of output of the rth type for the jth DMU, x_{ij} is the observed amount of input of the ith type for the jth DMU, r indicates the s different outputs, i denotes the m different inputs, and j indicates the n different DMUs.

The weights u_r and v_i in the objective function are chosen to maximize the value of the DMU's efficiency ratio subject to the less than unity constrains. These constrains ensure that the optimal weights for DMU_0 in the objective function does not imply an efficiency score greater than unity, either for itself or for any of the other DMUs.

The above DEA problem is a fractional linear program in which the numerator has to be maximized and the denominator minimized simultaneously, i.e. the problem has an infinite number of solutions. To solve the model it is first necessary to convert it into linear form by following a transformation developed by Charnes and Cooper (1962) for fractional programming. It allows the introduction of a constant

$$\sum_{i=1}^{m} v_i x_{i_0} = 1, \tag{5.5}$$

meaning the sum of all inputs is set to equal one. The obtained linear programming problem that is equivalent to the linear fractional programming problem (5.1) – (5.4) for DMU_0 can be written as:

$$\max_{u} z_0 = \sum_{r=1}^{s} u_r y_{r_0},, \tag{5.6}$$

$$\sum_{r=1}^{s} u_r y_{r_j} - \sum_{i=1}^{m} v_i x_{i_j} \le 0, j = 1,2,..., n, \tag{5.7}$$

$$\sum_{i=1}^{m} v_i x_{i_0} = 1, \tag{5.8}$$

$$u_r \ge 0, \quad r = 1,2,\ldots,s, \tag{5.9}$$
$$v_i \ge 0, \quad i = 1,2,\ldots,m. \tag{5.10}$$

The CRS assumption is only appropriate when all DMUs are operating at an optimal scale. Imperfect competition, constraints on finance, leverage concerns, certain prudential requirements, etc. may cause a DMU not to operate at optimal scale. The fact that banks face non-constant returns to scale has been documented empirically by, among others, McAllister and McManus (1993), and Wheelock and Wilson (1999). To overcome this problem a DEA model with variable returns to scale has been developed. In this model the variables of technical efficiencies are measured which are confounded to scale efficiencies. The convexity constrain is added to the standard CCR model:

$$\sum_{j=1}^{n} \lambda_j = 1. \tag{5.11}$$

The input-oriented VRS for the DMU_0, firstly introduced in Banker *et al.* (1984), can be consequently written as:

$$\min_{\lambda} z_0 = \Theta_0, \tag{5.12}$$

$$\sum_{j=1}^{n} \lambda_j y_{r_j} \ge y_{r_0}, r = 1,2,..., s, \tag{5.13}$$

$$\Theta_0 x_{i_0} - \sum_{j=1}^{n} \lambda_j x_{i_j} \ge 0, i = 1,2,..., n, \tag{5.14}$$

$$\sum_{j=1}^{n} \lambda_j = 1, \tag{5.15}$$

$$\lambda_j \ge 0, \quad j = 1,2,\ldots,n, \tag{5.16}$$

where the technical efficiency of DMU_0 is denoted by Θ_0, and λ_j indicates weight of the jth DMU. Moreover, $\lambda = (\lambda_1, \lambda_2, ..., \lambda_n)$, $\lambda \ge 0$, is the vector of weights obtained by individual DMUs. Thus, it is an n-dimensional vector of the model's variables. Whereas the DMU with technical efficiency $\Theta_j < 1$ is considered as inefficient, the efficiency $\Theta_j = 1$ shows the efficient DMU placed on the efficiency frontier. The BCC model eliminates the scale part of efficiency from the analysis and therefore the CCR efficiency score for each DMU will not exceed the BCC efficiency score, which is intuitively clear since the BCC model analyses each DMU locally, i.e. compared to the subset of DMUs that operate in the same region of returns to scale, rather than globally. Thus, the BCC efficiency scores are also called pure technical efficiency scores. Since we perceive assumptions of the CCR model to be in conflict with reality in banking industry, this study applies the BCC model for empirical analysis expecting more robust results.

Review of Relevant Literature on Banking Efficiency

Efficiency and financial performance of banks and other financial institutions are very frequently discussed topics in economic literature. Sherman and Gold (1985) were one of the first researchers to use the nonparametric approach to evaluate and compare the performances of banks. Berger and Humphrey (1997) surveyed 130 studies that apply frontier efficiency analyses to financial institutions in 21 countries. They report that the majority of these studies are confined to the U.S. banking sector, and call for the need to do further research in this area outside the United States. Since then, more than 60 empirical studies on banking efficiency have been published and their scope has expanded to more countries including transition ones. However, the rapid development of banking sectors and integration process make the previous studies out-of-date very quickly. Therefore, there is a permanent need for further cross-country analysis of banking efficiency.

Further, the text provides a brief review of empirical literature estimating efficiency of banks in the countries included in this chapter. The majority of studies cited do not only estimate the efficiency of banks but also address some issues such us influence of foreign ownership, privatisation, or concentration on efficiency. Many papers investigate determinants of bank efficiency distinguishing the internal and environmental variables. In this review, however, the emphasis is mainly put on the results of efficiency estimation and the rest of the findings are considered as irrelevant for the present study.

National Studies on Banking Efficiency

The first comprehensive study on Greek banks efficiency was Christopoulos *et al.* (2002) covering the period 1993–98. The empirical results show that larger banks were less efficient than smaller ones. Also, it is found that economic performance, bank loans and investments were positive related to the cost efficiency of the Greek commercial banking sector. Cost efficiency in Greek banking was evaluated also in Kamberouglou *et al.* (2004) extending the time period to 1993–99. The results obtained indicated that mean efficiency did not exceed 60 per cent and some evidence was provided that bank size, type of ownership and risk behaviour may explain differences in measured efficiency scores. Efficiency of Portuguese banks was estimated in Canhoto and Dermine (2000). The banking efficiency was evaluated for the period 1990–95 applying DEA. The results demonstrate an improvement in efficiency mostly driven by technological change. Considering CRS, the average efficiency increased from 59 per cent in 1990 to 84 per cent in 1995. A rise from 73 per cent to 93 per cent was detected, allowing VRS.

Portuguese banks also comprised datasets in several cross-country studies. For instance Lozano–Vivas *et al.* (2001) used 1993 data of 10 European banking industries. Their estimation of efficiency employing DEA led to results that Portuguese banks had a mean efficiency of 15.99 per cent in standard input-output model and 79.87 per cent when national environmental variables were incorporated. The average efficiency score of the whole sample was 28.23 per cent and 62.14 per cent, respectively. Carbo *et al.* (2002) applied the stochastic frontier approach (SFA) on a large sample of European savings banks between 1989 and 1996. Portugal's saving banks were classified as the second worst in Europe (just ahead of Finnish banks) while their mean efficiency over the period was 70.8 per cent and the average of all national sectors was 78.2 per cent. Nevertheless, the enhancement from 65.1 per cent in 1989 to 72.5 per cent in 1996 was revealed in Portugal. Weill (2004) analyzed the relationship between competition and efficiency in banking on a sample of 12 EU-member countries, including Greece and Portugal, during the period 1994–99. The most striking result is the improvement in efficiency for all countries, whilst the most significant movement of 22.77 percentage points appeared in Greece, catapulting the country from the absolute bottom (efficiency of 50.98 per cent) to the middle part of the overall standings (efficiency of 73.75 per cent). The Portuguese banking industry also recorded a noticeable progress of 20.62 points departing from 54.61 per cent in 1994 and achieving the level of 75.23 per cent in 1999.

Moving our attention now to banking in the CEE-9 countries, the most extensively analyzed banking sector is that of Poland. Besides cross-country studies, there are also three papers concentrating only on the country's market. Pawlowska (2003) applied DEA in examining of the impact of mergers and acquisitions (M&A) on efficiency of banks in Poland in the period 1997–2001. A generally increasing level of efficiency is reported and the improvement of efficiency of banks involved in the M&A process is noticeable. Moreover, size was found as an important factor in explaining efficiency, since the majority of efficient banks were categorized as very large and large banks. Although the efficiency of Poland's bank industry was also investigated using DEA in Havrylchyk (2004), the results indicate that bank efficiency did not improve during 1998 and 2000. Nevertheless, foreign banks were found to be more efficient than their domestically owned counterparts. On the contrary, Nikiel and Opiela (2002) employed a parametric approach and explored the possibility that customer type, rather than foreign ownership and size, explains efficiency. They found that foreign banks servicing foreign and business customers are more cost-efficient and less profit-efficient than other banks in Poland. The Czech banking sector was investigated solely in Taci and Zampieri (1998) using the distribution free approach, one of the parametric methods. The conclusion was that private banks have a higher mean efficiency score, supporting rapid privatisation. Hasan and Marton (2003) used the SFA to estimate profit and cost efficiency of Hungarian banks during the period 1993–98. They found an improvement of both types of efficiency. While the cost efficiency increased from 62.08 per cent to 77.61 per cent, the profit efficiency increased from 57.69 per cent to 73.94 per cent. To our knowledge there is no other empirical work focusing on bank efficiency in solely one of the CEE-9 countries.

Cross-country Studies on Banking Efficiency

Banking efficiency in the V4 countries during 1999 and 2003 is analyzed in Stavárek (2005a) and Stavárek (2005b). Although the two studies employ different estimation techniques – SFA and DEA respectively – the findings were found to be very consistent. Overall, the results suggest that the Czech banking sector is the most efficient, followed by the Hungarian with a marginal gap. For instance Stavárek (2005b) reports the average efficiency of the V4 region in 2003 to be 79.99 per cent, efficiency in the Czech Republic 88.01 per cent, in Hungary 84.31 per cent, in Poland 78.58 per cent, and in Slovakia 67.69 per cent using the BCC model. Slovakia's banking sector was recognized as the least efficient. Although there has been an improvement in levels of efficiency in all countries since 1999, its intensity seemed to be poor. Regarding chronology, the first comprehensive cross-country study on banking efficiency in CEE countries was Grigorian and Manole (2002). The dataset consisted of banks from 17 countries and the period studied was 1995–98. Using DEA, the Czech and Slovenian banking sectors were identified as the most efficient followed by Bulgaria, Hungary, Poland and Slovakia. Romanian banks obtained the lowest average efficiency among CEE-9 countries. The efficiency scores in 1998 varied from 51.1 per cent (Romania) to 79.9 per cent (Czech Republic).

Yildirim and Philippatos (2002) examined the cost and profit efficiency of banking sectors in 12 transition countries of the region in 1993–2000 by alternative parametric approaches. The mean efficiency of all banks and all years was 70 per cent in the case of cost efficiency and 55.3 per cent in profit efficiency. Whereas the national cost efficiency was below the regional average in Estonia, Latvia, Lithuania and Slovakia and the differences were rather marginal, the profit efficiency scores had a wider range and were lower than the regional average in Hungary, Poland and Romania. Bulgaria was not included in the analysis. Matoušek (2004) employed the Distribution Free Approach to compare cost efficiency in eight EU accession countries in 1994–2001. The highest average efficiency scores were assigned to Latvia and Slovenia while the estimated efficiency was 75 per cent and 71 per cent respectively. On the other hand the banking systems with the lowest efficiency were in Poland and Lithuania. The estimated efficiency for Poland was only 59 per cent and for Lithuania 61 per cent. Fries and Taci (2005) estimated cost efficiency of banks in 15 post-Communist European countries during the period 1994–2001 using SFA and two alternative models, with and without country-level factors. The average bank efficiency levels estimated by the two models varied from 47 per cent in the Czech Republic to 85 per cent in Estonia and from 42 per cent in Bulgaria and the Czech Republic to 78 per cent in Kazakhstan, respectively. The Slovak banking sector proved to be the most efficient banking sector among the CEE-9 countries.[8] Using data from 1996 to 2000, Bonin *et al.* (2005) investigated the effects of ownership, especially by a strategic foreign owner, on bank efficiency for 11 transition countries. They found that foreign-owned banks are more cost-efficient than other banks and that they also provide better service, in particular, when they have a strategic foreign owner. Estimations of the efficiency level in the countries analyzed are not provided in the paper.

Only two studies created a mixed estimation set of transition as well as developed European banking sectors. Stavárek and Polouček (2004) analyzed banks from V4 countries along with banks from Belgium and Finland in 2000 and 2001. They applied four models differing in the assumption of returns to scale and input-output specification and came to the general conclusion that banks from Finland and Belgium are more efficient than banks from V4 countries. The gap varied from roughly four percentage points in the Czech Republic to more than 12 points in Slovakia. Weill (2003) measured cost efficiency on sample of banks from 11 Western European and six Eastern European countries with the SFA of two years, 1996 and 2000. The cross-country analysis showed in fact that Western countries had efficiency score medians ranging from 61.48 per cent for Portugal to 75.63 per cent for the United Kingdom, while the medians for Eastern countries ranged from 45.09 per cent for Slovakia to 73.24 per cent for the Czech Republic. Among Western countries, Greece and Portugal had the least efficient banking sectors. Among Eastern countries, it appeared that Czech banks were as cost efficient as most efficient EU banks, while Hungarian banks dominated the banks of the least efficient EU banks, namely Greek and Portuguese banks. Furthermore, the banks originating from the four other Eastern countries (Latvia, Poland, Slovakia, and Slovenia) clearly underperformed the banks of EU countries.

This study differs from the two mentioned above in three ways. First, to evaluate the level of bank efficiency, the most up-to-date available data are employed and the period analyzed is extended to the year of the EU enlargement. Second, the investigation concentrates on banking intermediation instead of cost efficiency or production process since we consider transformation of deposits to credits and loans as the primary function of banks. Third, we strictly distinguish four groups of countries according to the degree achieved in European integration and economic levels to realize whether the differences in bank efficiency correspond to such segmentation.

Data and Selection of Variables

The analysis is based on data of banks representing more than 90 per cent of the total banking assets in all countries. Since the sample period selected was 2001–04, i.e. years covering the final stage of transformation free of instability, arguments concerning reliability of data and indicators may be considered as groundless. While describing the data, it is necessary to note that composition of the dataset changed slightly over the period analyzed because some of the banks ended their operation and data on several banks from other CEE-9 countries are not available for all these years. Therefore, the sample contains 122 banks in 2001, 126 banks in 2002, 125 banks in 2003, and 124 banks in 2004.[9] All data were extracted from the banks' official end-of-year unconsolidated balance sheets and financial statements based on international accounting standards. All data presented in value terms of local currencies were converted into EUR as a reference currency following the purchasing power parity hypothesis. For the conversion, we used "Index of purchasing power of the Euro – Annual data" calculated and reported by Eurostat. We analyzed only commercial banks (some of them originally savings banks) that operate as independent legal entities. All foreign branches, building societies, mortgage banks, specialized banks or credit unions were excluded from the estimation set.

In banking literature, there is a considerable disagreement on the perception of the banking activities' principles and on the explicit definition and measurement of banks' inputs and outputs. A fundamental difficulty arises in the treatment of bank deposits. Long-lasting debate in the literature surrounds the input-output status of deposits. Traditionally, deposits are regarded as the main ingredients for loan production and the acquisition of other earning assets. On the other hand, high value-added deposit products, like integrated savings and checking accounts, investment trusts and foreign currency deposit accounts tend to highlight the output characteristics of deposits. Indeed, high value-added deposit services are an important source of commissions and fee revenues for specialized commercial banks such as trust and private banks. In the context of these specialized institutions, one cannot afford to ignore the output nature of deposits. Extending this argument further, one might contend that the classification of deposits should therefore depend on the structure and characteristics of banks in the representative sample and be viewed in the regulatory context of the country in question. For example, since the magnitude of high value-added deposits is relatively small compared to time and savings deposits in CEE-9 countries, there may be more reasonable to regard deposits as inputs in these circumstances.

Three main approaches have been developed to define the input-output relationship in financial institution behaviour in the previous literature. Firstly, the production approach (Sherman and Gold, 1985) views financial institutions as producers of deposit and loan accounts, defining output as the number of such accounts or transactions. This method usually defines inputs as the number of employees and capital expenditures on fixed assets. Second, the intermediation approach (Sealey and Lindley, 1977) stems directly from the traditional role of financial institutions as intermediaries that convert financial assets from surplus units into deficit units. Operating and interest costs are usually the major inputs, whereas interest income, total loans, total deposits and non-interest income form the principal outputs. Third, the asset approach recognizes the primary role of financial institutions as creators of loans. In essence, this stream of thought is a variant of the intermediation approach, but instead defines outputs as the stock of loan and investment assets (Favero and Papi, 1995).

The intermediation approach seems to have dominated empirical research in this area and thus, we adopt for the definition of inputs and outputs the original approach proposed by Sealey and Lindley (1977) with a small modification. Their definition assumes that the bank collects deposits to transform them, using labour and capital, into loans. We determined the appropriate number of inputs and outputs with respect to the dataset size and consequently employed three inputs (labour, capital, and deposits), and two outputs (loans and net interest income).[10] We measure labour by the total personnel costs (*PC*) covering wages and all associated expenses, capital by the net book value of fixed assets (*FA*), deposits by the sum of demand and time deposits from customers and interbank deposits and sources obtained by bonds issued (*TD*). Loans are measured by the net value of loans to customers and other financial institutions (*TL*) and net interest income as the difference between interest incomes and interest expenses (*NII*).

Table 5-12 Descriptive statistics of inputs and outputs (2001–2004, in EUR)

	TD	PC	FA	TL	NII
			2001		
Mean	3 535 583	61 566	100 077	2 788 150	117 190
Median	686 201	12 677	21 075	505 603	21 539
Standard deviation	8 028 022	125 565	194 570	6 785 717	241 265
Min	25 067	338	461	11 229	-221
Max	54 695 000	774 735	1 311 444	47 189 221	1 506 384
			2002		
Mean	3 544 246	56 268	94 335	2 907 279	118 361
Median	693 189	13 589	20 736	529 119	25 795
Standard deviation	8 064 031	110 467	175 051	7 027 006	225 442
Min	8 989	254	875	13 515	265
Max	55 733 000	786 496	1 132 094	49 520 081	1 326 748
			2003		
Mean	3 895 045	60 430	88 197	3 165 955	123 158
Median	908 349	14 978	23 388	764 208	35 915
Standard deviation	8 742 487	116 287	164 430	7 346 581	224 530
Min	18 626	466	1 116	17 520	849
Max	62 904 000	864 032	1 129 018	53 579 445	1 466 011
			2004		
Mean	3 979 518	62 309	84 061	3 360 894	125 707
Median	980 072	15 277	22 646	758 830	38 318
Standard deviation	8 878 020	118 913	162 803	7 201 419	222 993
Min	20 114	471	1 079	19 666	1 005
Max	65 441 803	901 552	1 126 525	56 004 331	1 527 628

Source: Author's calculations

The main modification of the traditional intermediation approach is the absence of investment (financial) assets on the side of outputs. This part of banks' assets is excluded because the majority of banks' investments in CEE-9 countries are allocated in treasury bills and government bonds and we do not perceive this as pure intermediation that finances customers' investment and consumption needs. The second modification is motivated to accent not only the volume of the intermediation process but also its quality and profitability. Thus, the *NII* is added on the output side of the model. See Table 5-12 for a descriptive statistics of all inputs and outputs calculated for the entire sample of banks.

Empirical Results

Following the methodology described, we evaluated the efficiency of all banks in the estimation set and calculated DEA efficiency scores obtained by running a program for the BCC model. We used the EMS software, version 1.3.0, by Holger Scheel for the DEA scores calculation. To avoid any input or output being totally ignored in determining efficiency, the constraints specified in equations (5.9) and (5.10) were modified to weights equal to or greater than 0.001. The specification of the BCC model was modified analogically. We pooled the cross-country data and used them to define a common best-practice efficiency frontier. This allowed us to focus on determining the relative differences in performances across banking industries. The same approach was previously followed by Berg *et al.* (1993), Pastor *et al.* (1997), Grigorian and Manole (2002), Casu and Molyneux (2003) or Stavárek (2004). Table 5-13 reports the elementary descriptive statistics of the efficiency scores obtained relative to the entire sample.

It is possible to detect an improvement of average efficiency between 2001 and 2004. The mean efficiency scores seem to be in general accordance with results of the above surveyed studies. Since the development of efficiency may be examined in changes of frequency distribution, graphs in Figure 5-1 illustrate the frequency distribution of efficiency scores over the applied period of analysis.

Table 5-13 Descriptive statistics of efficiency scores (2001–2004, in %)

	2001	**2002**	**2003**	**2004**
no. of DMUs	122	126	125	124
no. of efficient DMUs	5	6	9	10
Mean	60.11	64.93	74.93	79.21
Median	57.29	66.45	75.79	80.07
Standard deviation	21.67	18.05	17.81	17.13
Min	12.47	7.86	22.23	25.94
Max	100.00	100.00	100.00	100.00

Source: Author's calculations

Fig. 5-1 Frequency distribution of efficiency scores (2001–2004)

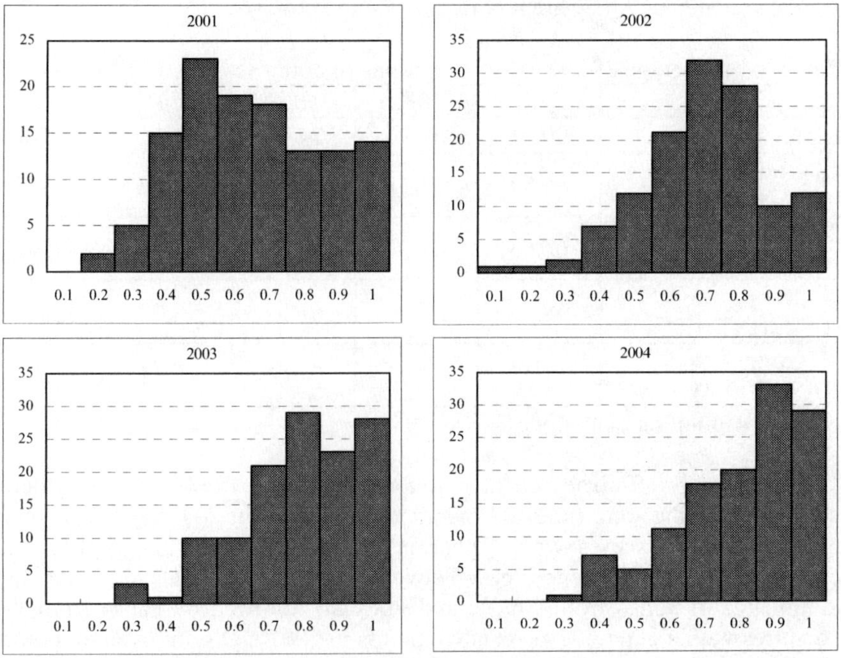

Source: Author's calculations

The improvement of efficiency can be identified in a shift of the cluster comprising most DMUs from 0.50–0.70 to 0.08–1.00 during the period analyzed. The number of DMUs whose efficiency came under the interval 0.00–0.40 was also reduced significantly in 2003 and 2004. In comparison with findings of Berger and Humphrey (1997) the figures also show signs of average performance. They surveyed, as mentioned earlier, 130 studies (122 of which were focused on depository financial institutions), applying frontier efficiency analysis (using parametric as well as non-parametric methods) to financial institutions in 21 countries. They drew to the conclusion that the mean value of average efficiencies was 0.79, with a standard deviation of 0.13, and a range of 0.31 to 0.97. Considering only 69 applications of non-parametric techniques, the mean average efficiency was 0.72, with a standard deviation of 0.17. Results of the present study are not poles apart.

Regional and National Differences in Efficiency

To observe differences in average efficiency among the four groups analyzed the mean efficiency scores of traditional EU-member countries, new

EU-member states comprising V4 and B3 countries, and candidate countries were calculated and they are reported in Table 5-14.

Table 5-14 Average efficiency in the groups of countries (2001–2004, in %)

	2001	2002	2003	2004	change
Entire sample	60.11	64.93	74.93	79.21	31.78
1st group (GRE, POR)	84.59	77.71	88.18	90.62	7.13
2nd group (CZE, HUN, POL, SVK)	62.63	65.93	76.79	82.95	32.44
3rd group (EST, LAT, LIT)	48.85	52.16	61.82	66.70	36.54
4th group (BUL, ROM)	41.32	64.52	72.41	75.33	82.31

Source: Author's calculations

The average efficiency of the entire sample was exceeded by two groups consisting of the long-time EU-member states and the V4 countries. Their mean efficiency scores were higher in all years. Our results support the existence of an efficiency gap between the groups analyzed with the dominance of banks from Greece and Portugal followed by banks from V4 countries with a gap of 22 percentage points in 2001 and roughly eight points in 2003 and 2004. The relative position of the two remaining groups swapped in 2002 when banks from two candidate countries surpassed banks from the Baltic States in terms of average efficiency. Results of efficiency estimation in 2004 confirmed this situation since the efficiency gap between the two groups was almost nine percentage points.

Moreover, Table 5-14 gives evidence to the general trend of increasing efficiency manifested in all regions. However, the pace of growth differs among groups significantly and one can interpret it that higher average efficiency score in the beginning of the period predestinated slower growth of efficiency in following years. Traditional EU-member countries recorded the slowest growth caused mainly by the substantial drop in average efficiency in 2002. Banks from the new EU-member states gathered in two groups experienced relatively the same increase in efficiency. Whereas the growth rate in the V4 countries was 32.44 per cent, banks from the Baltic region improved efficiency by 36.54 per cent. Summarizing all findings, standings of the groups according to average efficiency copies the hierarchy in terms of economic development and achieved stage of integration with the exception of the C2 countries which took third place in last three years. All transition regions speeded up the catch-up process in banking efficiency and the initial gaps were reduced considerably. Such a development can be considered as a reason to reject the hypothesis that inefficiency of banking intermediation in the new EU-member and candidate countries with no progress hampers economic growth and the convergence process.

We also computed average efficiency of all banking industries to provide more comprehensive results investigating whether the relative positions of banking sectors correspond with the standing of the respective group. The national average efficiency scores along with the changes over four years are depicted in Table 5-15. Taking into account results of the BCC model in 2004, the leading position of the traditional EU-members group was verified by the Portuguese banking sector as the most efficient followed by the Greek sector. Likewise, the second position of the V4 countries was confirmed by the results of the Czech, Hungarian and Polish banking sectors classified as third, fifth and sixth most efficient industries, respectively.

Table 5-15 Average efficiency in national banking sectors (2001–2004, in %)

	2001	2002	2003	2004	change
Entire sample	60.11	64.93	74.93	79.21	31.78
Greece	78.54	72.66	86.19	89.44	13.88
Portugal	91.52	82.26	89.98	91.79	0.30
Czech Republic	63.90	77.17	85.32	88.10	37.87
Hungary	64.40	70.30	83.26	86.28	33.98
Poland	69.54	65.70	75.13	77.81	11.89
Slovakia	43.72	47.92	63.63	72.69	66.26
Estonia	63.14	65.94	83.97	87.98	39.34
Latvia	40.24	51.03	55.08	61.42	52.63
Lithuania	50.70	44.97	56.41	60.87	20.06
Bulgaria	37.40	63.07	70.87	73.48	96.47
Romania	45.80	65.97	73.95	76.92	67.95

Source: Author's calculations

It is worth noting that in 2004, banks from three new EU-members analyzed in this paper which have most developed economies and the highest value of GDP per capita, i.e. Czech Republic, Hungary, and Estonia, brought their efficiency very close to the level estimated in two EU15 member states included in this study. One can see the gap of approximately 1.3 to 5.5 percentage points as rather marginal confirming that banking sectors of the most advanced new EU-members and the less developed EU15 economies have already considerably converged. Similarly with banks from the three most efficient new EU-member banking sectors, Bulgarian and Romanian banks achieved or even exceeded levels of banking industries of some of their forerunners. Departing from the bottom of standings in 2001, the extremely rapid growth of efficiency caused banks in Bulgaria and Romania to overperform their Slovak, Latvian and Lithuanian counterparts by three to 16 percentage points obtaining average efficiency a little bit lower than the efficiency of Poland's banks in 2004.

Analyzing the catch-up process from a national perspective, we have to consider the pace of the efficiency growth. The growth rates have a very wide range and vary from 96.47 per cent in Bulgaria to 0.30 per cent in Portugal.[11] The second slowest growth of efficiency between 2001 and 2004 was recorded in Poland. The 11.89 per cent growth achieved is substantially below the entire sample's average as well as below the regional average. Such a result is absolutely in accordance with the development of other key indicators showing Polish banking sector as the most problematic among V4 countries. Table 5-5 exhibits that banks in Poland had the highest share of NPL in credit portfolios, the highest interest spread, and the lowest profitability in the Visegrad region. A growth slower than the entire sample's average was also calculated in Greece and Lithuania. The catch-up process in other countries was fully accomplished since their registered growth rates exceeded the average improvement of their forerunning group.

The results suggest that there is a gap in efficiency between developed banking sectors and the majority of the new EU-member and candidate countries. Moreover, accepting conclusions of Weill (2003) or Stavárek and Polouček (2004), one can expect that involving of other EU15 banks into the dataset should result in generally lower efficiency of CEE-9 banks than estimated in the present study. The efficiency gap may be explained either by key indicators of the banking industries presented and discussed in the first section of this chapter or by some incidental outcomes of the efficiency estimation. Further on, we apply both approaches whilst some important facts about lending policy in Slovakia, Poland. Latvia, Lithuania, Bulgaria, and Romania are first elaborated, and secondly the weaknesses of banks detected in efficiency estimation.

Although the financial intermediation in Slovakia measured as total banking assets to GDP stood at almost 87.5 per cent in 2004, and is thus relatively high compared to other CEE-9 countries, the loans to private sector as a percentage of GDP reached only 33 per cent and had been continuously falling until 2002. This is due to the fact that formerly state-owned banks that dominate the banking market in all areas are still struggling to come to terms with the rough and tumble events of recent years, reflected in a very cautious lending policy. On the other hand, there has always been a growth of deposits resulting in a stable ratio of the private sector deposits on GDP that had been fluctuating around 60 per cent until 2002. The main reasons for that are the very strong banking traditions and the relatively low rates of inflation during the transition years that have not eroded the value of financial assets. Such an overhang of deposits with respect to lending activity added a further element to the intermediation inefficiency issue. Nevertheless, 2003 appeared to be a turning point for the Slovak banking sector recalling the aforementioned sharp raise in efficiency.

The unfavourable business climate in Poland[12], which affects banks both via weaker demand for banking services and indirectly via the borrower's ability to service a loan, not only led to a deterioration in profitability indicators over the years 2002–03, but also the level of financial intermediation (total bank assets to GDP) declined from 2001 to 2004.[13] Due to the slump in demand for loans resulting from a weaker economic environment, lending activity has recently been sluggish. Domestic currency lending has stagnated due to the banks' conservative lending policy, keeping interest rates on zloty-denominated loans relatively high and prompting the banks to increase their purchase of low-risk government bonds. By contrast, low interest rates on loans denominated in foreign currency triggered a rise in foreign exchange loans. The share of NPL in total loans, which was already rather high in Poland, increased from its historical low of 10.5 per cent in 1997 to 22.2 per cent in 2003, thus surpassing the figure recorded for 1995. Such developments limited the banking efficiency in Poland to more substantial growth.

Two of the Baltic States – Latvia and Lithuania – obtained the lowest average efficiency scores in 2004. However, the efficiency growth of more than 52.5 per cent in Latvia clearly signalled a great deal of catch-up potential. Such prospects were supported by strong economic growth, robust domestic demand, decreasing spreads and strong FDI inflows which led to a major upswing in lending in all B3 countries. Moreover, despite impressive growth rates of disbursed loans, private sector lending climbed to 40 per cent and 48 per cent of GDP in Estonia and Latvia respectively at yearend 2004. In Lithuania, it only managed to rise to 24 per cent of GDP, which is a mere one-fifth of the EU15 level. The more extensive improvement of Lithuanian banks' efficiency was prevented by the massive appreciation of the litas vis-à-vis U.S. dollar since roughly one fourth of the banking assets and liabilities were denominated in USD. This reflected the pegging of Lithuanian currency to the USD for many years within the framework of the currency board. Since the general economic conditions have had a predominantly positive impact on banking efficiency, the sources of Latvia's and Lithuania's banks' inefficiency should be primarily sought in the quality of the lending process and managerial skills.

Lower efficiency in the Balkans stems from the banks' very cautious approach to lending, which is not surprising, given the difficulties in reinforcing creditor rights, uncertainties in obtaining information and hesitant reforms in the corporate sector. In addition, banks are still struggling to digest the shock from the recent banking crises. Low-risk businesses such as foreign exchange and interbank transaction or purchase of government bonds are preferred, which leads to a crowding out of the private sector, especially small and medium-sized enterprises. Moreover, banks are left far more prone to unexpected exchange rate fluctuations. The credit institutions' exceptionally circumspect approach to extending credit is also reflected by the maturity structure of the loan portfolio since half of the total loans disbursed to the private sector are short-term, that is, with maturity of less than one year. The risk aversion towards lending that adversely affects efficiency is also underscored by the high capital adequacy in Bulgarian and Romanian banking sectors substantially exceeding the limits as well as common standards. However, both C2 countries have made a significant progress in reforming their financial sectors and 2002 was the year of an extraordinary increase in banking efficiency.

One of the important advantages of DEA that attracts analysts and managers is its ability to identify the potential improvement for inefficient DMUs. For the inefficient DMUs, DEA compares the DMU with a convex combination of DMUs located on the frontier and enables the analyst to indicate the sources and the level of inefficiency for each of its inputs and outputs. The indicated targets, which are shown to the inefficient DMUs as models, are their actual peer units; therefore, the results are more likely to be accepted by the managers of these DMUs. One of the possible approaches to identify exactly the causes of inefficiency is the analysis of weights assigned to inputs and outputs. The lower the weight assigned the greater effort to minimize impact of the respective input or output on the efficiency score. Thus, inputs and outputs with the lowest weights can be labelled as sources of the DMU's inefficiency. Because the input-oriented model is applied in this study, we restrict our attention on the inputs of banking intermediation. To conserve space, separate discussions on each bank's weaknesses are substituted by a summary on a national basis.[14] Identification of the sources of inefficiency may help remove some obstacles on the way to catch to more efficient countries in the banking intermediation.

Estimation of the Portuguese banks' efficiency yielded results that are far from any kind of generalisation. The causes of inefficiency differ among banks and nearly no unifying element can be found. Although such diversification of weaknesses on the input side is obvious also in Greece, one may consider personal costs in the Greek banking industry as high with respect to the output capacity since half of the Greek banks obtained the lowest possible weight of the personal costs input. On the other hand, the CEE-9 banking sectors are more uniform in recognizing the inefficiency sources. Fixed assets proved to be the most significant factor pushing the efficiency down in seven banking sectors (Czech Republic, Slovakia, Estonia, Latvia, Lithuania, Bulgaria and Romania). Moreover, the significantly negative impact of FA can be observed also in Poland where FA was the primary cause of inefficiency also in 2002. Banks in the CEE-9 countries dispose of property, mainly in the form of real estate, which is excessive with respect to the market size and is not able to generate sufficient output. Besides the FA, banking efficiency was influenced negatively by personal costs. This input was found as the main factor aggravating efficiency in Hungary and Poland. Such a result conforms to the relatively lower concentration of the Hungarian and Polish markets documented in Tables 5-4 and 5-5. Since there are more banks serving the whole market more staff have to be employed. Consequently, due to limited market shares the employees' output potential is not fully replenished. Moreover, the majority of Romanian banks were also negatively affected by the PC. Table 5-16 summarizes the main sources of inefficiency (inputs with the lowest average weight) in all banking sectors and years analyzed.

Table 5-16 Main sources of banking inefficiency (2001–2004)

	2001	2002	2003	2004
Greece	PC	PC	PC	PC
Portugal	PC	FA	FA	FA
Czech Republic	FA	FA	FA	FA
Hungary	FA	PC	PC	PC
Poland	PC	FA	PC	PC
Slovakia	FA	FA	FA	FA
Estonia	FA	FA	FA	FA
Latvia	FA	FA	FA	FA
Lithuania	FA	PC	FA	FA
Bulgaria	FA	FA	FA	FA
Romania	PC	PC	PC	PC

Source: Author's calculations

Examination of the Issue of a Bank's Size

We are aware of the fact that averaging without any respect to the size of banks causes loss of information, and therefore, we implemented in our analysis a size-adjusted average efficiency (*SEA*) calculated as:

$$SEA = \sum_{j=1}^{n} w_j \Theta_j, \tag{5.17}$$

where *SEA* is the size-adjusted average efficiency, w_j is the weight computed as a share of jth DMU's assets on total assets of all estimated DMUs from a particular country, Θ_j is the observed efficiency for the jth DMU, and j

indicates the different *n* DMUs. Results of the *SEA* calculation for all banking sectors are portrayed in Table 5-17.

Table 5-17 Average size-adjusted efficiency (SAE) in national banking sectors (2001–2004, in %)

	2001	2002	2003	2004	change
Greece	86.76	76.30	88.29	91.27	5.20
Portugal	98.91	91.66	90.97	93.34	-5.63
Czech Republic	75.35	79.57	84.68	89.01	18.13
Hungary	70.57	70.49	82.33	87.40	23.85
Poland	79.34	67.22	75.95	76.54	-3.53
Slovakia	39.10	43.81	55.40	66.89	71.07
Estonia	59.24	62.03	88.75	91.05	53.70
Latvia	44.50	53.48	61.14	66.25	48.88
Lithuania	40.38	46.70	63.11	68.31	69.17
Bulgaria	32.61	63.82	72.39	75.84	132.57
Romania	53.33	54.91	67.37	72.75	36.41

Source: Author's calculations

The *SEA* indicator may be used to investigate whether size of a bank matters in explaining differences in the efficiency achieved. To proceed in this kind of analysis we have to compare *SAE* with a "simple" average efficiency. If the difference is positive the larger banks over-perform the smaller banks and vice versa. The higher the absolute value of the difference, the more significant is the gap in efficiency between large and small banks. See Table 5-18 for differences calculated for all banking sectors.

The results indicate that the absolute value of differences between two types of average efficiency decreased during the period under study and it exceeded five percentage points only in two countries in 2004 compared with seven countries in 2001. In other words, performance of larger and smaller banks became more equalized and the size of a bank did not significantly account for variances in efficiency among banks. Considering results from 2004, the difference is positive in eight out of eleven banking sectors suggesting better performance of larger banks.[15] Such a finding is evident mainly in the B3 countries and it is worth noting that the difference was negative in Estonia and Lithuania in 2001.

Table 5-18 Differences between SAE and average efficiency (2001–2004, in percentage points)

	2001	2002	2003	2004
Greece	8.22	3.64	2.10	2.32
Portugal	7.39	9.40	1.00	1.55
Czech Republic	11.45	2.40	-0.64	0.91
Hungary	6.17	0.19	-0.93	1.12
Poland	9.81	1.51	0.82	-1.27
Slovakia	-4.63	-4.10	-8.23	-5.80
Estonia	-3.90	-3.91	4.78	3.07
Latvia	4.26	2.45	6.06	4.83
Lithuania	-10.31	1.73	6.70	7.44
Bulgaria	-4.78	0.74	1.52	2.36
Romania	7.53	-11.07	-6.58	-4.17

Source: Author's calculations

Recall that the CCR efficiency score is a product of technical and scale efficiency, and BCC measures purely technical efficiency; thus, the ratio of the efficiency scores:

$$S_j = \frac{\Theta_{j,CCR}}{\Theta_{j,BCC}} \tag{5.18}$$

yields a measure of the relative scale efficiency of bank j. If $S_j = 1$, this means that bank n is operating at the most efficient scale size. If it is less than one, this means there is scale inefficiency for bank j. Thus, $(1-S_j)$ represents the relative scale inefficiency of a bank. The units that are CCR-efficient will also be scale-efficient, since scale was already factored in the CCR model. Thus, the two are equal. The units that are BCC-efficient, but inefficient in the CCR model, have a scale inefficiency. Since they were technically efficient, all of the inefficiencies picked up by CCR are due to scale. However this ratio does not indicate whether the banks with scale inefficiency are too small or too big. To detect not only the extend of scale inefficiency but also its orientation we modified the ratio and replaced the CRS efficiency by non-decreasing returns to scale (NDRS) efficiency and VRS efficiency by the non-increasing returns to scale (NIRS) efficiency score:

$$S_j = \frac{\Theta_{j,NDRS}}{\Theta_{j,NIRS}}. \tag{5.19}$$

Consequently, the scale inefficiency higher than zero denotes too large bank and inefficiency lower than zero identifies too small bank from the point of view of the input-oriented DEA model. Average scale inefficiencies of all banking sectors are presented in Tables 5-19 and 5-20. Moreover, the table shows average size-adjusted scale inefficiency (*SASI*) taking into account the size of the bank and its market power in the country's banking sector. This indicator can shed some light on the issue whether the size of a bank is related to the scale inefficiency. *SASI* is calculated analogically with the equation (5.17) and can be formally written as:

$$SASI = \sum_{j=1}^{n} w_j SI_j, \tag{5.20}$$

where *SASI* is the size-adjusted average efficiency, w_j is the weight computed as a share of jth DMU's assets on total assets of all estimated DMUs from a particular country, SI_j is the observed scale inefficiency for the jth DMU calculated as $1\text{-}S_j$, and j indicates the different n DMUs. If the SASI is higher than the average scale inefficiency the larger banks suffer from the scale inefficiency more than the smaller banks and vice versa.

Table 5-19 Scale inefficiency in banking sectors (2001–2002, in %)

	2001		2002	
	scale ineff.	**SASI**	**scale ineff.**	**SASI**
Greece	16.79	47.61	13.95	19.65
Portugal	41.73	48.60	13.48	24.77
Czech Republic	20.79	42.03	5.71	14.55
Hungary	22.06	31.87	6.67	11.60
Poland	24.47	44.19	8.81	17.71
Slovakia	12.04	21.70	3.61	7.63
Estonia	-2.82	26.50	3.21	8.25
Latvia	4.31	11.41	1.90	2.55
Lithuania	-34.65	12.53	3.41	5.72
Bulgaria	-6.19	7.51	2.98	5.32
Romania	11.35	30.43	6.88	15.88

Source: Author's calculations

Table 5-20 Scale inefficiency in banking sectors (2003–2004, in %)

	2003		2004	
	scale ineff.	**SASI**	**scale ineff.**	**SASI**
Greece	21.94	25.93	24.08	26.67
Portugal	19.63	24.60	20.44	25.03
Czech Republic	14.93	23.75	16.72	24.90
Hungary	16.86	22.54	17.55	23.31
Poland	14.49	23.54	13.60	24.77
Slovakia	5.88	16.91	8.93	17.80
Estonia	-0.16	19.18	2.41	15.48
Latvia	4.25	9.60	3.21	7.72
Lithuania	3.04	10.93	4.42	11.24
Bulgaria	2.88	6.97	1.57	8.16
Romania	4.65	17.50	6.13	20.05

Source: Author's calculations

The results presented on scale inefficiency clearly show some common findings for the entire sample. First, all scale inefficiencies are positive in 2004 suggesting the banks are too large with respect to their real output production. Second, countries analyzed can be divided into two groups according to the level of scale inefficiency using results from 2004. The first group generally consists of banking sectors with efficiency higher than average and scale inefficiency varying from 13.60 to 24.08 per cent. The second group overwhelmingly comprises banking sectors with efficiency lower than average and scale inefficiency ranging between 1.57 and 8.93 per cent. One can point out that higher average efficiency goes concurrently with higher scale inefficiency.[16]

High scale inefficiency in Greece and Portugal stems from the fact that banks in these countries maintain an extensive network of bank branches compared to the number of branches in the CEE-9 countries.[17] This traditional structure, common in EU15 (50 bank branches per 100,000 inhabitants), is very efficient in collecting deposits (input side of banking intermediation) but not so in disbursing loans (output side of banking intermediation). Thus, a better utilisation of existing size or its consolidation may contribute to the decline of scale inefficiency. On the contrary, banks in B3 or C2 countries operate at almost optimal size and their efficiency gap is therefore primarily caused by technical inefficiency frequently assigned to the shortage of managerial skills. Third, the scale inefficiency decreased in all countries except Greece. This development may be attributed to the ongoing restructuring of banks after privatisation, successful expansion of purely foreign-owned and middle-sized banks to the retail segment of the market and positive trends in economic environment. Fourth, the *SASI* figures unambiguously show that the problem of inadequate size refers especially to large banks. It is also absolutely evident that this issue gains strength in the CEE-9 countries where the difference between SASI and the average scale inefficiency are in many cases very close or surpassing the level of ten percentage points.

Conclusion

This study aimed to estimate and compare efficiency of banking intermediation in eleven countries representing four relatively homogenous groups of countries at different stages of European integration and economic development during the period 2001–04. We also analyzed the linkage between efficiency and bank size by calculating size-adjusted efficiency and the issue of the optimal bank size was investigated by incorporating scale inefficiency.

The results of efficiency estimation suggest that there exists an efficiency gap for banks in the CEE-9 countries in comparison to banks from Greece and Portugal representing the least developed EU15 countries. The hierarchy of groups in terms of banking efficiency mostly concurs with that in terms of economic development and the stage achieved towards European integration. We registered a substantial improvement of efficiency in all regions of new-member and candidate countries boosting the convergence process and placing the average efficiency of some CEE-9 countries near efficiency levels of Greece and Portugal. However, favourable performance of transition countries is weakened by a high range of the country's efficiency means. In particular, whereas the Czech banking sector's average efficiency almost equals the efficiency in Greece, the Slovak banking sector, as the other representative of the V4 region, was evaluated as the third least efficient of all countries. Similarly, Estonian banks achieved in 2004 an average efficiency of only one and half percentage points lower than the same indicator in Greece. At the same time, Latvia and Lithuania obtained an average efficiency score that was almost 20 percentage points lower than the entire sample's mean and were consequently classified as the least efficient banking sectors. Therefore, these are the only two countries where the low efficiency of banking intermediation could hamper economic growth and the convergence process. In Lithuania, such a conclusion is amplified by a considerably slow growth of efficiency between 2001 and 2004.

Another crucial problem in the CEE-9 countries is the noticeably high scale inefficiency of large banks. These banks are too big with respect to their real output production and the road towards higher efficiency does not lead through establishing of new branches and engaging of new employees. This conclusion is extremely important in the context of generally lower number of bank branches and consequently lower direct accessibility of banking services in the CEE-9 countries as compared to EU15. Therefore, large banks may either consolidate the input base or make progress in its utilisation. Closing branches is highly improbable because of the recent expansion of medium-sized banks in the retail market, and large banks are not likely to loose their market share. Likewise, the consolidation can not be done by a wave of mergers. Nearly all large banks in the CEE-9 countries are owned by strategic foreign investors and it is absolutely out of the question to proceed with a merger of daughter banks without the same process involving the parent institutions. Thus, the adequate approach to improve efficiency is the better utilisation of existing inputs in financial intermediation. A complex menu of banking products and services of the highest quality is the only possibility to attract well-renowned and long-established companies and manufacturers which are the most credible and sought after bank customers. Since this market segment is extremely competitive, credit institutions should extend their lending activities particularly in the household sector as well as and small and medium-sized enterprises.

References

Andronova-Vincelete, G. 2001. Bulgarian Banking Sector Development, Post-1989. *Southeast European Politics* 2(1):4–23.

Balcerowicz, Ewa and Andrzej Bratkowski. 2001. *Restructuring and Development of the Banking Sector in Poland. Lessons to Be Learnt by Less Advanced Transition Countries.* CASE Reports No. 44. Warsaw: CASE.

Banker, R.D., A. Charnes and W.W. Cooper. 1984. Some Models for Estimating Technical and Scale Inefficiencies in Data Envelopment Analysis. *Management Science* 30(9):1078–92.

Berg, A., F.R. Forsund, L. Hjarmansson and M. Suominen. 1993. Banking Efficiency in the Nordic Countries. *Journal of Banking and Finance* 17(2/3):371–88.

Berger, A.N. and D.B. Humphrey. 1997. Efficiency of Financial Institutions: International Survey and Directions for Future Research. *European Journal of Operational Research* 98:175–212.

Bonin, J., I. Hasan and P. Wachtel. 2005. Bank performance, efficiency and ownership in transition countries. *Journal of Banking and Finance* 29(1):31–53.

Bonin, John and Paul Wachtel. 2002. *Financial Sector Development in Transition Economies: Lessons from the First Decade.* BOFIT Discussion Paper 9/2002. Helsinki: BOFIT.

Bruckbauer, Stefan, Sándor Gárdó and Lisa Perrin. 2004. *Banking in CEE*. Wien: Bank Austria Creditanstalt.

Canhoto, Ana Maria and Jean Dermine. 2000. *A Non-Parametric Evaluation of Banking Efficiency in Portugal, New vs. Old Banks. Working Paper No. 2000/03/FIN*. Lisbon: Univesidade Católica Portuguesa.

Carbo, S., E.P.M. Gardener and J. Williams. 2000. Efficiency and Technical Change in Europe's Savings Banks Industry. *Revue de la Banque* 6(2):381–94.

Casu, B. and P. Molyneux. 2003. A Comparative Study of Efficiency in European Banking. *Applied Economics* 35(17):1865–76.

Charnes, A. and W.W. Cooper. 1962. Programming with Linear Fractional Functions. *Naval Research Logistic Quarterly* 9(304):181–6.

Charnes, A., W.W. Cooper and E. Rhodes. 1978. Measuring the Efficiency of Decision Making Units. *European Journal of Operational Research* 2(2):429–44.

Chritopoulos, D.K., S.E.G. Lolos and E.G. Tsonias. 2002. Efficiency of the Greek banking system in view of the EMU: a heteroscedastic stochastic frontier approach. *Journal of Policy Modelling* 24(9):813–29.

Demel, Walter, Stefan Maxian and Helena Horská. 2005. *CEE Banking Sector Report*. Vienna: Raiffeisen Zentralbank Österreich AG.

European Central Bank. 2004. *Report on EU banking structure*. Frakfurt am Main: Euroepan Central Bank.

————. 2005a. EU banking sector stability. Frakfurt am Main: Euroepan Central Bank.

————. 2005b. EU banking structures. Frakfurt am Main: Euroepan Central Bank.

Farrell, M.J. 1957. The Measurement of Productive Efficiency. *Journal of the Royal Statistical Society (Series A)* 120(2):253–81.

Favero, C.A. and L. Papi. 1995. Technical Efficiency and Scale Efficiency in the Italian Banking Sector: A non-parametric Approach. *Applied Economics* 27(3):385–95.

Fries, Stephen and Anita Taci. 2002. *Banking Reform and Development in Transition Economies*. EBRD Working Paper No. 71. London: EBRD.

————. 2005. Cost efficiency of banks in transition: Evidence from 289 banks in 15 post-communist countries. *Journal of Banking and Finance* 29(1):55–81.

Golajewska, Marta and Pawel Wyczański, eds. 2002. *Stability and Structure of Financial Systems in CEC5*. Warsaw: National Bank of Poland.

Grigorian, David A. and Vlad Manole. 2002. *Determinants of Commercial Bank Performance in Transition: An Application of Data Envelopment Analysis. (World Bank Policy Research Paper 2850)*. Washington, D.C.: World Bank.

Hájková, D., J. Hanousek and L. Němeček. 2002. The Czech Republic's Banking Sector: Emerging from Turbulent Times. *BIS Papers* 7(1):55–74.

Hansson, Ardo H. and Triinu Tombak. 1999. Banking Crises in the Baltic States: Causes, Solutions and Lessons. In *Financial Sector Transformation: Lessons from Economies in Transition*, ed Mario I. Blejer and Marko Škreb, 195–236. Cambridge: Cambridge University Press.

Hasan, I. and K. Marton. 2003. Development and efficiency of the banking sector in a transitional economy: Hungarian experience. *Journal of Banking and Finance* 27(12):2249–71.

Havrylchyk, Olga. 2004. *Efficiency of the Polish Banking Industry: Foreign versus Domestic Banks.* Paper presented at the conference Economic, Econometric and Cross-Disciplinary Aspects of European Union Enlargement at EUI Florence on May 13–14, 2004.

Kamberouglou, Nicos C., Elias Liapis, Georgie T. Simigiannis and Panagiota Tzamourani. 2004. *Cost Efficiency in Greek Banking.* Working Paper No. 9. Athens: Bank of Greece.

Kulhánek, Lumír, Stanislav Polouček and Daniel Stavárek. 2004. The Financial and Banking Sectors in Transition Countries. In *Reforming the Financial Sector in Central European Countries*, ed Stanislav Polouček, 1–32. Houndmills, Basingstoke, Hampshire: Palgrave Macmillan.

Leibenstein, H. 1966. Allocative Efficiency vs. "X-Efficiency". *American Economic Review* 56(3):392–415.

Lozano–Vivas, A., J.T. Pastor and I. Hasan. 2001. European Bank Performance Beyond Country Borders: What Really Matters? *European Finance Review* 5(1–2):141–65.

Matoušek, Roman. 2004. *Efficiency and Scale Economies in Banking: Empirical Evidence from Eight Accession Countries.* Paper presented on XIV. Conference A.I.S.S.E.C. in Naples, 27–28 February, 2004.

McAllister, P.H. and D. McManus. 1993. Resolving the Scale Efficiency Puzzle in Banking. *Journal of Banking and Finance* 17(2/3):389–406.

Nikiel, E.N. and T.P. Opiela. 2002. Customer Type and Bank Efficiency in Poland: Implications for Emerging Market Banking. *Contemporary Economic Policy* 20(3):255–71.

Pastor, J.T., A. Lozano and J.M. Pastor. 1997. *Efficiency of European Banking Systems: A Correction by Environmental Variables.* Valencia: IVIE.

Pawlowska, Malgorzata. 2003. *The Impact of M&A on Technical Efficiency, Scale Efficiency and Productivity Change in the Polish Banking Sector: a Non-Parametric Approach.* Materialy i Studia – Paper No. 29. Warsaw: National Bank of Poland.

Sealey, C.W. and J.T. Lindley. 1977. Inputs, Outputs and a Theory of Production and Cost at Depository Financial Institutions. *Journal of Finance* 32(8):1251–66.

Sherman, D.H. and F. Gold. 1985. Bank Branch Operating Efficiency: Evaluation with Data Envelopment Analysis. *Journal of Banking and Finance* 9(3):297–315.

Polouček, Stanislav, ed. 2004. *Reforming the Financial Sector in Central European Countries.* Houndmills, Basingstoke, Hampshire: Palgrave Macmillan.

Stavárek, D. 2004. Banking Efficiency in Visegrad Countries Before Joining the European Union. *European Review of Economics and Finance* 3(3):129–67.

————. 2005a. Efficiency of Central European Banks in 1999–2003: A Stochastic Frontier Approach. *Acta Academica Karviniensia* 6(1): 224–37.

————. 2005b. Zprostředkovatelská činnost bank ve střední Evropě: Část I.– Mezinárodní analýza efektivnosti. *Ekonomie a Management* 8(1): 33–53.

Stavárek, Daniel and Stanislav Polouček. 2004. Efficiency and Profitability in the Banking Sector. In *Reforming the Financial Sector in Central European Countries*, ed Stanislav Polouček, 75–135. Houndmills, Basingstoke, Hampshire: Palgrave Macmillan.

Szapáry, György. 2001. *Banking Sector Reform in Hungary: Lessons Learned, Current Trends and Prospects.* NBH Working Paper 2001/5. Budapest: National Bank of Hungary.

Taci, Anita and Emilia Zampieri. 1998. *Efficiency in the Czech banking sector.* CERGE-EI Discussion Paper No. 4/98. Prague: Charles University.

Tkáčová, D. 2001. Banking Sector in the Slovak Republic. Development, Restructuring and Privatisation. *BIATEC* 9(8–10):38–40.

Tsantis, Andreas. 1997. Developments in the Romanian Banking Sector. In *The New Banking Landscape in Central and Eastern Europe: Country Experiences and Policies for the* Future, 167–216. Paris: Organisation for Economic Co-operation and Development.

Vujcic, B. and I. Jemric. 2002. Efficiency of Banks in Croatia: A DEA Approach. *Comparative Economic Studies* 44(1):169–93.

Weill, Laurent. 2003. *Is There a Lasting Gap in Bank Efficiency between Eastern and Western European Countries?* Paper presented at the 20th Symposium on Monetary and Financial Economics in Birmingham, June 2003.

————. 2004. On the Relationship Between Competition and Efficiency in the EU Banking Sectors. *Kredit und Kapital* 37(3):329–52.

Wheelock, D.C. and P.W. Whilson. 1999. Technical Progress, Inefficiency, and Productivity Change in U.S. Banking, 1984–1993. *Journal of Money, Credit, and Banking* 31(2):212–34.

Yildirim, Semih H. and George C. Philippatos. 2002. *Efficiency of Banks: Recent Evidence from the Transition Economies of Europe – 1993–2000.* Paper presented at EMFA Meeting 2002 in London.

Notes

1 The research behind this paper is supported by the Czech Science Foundation within a project no. GAČR 402/05/2758 "Integration of the financial sector of the new EU member countries into the EMU".

2 See Chapter One or Polouček (2004) for more about structure of the financial sector in selected European countries.

3 The annual growth rates of the real GDP in Greece were 4.3 per cent in 2001, 3.6 per cent in 2002, 4.5 per cent in 2003, and 4.1 per cent in 2004. The Portuguese economy grew in the real terms by 1.7 percent in 2001, 0.4 per cent in 2002, -1.1 per cent in 2003, and 1.0 per cent in 2004.

4 For more about banking sector transformation in transition countries, see Kulhánek *et al.* (2004), Bonin and Wachtel (2002) or Fries and Taci (2002) among others.

5 Both figures do not include institutions from the cooperative sectors.

6 Consolidation of the Czech banking sector is discussed for instance in Hájková *et al.* (2002), Hungary's consolidation program is analyzed in Szapáry (2001), Balcerowicz and Bratkowski (2001) pay attention on the Polish consolidation and Tkáčová (2001) deals with banking sector stabilisation in Slovakia. An in-depth analysis of banking sector transformation in Bulgaria and Romania is provided in Andronova–Vincelete (2001) and Tsantis (1997) respectively. Analysis of causes, lessons and solutions of the banking crises in the Baltic States is provided in Hansson and Tombak (1999).

7 For an in-depth description of the concept of efficiency and differences between efficiency, productivity and profitability see Stavárek and Polouček (2004).

8 Such conclusions are in conflict with a top position of the Czech banking sector and generally low efficiency of Slovak banks endorsed by the results of the aforementioned studies.

9 In particular, the dataset consists of eight Greek, seven Portuguese, 15 Czech, 16 Hungarian, 26 Polish, 12 Slovak, six Estonian, 10 Latvian, eight Lithuanian, eight Bulgarian, and seven Romanian banks in 2001. In 2002, the dataset comprises nine Greek, 10 Portuguese, 15 Czech, 12 Hungarian, 21 Polish, 12 Slovak, six Estonian, 10 Latvian, eight Lithuanian, 12 Bulgarian, and 12 Romanian banks. In 2003, nine

Greek, 10 Portuguese, 12 Czech, 14 Hungarian, 21 Polish, 12 Slovak, six Estonian, 10 Latvian, eight Lithuanian, 12 Bulgarian, and 12 Romanian banks were included in the dataset. In 2004, the analysis was based on data from nine Greek, 10 Portuguese, 12 Czech, 14 Hungarian, 20 Polish, 12 Slovak, six Estonian, 10 Latvian, eight Lithuanian, 12 Bulgarian, and 12 Romanian banks.

[10] Under the non-parametric approach which will be implemented in our empirical analysis, increasing the number of variables reduces the number of technically inefficient observations. Therefore, in order to minimize this possible drawback of the methodology, we restricted our choice of variables to a three-input, two-output model.

[11] The decrease in efficiency of Portuguese banks may partly stem from the economic recession in Portugal which started in 2002 and extended throughout 2003.

[12] Poland experienced stagnation in 2001 and 2002, budget deficit surpassed the Maastricht criterion of 3 per cent of GDP in all four years analyzed, the FDI inflow slackened in 2002 and 2003, and gross foreign debt exceeded 45 per cent of GDP in 2003.

[13] The comparatively low level of financial intermediation is emphasized by the low penetration of banking services. Only 65 per cent of Poles over the age of 18 have a bank account, and only 53 per cent of all account holders use bank cards.

[14] Results of estimation including names of banks analyzed and their efficiency scores, weights or data may be provided by the author upon request.

[15] It is quite a common finding for many other studies that smaller banks dominate the frontier in the CCR model, while in the BCC model, frontier banks are on average much larger (e.g. Berg *et al.* (1993) or Vujcic and Jemric (2002) came to the same conclusion).

[16] There are two exemptions. First, Polish banks' average efficiency was below the entire sample's average and their average scale inefficiency exceeded the sample's average in 2004. Second, situation of Estonian banks was absolutely opposite in 2004.

[17] In 2004, there were 3,403 branches in Greece, 5,408 branches in Portugal, 1,785 branches in the Czech Republic, 1,015 branches in Hungary, 3,084 branches in Poland, 1,113 branches in Slovakia, 203 branches in Estonia, 583 branches in Latvia, 758 branches in Lithuania, 689 branches in Bulgaria, and 2,864 branches in Romania. The difference between the Western and Eastern zone become even more evident if the ratio of bank braches' number on 100,000 inhabitants is calculated.

CHAPTER SIX

CROSS-BORDER BANKING MERGERS AND ACQUISITIONS IN EUROPE: AN EMPIRICAL INVESTIGATION

The European banking landscape has experienced a profound restructuring since the mid 1980s and still is substantially changing. The change has been driven by a tremendous technological progress, the ongoing national and European deregulation, the implementation of the European Monetary Union (EMU), and ongoing globalisation (Bank for International Settlements, 2001). In most countries, the gradual elimination of barriers to international capital flows, jointly with a general relaxation of barriers to operating across geopolitical borders have made possible the ongoing expansion of international financial institutions. Allowing the production of financial services at large distances from the home country headquarters, the new communications, information, and financial technologies have helped banking institutions take advantage of these relaxed geopolitical barriers. As well, the globalisation of non-financial economic activity has increased the demand for the services of multinational financial institutions, capable of following customers operating in foreign countries.

For a number of reasons, domestic banking mergers and acquisitions (M&As) have long outnumbered cross-border operations in European countries. First, most countries have historically used regulations to discourage foreign entry – for example, requiring foreign banks to hold excess amounts of capital, or requiring branches of foreign banks to adhere to both home and host country regulations. Second, the difficulty of operating in a foreign country is also due to the differences in language, business customs, laws and problems associated with distance that devalued such investments. Third, domestic banks might form combinations in order to gain the scale needed to make future cross-border acquisitions themselves or to compete more effectively against potential foreign entrants (Berger *et al.*, 2004).

The experience of the European community constitutes a unique case for the investigation of cross-border banking activity and foreign investments. The Treaty of Rome in 1957 created the basis for the existence of a European common market. The First Banking Co-ordination Directive of 1977 created a framework for a single European banking market by eliminating differences in banking regulations and practices across the Member States of the European Union (EU).

A license from the national authority was needed in most countries to operate in the market. The Second Banking Co-ordination Directive of 1989 introduced a single banking license for operating across the EU, aimed at liberalizing the trade of financial services across Europe. Therefore, a bank authorized to operate in a member country could operate in any other member countries without any further local authorisation. However, national European governments can not formally allow foreign banks entry that involves the acquisition of domestic banks.[1] Given the important obstacles to cross-border banking activity, some studies (Berger *et al.*, 1999; Boot, 2003) outline the limited relevance of the traditional economic rationale to explain the banking movements abroad. In this respect, the recent research tried to provide an alternative argument, specific to the international banking growth strategies. On the other hand, the recent changes in the macro environment suggest that pan-European consolidation is likely to accelerate. The European Central Bank and European Commission are actively pushing for the creation of an integrated financial system to better allocate capital across Europe and increase competition in banking services. Moreover, regulatory harmonisation has increased significantly compared with the last ten years (Basel II, IAS/IFRS) making accounts much more transparent and reducing "regulatory" risks. In this context, consolidation activity among European banks significantly increased within the last decade and in particular within the last two years.

In this chapter, we study the determinants of cross-border banking M&A activity in Europe, given the context of the recent phase of banking internationalisation. Using the data of banking M&A activities over the period 1987–2004, we perform the analysis of countries' characteristics in order to explain cross-border investments by banking institutions in Europe. Our contribution consists in distinguishing between investing countries and the target countries of foreign banking acquisitions. Considering the theory of comparative advantage, we have tested whether some of the countries have advantages in receiving banking FDI or investing abroad via cross-border M&As.

The remainder of the chapter is organized as follows. The next section highlights the previous empirical evidence on cross-border banking activity and sets up the theoretical background for the empirical analysis of M&As trends. Section 2 describes the data set and presents the results of empirical analysis on the determinants of cross-border banking M&A activity in European countries. In the last section, we conclude about policy implications of our results.

Theoretical and Empirical Research on Cross-Border Banking

Important research on banking consolidation in Europe examined the external factors that facilitate European banking integration and consolidation. These factors include: (i) globalisation of the international financial system due to the liberalisation of international capital movements and financial deregulation within countries; (ii) major technological advances, particularly in the field of data processing; (iii) improvements in the cross-border regulatory environment linked to the Single Market Programme and the introduction of the Euro. Other studies focus on the motivations of banks to expand in foreign markets and the obstacles that they face to be as efficient and competitive as the domestic institutions.

Theoretical Background of Cross-Border Banking Activity

Previous research has emphasized the importance of barriers to entry as the main determinant of cross border banking movements. Regulatory restrictions in the host country have often been mentioned as a barrier to entry in multinational banking. A pre-requisite for entering a foreign country is, obviously, the national authority's approval of the entry. As previously noted, regulatory barriers were formally removed within the EU through the Second Banking Directive. Nevertheless, factors, such as the existence of hidden restrictions, as well as non-regulatory barriers could at least partially isolate national banking sectors from competition (Blandon, 2000). Many theoretical and empirical studies focused on the motivations of international banking. According to the results of research on international banking activity, the banking motivations to expand in foreign markets (through M&As) can be classified in four main rationales: (i) servicing exporters from the home country; (ii) servicing foreign subsidiaries of home country clients; (iii) participating in the host county's capital market; (iv) participating in the host country's banking system or banking consolidation process.

The main motive for banking foreign banking investment (FDI) is to provide banking services to the home country's clients. The range of banking services typically offered would include the providing of information about the general and economic conditions for doing business in a particular foreign country and, above all, the collection of receivables for home country exporters. The rationale for this behaviour would be the need to preserve existing banking relationships in the home country before they could be eventually substituted by a new banking relationship (Williams, 1997). Following the banking clients' multinational expansion has been widely considered as the main motivation of cross-border banking movements.

Grubel (1977) applied the theories of FDI and international trade to the internationalisation of banks providing the theoretical explanation. According to this explanation, multinational banks go abroad to service their domestic customers who have gone abroad. Information asymmetries regarding local banks about the client's financial needs would constitute the main ownership advantage for the foreign bank. The Eclectic theory provides the theoretical framework of international banking based on three concepts: ownership advantage, location advantage, and internalisation advantage. The presence of these advantages allows the foreign bank to overcome the advantages possessed by the domestic banks due to incumbency. Given the basic characteristics of the financial services industry, the eclectic framework predicts that banking institutions are more likely to move across international boundaries via FDI rather than by cross-border trade.

Ownership advantages are resources or production processes to which firms in the host countries do not have access. These proprietary assets that are typically knowledge-based represent a crucial factor to prompt FDI. This is due to the possibility of moving knowledge-based assets across great distances at low cost, and applying them to multiple plants at low marginal cost. These advantages in the form of intangible, customer-specific, and knowledge-based assets are important for providing credit to small and medium sized enterprises.

Location advantages are conditions in the host country that make it profitable for a multinational enterprise to produce in the host country rather than producing at home and export to the host country (Berger *et al.*, 2004). Some examples of location advantage are cheap factor prices in the host country, high transportation costs, import quotas and tariffs, and better access to the host country customers. The factors relative to location advantages in multinational banking include differences in regulatory structures, the geographical dispersion of the bank's client base, leading to banks following their retail customers, information collection, and access to a skilled pool of labours.

Internalisation advantages are conditions which preclude a firm from simply licensing its "knowledge capital" to a host country firm. According to Casson (1990), the existing flow of information resulting from the bank-client relationship would not be pre-empted by a potential competitor bank. The underlying hypothesis to this point of view is to consider the bank's information network and its infrastructure of skills that correspond to the personal contact, as one of the main advantages of a multinational bank. Therefore, owning information-gathering centres in a variety of locations can enhance these advantages. Williams (1997) considers the ability of the multinational bank to institutionalize and learn from this network of information as source of its comparative advantage. Banks have traditionally played a major role in domestic and international capital markets. The growing expansion of commercial banks towards the securities business should make this trend continue and even increase in the future.

Accordingly, some authors (Heinkel and Levi, 1992; Focarelli *et al.*, 2000) have suggested that banks will establish facilities abroad with the aim of participating in the host country's capital market. Hence, banks would funnel internationally the savings originated in the home country through cross-border acquisitions and have easier access to the domestic customers. The greater possibilities of diversification available at an international level would justify this behaviour. Participating in the host country banking consolidation should be a straightforward motivation for cross-border acquisitions. Accordingly, banks would enter in foreign countries to carry out the typical commercial banking activities, i.e. lending and accepting deposits. The less concentrated foreign markets are more likely to be the targets of cross-border banking investments.

Previous Evidence on International Banking Activity

Previous research on international banking provides empirical evidence on the following issues: (i) limited economies of scale and synergies achieved on cross-border M&As; (ii) difficulties associated with cross-border banking activity, (iii) low performance of international banks in foreign markets; (iv) strategic rationale of international banking growth. The empirical evidence on cross-border banking M&As confirms the consensus view that cross-border deals add limited value. The academic research on cross-border acquisitions of financial institutions in developed countries suggests mediocre post-merger financial performance at best. Examining cross-border operations in Europe, Beitel and Schiereck (2001) found that the associated combined bidder and target value changes were generally zero or negative, compared with domestic mergers, in which combined values were positive on average.

A study of U.S. M&As provides some evidence consistent with fewer benefits from cross-border M&As. De Long (2001) found that mergers combining two firms from different geographic areas created less shareholder value. Similarly, the risk-reduction benefits from cross-border bank mergers seem to be no insignificant as they have little impact on the volatility of stock returns as proved by Amihud *et al.* (2002). Whereas most of the empirical studies on efficiency of foreign banks in developed countries found that domestically owned banks are more efficient, Berger *et al.* (2000) show the possible exception for U.S. banks. In a European study, Vander Vennet (1996) found that foreign institutions have about the same efficiency on average as domestic institutions while a few studies have shown the same evidence. The research on cross-border banking efficiency in developing countries finds different results from those in developed countries. Studying foreign banks in over 80 countries, Claessens *et al.* (2001) found that foreign-owned banks have relatively high profitability in developing countries.

The empirical studies provide evidence of limited gains from cross-border M&As. This result is due to the obstacles faced by foreign-owned institutions that limit their efficiency. Accordingly, Buch and DeLong (2004) found that the banks in highly regulated markets are less likely to be the targets of cross-border acquisitions. The results of their study suggest that cultural differences and distance tend to discourage these types of operations. Therefore, these kinds of structural factors act as barriers to cross-border lending and borrowing by banks, considering the results of Buch (2001, 2003).

Berger and Smith (2003) detected another obstacle related to the preferences of the customers for the services provided by the local banks. The domestically owned banks have the advantage of better knowledge of the local conditions and information about domestic customers. In this respect, foreign affiliates of multinational corporations operating in European countries usually choose domestic banks for cash management, liquidity services, and short-term financing. Other studies have argued that cross-border consolidation within Europe may be deterred by political factors, cultural differences, the use of different payment and settlement systems, and remaining differences in capital markets, taxes, and regulations across the countries (Boot, 2003; Blandon, 2000).

Many empirical studies confirm the hypothesis of "following-the-client behaviour" as driving factor of banking internationalisation (Grosse and Goldberg, 1991, Wengel, 1995; Brealey and Kaplanis, 1996). Concerning the latter argument, Casson (1990) found that U.S. banks expanded offshore to follow the expansion of U.S. manufacturing firms. This empirical research supports servicing home country exporters as a determinant of foreign banking expansion. However, the results of Stanley *et al.* (1993) and Seth *et al.* (1998) suggest that this strategy is not the only motivation explaining cross-border M&As. Focarelli and Pozzolo (2001) argued that this motivation is only relevant for small banks, while the behaviour of larger banks is determined by diversification polices. Previous research has revealed the existence of a large and well-developed capital market in the home country, as a determinant of banking expansion abroad. Accordingly, DePaula (2002) suggests that the internationalisation of banks could also be explained by the strategy of universal banks seeking to diversify their activities in the financial markets of the host country through the acquisition of majority, controlling stakes or the acquisition of minority. Hence, economic conditions in the home and the host countries seem to be the key determinants of the banking FDI.

The study of Focarelli *et al.* (2001) provides some evidence consistent with the explanation of banking internationalisation that is due to increased banking competition caused by financial deregulation. The results of their study suggest that countries with developed financial markets are more likely to be at the origin of cross-border M&As. The empirical evidence reveals that banks expand to countries where the potential economic growth is stronger and the banking sector is less efficient. De Félice and Revoltella (2003) provide some evidence consistent with the importance of the regulatory environment and the degree of concentration in the host country and the domestic country of the international bank as decisive factor of its strategies to go abroad. The results of Berger *et al.* (2004) provide empirical evidence of the international trade theories (theory of comparative advantage and the new trade theory) as a framework to explain cross-border financial M&As. They found that the characteristics of EU countries are determining factors of financial FDI having implications on the comparative advantage of foreign banks.

Empirical Evidence on Cross-Border Banking M&As in Europe

The purpose of our empirical tests is to investigate the patterns of FDI via cross-border banking M&As in Europe. Unlike most previous researchers, we focus our analysis only on international banking expansion in the main European countries.

European Banking M&As Trends

The data of M&A trends reported in Figure 6-1 show a significant M&A activity among large credit institutions in the run-up to and the early years of the EMU (1998–2000). During 2003, M&A activity in terms of value stabilised at levels comparable with those recorded in 2001 and 2002 (European Central Bank, 2004). Around 70 per cent of the entire transactions volume between 1985 and 2000 are related to nationally focused banking M&As. Thus, European banking institutions seem to consolidate their national markets first to become powerful enough to stand the arising competition of a single European market of financial services.[2]

Fig. 6-1 Volume of banking M&As in the EU (1990–2004, in USD bln)

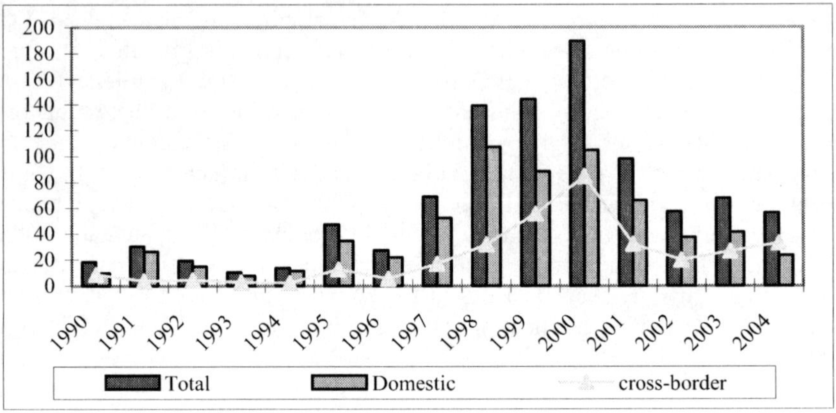

Source: Thomson Financial Securities, author's calculations

In 2004, the percentage of domestic M&A activity in the banking sector fell to 42 per cent of the total value of M&A transactions. The recent acquisition of Abbey National by Santander explains to some extent this new trend in the M&A activity of European banks. This transaction and the recent ongoing deals between Banco Bilbao Vizcaya Argentaria, ABN Amro and the Italian banks Banca Nazionale del Lavoro and Banca Antonveneta draws more attention to cross-border M&As and raises the question of future deals between EU financial institutions.

In order to identify the determinants of cross-border M&As in the EU, we focus our analysis on the investing and receiving countries of foreign banking investments. The data of M&As are taken from the Thomson Financial Securities Data database on M&As from 1985 to 2004. However, the regression analysis begins from 1987 due to data limitations for other variables. According to the assumption of Berger *et al.* (2004), we consider the M&As in foreign countries as outgoing banking investments and the M&As of foreign banks or credit institutions in a European country as incoming banking investments. These data for the EU banking sector as a whole are displayed in Figure 6-2 and reveal a net investing banking sector with an excess of outgoing investments.[3]

Fig. 6-2 Number of cross-border banking M&As in the EU (1985–2004)

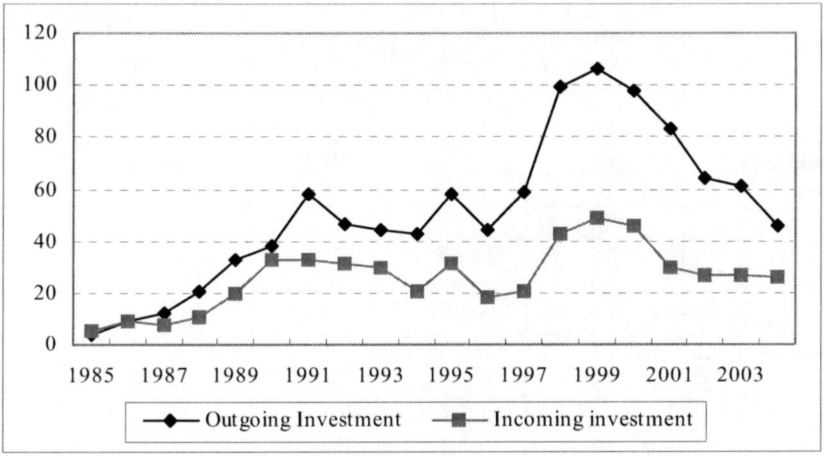

Source: Thomson Financial Securities, author's calculations

We examined the banking FDI in the old EU Member States (EU15) without restricting the target activity of cross-border banking M&As. This methodology of our data selection has the advantage of providing a geographic diversification indicator of banking activities. In this respect, we will test the effects of local countries characteristics on broadening banking scale and scope through cross-border M&As. Table 6-1 presents the number of M&As for the period 1985–2004 in all EU15 banking systems as an indicator of their net internationalisation and the frequency of cross-border banking investments in these countries. The aggregate transaction volumes of cross-border banking acquisitions are displayed in the Table 6-2. The data of cross-border banking activity reveals some EU15 banking systems as net investing and others countries as net receiving of banking FDI. Given the number of banking acquisitions in foreign markets, France, Belgium, Germany, Spain, Netherlands, Austria, Sweden, Luxembourg, and Finland had higher level of outgoing investments than banking FDI received. The second group of countries which predominantly received banking FDI includes Ireland, Italy, Portugal, UK, and Denmark. Nevertheless, Italy and the UK can be perceived as the net-investing countries if the volume of cross-border banking M&As is taken into consideration.

Table 6-1 Number of cross-border banking M&As in EU15 (1985–2004)

Country	(1) Incoming investment (Target)	Share in EU15 (%)	(2) Outgoing investment (Investor)	Share in EU15 (%)	(3)=(2)-(1) Net Investment
Austria	10	1.93	34	3.31	24
Belgium	24	4.62	108	10.52	84
Denmark	14	2.70	9	0.88	-5
Finland	8	1.54	11	1.07	3
France	75	14.45	309	30.09	234
Germany	30	5.78	111	10.81	81
Greece	11	2.12	11	1.07	0
Ireland	21	4.05	20	1.95	-1
Italy	54	10.40	51	4.97	-3
Luxembourg	8	1.54	15	1.46	7
Netherlands	19	3.66	44	4.28	25
Portugal	22	4.24	18	1.75	-4
Spain	74	14.26	122	11.88	48
Sweden	13	2.50	35	3.41	22
UK	136	26.20	129	12.56	-7
EU15	519	100.00	1027	100.00	508

Source: Thomson Financial Securities, author's calculations

The high volume of outgoing investments suggests the large scale of cross-border acquisitions in the EU15 countries. Although the number of transactions implies that Austria, France, Luxembourg, and Finland are investor countries, the volume of investment allow us to draw the opposite conclusion. This result is consistent with the hypothesis that the scale of cross-border deals in these countries affects their position as receiving or investing countries. Therefore, the high level of incoming banking FDI could explain these differences on analysis considering the number or the volume of cross-border acquisitions. Moreover, the differences between the number and the volume of M&As illustrate the importance of target and investing countries' characteristics as determinants of their internationalisation. In this respect, some countries receiving the banking FDI should have some comparative advantages which justify the high number of cross-border M&As in these countries.

Table 6-2 Volume of cross-border banking M&As in EU15 (1985–2004, in EUR mil)

Country	(1) Incoming investment (Target)	Share in EU15 (%)	(2) Outgoing investment (Investor)	Share in EU15 (%)	(3)=(2)-(1) Net Investment
Austria	8 933.8	5.78	3 787.4	1.54	-5 146.4
Belgium	3531	2.29	16 723.2	6.80	13 192.2
Denmark	7 247.2	4.69	2 017.6	0.82	-5 229.6
Finland	9105	5.90	8 178.1	3.32	-926.9
France	28 382.4	18.38	22 518.9	9.15	-5 863.5
Germany	8 927.7	5.78	37 968.5	15.43	29 040.8
Greece	2 105.4	1.36	1 054.0	0.43	-1 051.4
Ireland	4 599.6	2.98	3 256.9	1.32	-1 342.7
Italy	9 269.8	6.00	10 734.9	4.36	1 465.1
Luxembourg	3 812.7	2.47	1 491.3	0.61	-2 321.4
Netherlands	4 785.7	3.10	14 030.5	5.70	9 244.8
Portugal	6 060.9	3.92	2 735.0	1.11	-3 325.9
Spain	10 105.5	6.54	51 808.1	21.06	41 702.6
Sweden	2 578.1	1.67	12 529.9	5.09	9 951.8
UK	44 993.1	29.13	57 205.9	23.25	12 212.8
EU15	154 437.9	100.00	246 040.2	100.00	91 602.3

Source: Thomson Financial Securities, author's calculations

Therefore, there is a high potential for banking institutions operating in these countries to make cross-border acquisitions or to be attractive targets for cross-border M&As. As illustration, we note that the large European countries like France, UK, Spain, Germany, and Italy have the highest share of cross-border banking investment. This result suggests that the scale of M&A operations in these countries has been important. The domestic consolidation of European banking systems and the economic characteristics of their countries could be decisive factors in cross-border banking investments. The discussion about other determinants of cross-border banking movements within Europe is presented in next section. Given the results of analysis, we examine separately the number and the volume of cross-border banking M&As as different indicators of incoming and outgoing banking investments in EU15 countries.

Model, Data and Variables Used

To investigate the determinants of international banking investment in the EU15 countries, we test the following model using the data of cross-border M&As for the period 1987–2004:

$$MA_{it} = a + \sum_{i=1,N} \alpha_i Country_i dummies + \sum_{i=1,N} \beta_i x_{it} + \varepsilon_{it}, \qquad (6.1)$$

$$MA_{jt} = b + \sum_{j=1,N} \alpha_j Country_j dummies + \sum_{j=1,N} \beta_j x_{jt} + \varepsilon_{jt}, \qquad (6.2)$$

where $i = 1,N$ indexes the home country of banking FDI, $j = 1,N$ indexes the receiving country of banking FDI, $t = 1,T$ indexes the year the M&A was announced and x_{it}, x_{jt} denote the explanatory variables defined below.

We used two different dependent variables in regressions of the equation (6.1) measuring the outgoing FDI of banking institutions from country *i* in year *t*. The first one is $BKEXP_{it}$ and it is defined as the number of cross-border M&As by EU15 banks. The second dependent variable is $IVSOR_{it}$ constructed as the ratio of the volume of the outgoing cross-border banking M&As to the nominal GDP of the same country in the same year. Analogically, $BKIMP_{jt}$ and $IVREC_{jt}$ are the alternative dependent variables in equation (6.2). They are examined as indicators of inflow of banking FDI via M&As to country *j*. The number and the volume of the incoming cross-border M&As are used and, consequently, the volume was divided by the respective nominal GDP.[4] According to the methodology of Berger *et al.* (2004), normalizing the dependent variable by combined GDP adjusts for the economic size of both countries. Accepting the ceteris paribus assumption, one would expect that economically large countries are more likely to be at the origin of cross-border banking acquisitions, as well as being more attractive targets for foreign acquirers.

The explanatory variables x_{it} and x_{jt} correspond with the home and host countries characteristics of cross-border banking movements through M&A operations. These variables include indicators describing the economic and regulatory environment in these countries. Their elementary descriptive statistics are presented in Table 6-3.

- *DOMS*: The share of domestic operations in the total of banking M&A is considered as an indicator of domestic consolidation process in the country's banking industry.
- *PIBGRWTH*: annual GDP growth rate as an indicator of economic conditions in the home and the host countries of banking FDI.

- *LPIBCAP*: the natural log of GDP per capita is another indicator of economic environment.
- *EXPS*: the ratio of exports to GDP is an indicator of the non-financial firms' exports activity.
- *IMPS*: the ratio of imports to GDP reveals the importance of international firms' presence in the target country of banking FDI.
- *OPEN*: the ratio of total exports and imports to GDP which measures an economic openness.
- *INFL*: inflation rate in the home and the countries
- *SBD*: dummy variable indicating the year of the Second Banking Directive implementation. This variable takes the value 1 from the year that the Directive was implemented in the country and 0 before this year.
- *EURO*: dummy variable that takes value 1 if the country was member of the EMU.

Table 6-3 Descriptive statistics of the variables used

	Mean	**Standard deviation**	**Minimum**	**Maximum**
Dependent variables				
BKEXP	3.75	5.34	0	32
BKIMP	1.87	2.52	0	14
IVSOR	2.28	6.13	0	60.63
IVREC	2.33	10.13	0	138.11
Explanatory variables				
DOMS	0.43	0.26	0	1
PIBGRWTH	0.029	0.215	-0.062	0.156
LPIBCAP	0.43	0.22	3.413	4.840
IMPS	0.41	0.23	0.185	1.360
EXPS	0.42	0.28	0.163	1.530
INFL	0.034	0.03	-0.002	0.204
OPEN	0.81	0.53	0.350	2.880

Source: Author's calculations

We assume at a given date that two countries having similar observable characteristics will have approximately the same number of cross-border M&As. The coefficients α_i and α_j reveal the degree of comparative advantage of each country *i* and country *j* relative to Luxembourg regarding their outgoing and incoming banking FDI. On the basis of Principal Components Analysis considering the EU countries' characteristics, we find that compared to other countries of the EU15, Luxembourg is distinguished from two other homogeneous groups. Table 6-4 and Table 6-5 report the coefficients on the country *i* characteristics as determinants of the outgoing banking investment in the EU15 countries. Accordingly, Table 6-6 and Table 6-7 show the results regarding incoming M&A obtained from various specifications of the equation (6.2). The panel of data contains 270 observations for 15 European countries.

The aim of our study is to identify investing and receiving countries of banking FDI in the EU. This is the reason we investigate the determinant factors of outgoing and incoming investments. We assume that the country's characteristics increase the likelihood to be an origin of foreign banking expansion or a target of cross-border M&As. These characteristics define the comparative advantage of banking institutions in the EU15 countries to invest in foreign markets or to receive banking FDI.

Expected Signs

The signs of the equations (6.1) and (6.2) coefficients are predicted considering the previous empirical results and the literature discussed above. According to the new trade theory literature, banking FDI is more likely flow into and out of highly developed countries. This assumption implies positive coefficients on *LPIBCAP* and *PIBGRWTH*. Moreover, given the law of comparative advantage, the country environments that foster strong banking institutions are more likely to have a competitive advantage over their competitors in the destination market allowing them to invest abroad. This also implies positive signs on *LPIBCAP* and *PIBGRWTH*. Considering the hypothesis "to follow customer abroad" as motivation of banking FDI, we predict that international activity of non-financial firms would be positively correlated with cross-border banking activity. This assumption implies positive coefficients on $EXPS_i$ and $IMPS_j$. This suggests that non-financial firms' exporting and importing activities have a positive effect on cross-border banking investment. On the other hand, the new trade theory literature predicts higher level of FDI when import barriers to trade are present, which implies a negative coefficient on $OPEN_j$.

The low inflation rate represents another positive economic factor that would encourage cross-border banking investments. Thus, we expect a negative coefficient on *INFL* in different regressions of the two equations (6.1) and (6.2). The previous evidence on cross-border banking suggests that highly developed economies may also be more attractive for banking FDI. Therefore, one would expect the same sign of coefficients on the above variables in regressions relative to incoming banking investments. The hypothesis that high domestic banking consolidation may increase banking incentives to expand in foreign market suggests a positive correlation between the indicator of domestic banking consolidation process and the outgoing banking investments. However, the less concentrated banking markets with less advanced domestic consolidation process are more likely to be the targets of banking FDI, which implies a negative coefficient on $DOMS_j$.

In order to distinguish countries which are more likely to be the banking FDI investing or receiving country, we introduce $Country_i$ and $Country_j$ dummies in regressions tests. The positive coefficients on $Country_i$ dummies suggest the existence of comparative advantage for these countries to be the origin of cross-border banking M&As. On the other hand, the coefficients on $Country_j$ dummies reveal the comparative advantage of EU15 countries, which are more attractive to banking FDI. The Second Banking Directive aimed to liberalize the trade of financial services across Europe and increase the integration of the European banking market. In this respect, the coefficient on *SDB* would be positive controlling for the positive effect of the European banking integration on facilitation of the cross-border banking M&As. Regarding the contribution of the single currency Euro to encouragement of cross-border banking investment, we also expect a positive coefficient on *EURO*.

Estimation Results

Since the dependent variables are truncated at zero, the various versions of equations (6.1) and (6.2) are estimated using standard Tobit estimation techniques. The panel data contains 270 country-year observations (15 countries and 18 years). We exclude Luxembourg from the $Country_i$ and $Country_j$ dummies vectors to avoid perfect colinearity. Thus, the coefficients on the remaining country dummies are interpreted relative to Luxembourg.

The empirical results of different specifications of the equation (6.1) are reported in Table 6-4 and Table 6-5 showing the factors that determine the outgoing banking FDI in the EU15 countries. Using this methodology, we can test for the determinants of cross-border M&As conditional on the characteristics of countries that did and did not participate in mergers in any given year. The coefficients on $DOMS_i$ are statistically significant, and, contrary to our expectations, negative. This result suggests that the advanced domestic banking consolidation process does not systematically lead to intensive cross-border banking M&As activity. The positive coefficients on $PIBGRWTH_i$ are consistent with the empirical results of Berger *et al.* (2004) confirming the assumptions of the new trade theory. This result suggests that the home economy's growth rate has a positive effect on outgoing banking FDI. In other side, the coefficients on $INFL_i$ are negative but not statistically significant. Similarly, the negative coefficients are not statistically significant on $LPIBCAP_i$, which implies that the effect of home economic development on cross-border banking investment is less evident. Our empirical results show that the international activity of non financial firms has no effect on the cross-border banking activity. The coefficients on $EXPS_i$ and $OPEN_i$ are insignificant and do not give any evidence of "following customer abroad" as principal motivation of European banking expansion in foreign markets. The positive effect of Euro implementation on cross-border European banking investment is more evident than the effect of the Second Banking Directive. The coefficients on $EURO_i$ and SBD_i are positive but only the first one is statistically significant.

Table 6-4 Determinants of outgoing banking investment in terms of volume of M&As ($IVSOR_i$ as the dependent variable)

Variable	(1)	(2)	(3)
DOMS	-7.340***	-7.572***	-7.384***
PIBGRWTH	47.482*	55.802**	52.428**
LPIBCAP	-1.739	-0.685	-1.256
IMPS	0.863		
INFL	-41.870	-32.700	-36.481
EXPS		-8.941	
OPEN			-2.705
SBD	1.320	1.895	1.594
EURO	4.093***	4.872***	4.596***
UK	4.318	-4.830	-1.168
Germany	2.447	-6.010	-2.766
France	2.858	-6.116	-2.650
Belgium	2.493	-1.556	0.078
Spain	6.160	-2.793	0.692
Italy	3.030	-5.911	-2.508
Ireland	0.347	-4.138	-2.557
Portugal	1.160	-7.135	-3.685
Austria	-1.810	-9.244	-6.329
Finland	1.500	-6.610	-3.584
Netherlands	0.587	-5.148	-2.931
Greece	-3.011	-12.526	-8.610
Denmark	-2.042	-9.555	-7.122
Sweden	4.515	-2.980	-0.550
Constant	6.949	12.699	11.231

Note: *, **, *** denote significance at 10 per cent, 5 per cent, 1 per cent
Source: Author's calculations

The $Country_i$ dummies were introduced in different specifications of the equation (6.1) controlling for the comparative advantage of countries to determine banking FDI. The coefficients on all countries dummies are not statistically significant, considering the volume of cross-border banking M&As as the dependent variable This result suggests that, on average, banking institutions in these EU countries have no advantage or disadvantage relative to institutions from Luxembourg. Being eliminated from countries' dummies, Luxembourg is considered obviously as a benchmark for analyzing the comparative advantage of the others EU countries. The results are different if the number of cross-border M&As in the EU15 countries (alternative dependent variable) is applied in the estimations. To test the impact of no-financial international firms' activity on the banking FDI, we include different indicators of their activity as determinants of outgoing banking investments. According to the previous evidence, $IMPS_i$, $EXPS_i$ and $OPEN_i$ are included in various regressions of the equation (6.1) as reported in column (1), (2) and (3) respectively in Table 6-4.

Table 6-5 shows the estimated home $Country_i$ dummies from regressions (4), (6), and (7) considering the number of cross-border $M\&As_i$. France, Belgium and Spain dummies are positive and statistically significant in all regressions. The UK and Germany dummies coefficients are also statistically significant and positive in two regressions. This result suggests that, on average, banking institutions from Germany, UK, France, Belgium and Spain have a comparative advantage at investing in foreign markets relative to Luxembourg banks. This is also the case of Italian banks if the positive coefficient on the Italy dummy from regression (4) is taken into account. The rest of the countries have no advantage or disadvantage comparing with Luxembourg. The size of the banking industries in these countries could explain the absence of comparative advantage that affect the capacity of banks to invest abroad. Regarding the coefficients on $PIBGRWTH_i$ and $LPIBCAP_i$, the home economy's growth rate and the home country's economic development has no effect on the number of cross-border banking M&As. This result is partly due to the particularity of European countries, which are highly developed. However, we found that the low home country's inflation rate has a positive effect on banking FDI via cross-border M&As. The negative and statistically significant coefficient on $INFL_i$ suggests that this indicator of a country's economic environment is an important driving factor of cross-border banking M&A activity.

Table 6-5 Determinants of outgoing banking investment in terms of number of M&As ($BKEXP_i$ as the dependent variable)

Variable	(4)	(5)	(6)	(7)
DOMS	-3.445**	-1.973**	-3.525**	-3.460**
PIBGRWTH	-14.035	-4.925	-8.471	-11.836
LPIBCAP	1.212	-0.493	1.773	1.354
IMPS	5.133	-1.969*		
INFL	-33.880**	-12.985	-28.836*	-32.346*
EXPS			-2.081	
OPEN				0.973
SBD	1.630**	1.629***	1.909**	1.711**
EURO	0.992	1.057**	1.546*	1.225
UK	14.069**		7.860	11.580**
Germany	12.704**		6.761	10.230*
France	23.934***		17.663***	21.340***
Belgium	9.564***		6.799**	8.471***
Spain	14.766**		8.585*	12.241**
Italy	10.542*		4.252	7.921
Ireland	5.567		2.185	4.076
Portugal	7.399		2.010	5.356
Austria	6.124		0.972	4.021
Finland	4.675		-1.148	2.198
Netherlands	6.484		2.452	4.816
Greece	6.409		0.170	4.011
Denmark	3.714		-1.616	1.636
Sweden	7.883		2.553	5.793
Constant	-12.042	6.555	-7.133	-9.563

Note: *, **, *** denote significance at 10 per cent, 5 per cent, 1 per cent
Source: Author's calculations

Regarding the other factors that determine banking expansion in foreign markets; the estimated coefficients on $EXPS_i$ and $OPEN_i$ provide no empirical evidence of banking motivation strategy to follow non-financial firms abroad. Contrary to our predictions about the necessity to consolidate the domestic banking industry before investing in foreign markets, the coefficient on $DOMS_i$ is negative. This result is partly due to the method of calculating the concentration indicator, which implies a negative correlation with the number of cross-border M&As. The low degree of banking concentration compared to the important cross-border banking investment in some European countries is another possible explanation for this surprising result.

Estimation results of the determinants of incoming banking FDI realized via M&As are provided in Table 6-6 and Table 6-7. The negative and statistically insignificant coefficient on the domestic market consolidation indicator $DOMS_j$ is consistent with the predictions of larger potential of consolidation in countries whose banking industries are less concentrated and therefore more likely to be the targets of cross-border M&As. The coefficients on economic environment indicators $PIBGROWT_j$, $LPIBCAP_j$, and $INFL_j$ are generally negative for all regressions of the equation (6.2) but not significantly significant. This result suggests that the host economy's growth rate has no effect on the value of incoming banking FDI. Moreover, the host country's inflation rate seems not to be an attractive incentive for cross-border banking activity across Europe. The positive coefficient on $IMPS_j$ is consistent with the hypothesis of customer following behaviour as motivation of cross-border banking movements through M&As. The coefficient on $OPEN_j$ is also positive and significantly different from zero for all regressions of the equation (6.2). This implies that the degree of host country's openness has positive effect on the volume of incoming baking investment via M&As.

All the $Country_j$ dummies, except the Belgium dummy from the regression (1) displayed in Table 6-6, have positive and statistically significant coefficients. This result suggests that only Belgium could have no advantage at receiving banking FDI comparing to Luxembourg. However, the other EU countries have a comparative advantage and should be more attractive to cross-border banking M&As. Moreover, the empirical results relative to the number of cross-border banking M&As confirm the existence of this comparative advantage for the UK, France, Germany, Spain, Italy, Ireland, Germany, Portugal, and Netherlands. See Table 6-7 for the statistically significant and positive coefficients of the mentioned $Country_j$ dummies. The rest of the $Country_j$ dummies are also positive but not statistically different from zero. Thus, Austria, Finland, Greece, Denmark, and Sweden are less attractive to banking FDI than Luxembourg or the other EU15 countries.

Table 6-6 Determinants of incoming banking investment in terms of volume of M&As ($IVREC_j$ as the dependent variable)

Variable	(1)	(2)	(3)	(4)
DOMS	-5.490	-5.424	-2.654	-2.725
PIBGRWTH	-22.445	-28.015	23.913	23.325
LPIBCAP	-0.702	-0.534	0.832	0.826
IMPS		64.173***	6.654**	
INFL	-66.614	-63.968	6.757	8.016
OPEN	26.289**			3.033*
SBD	0.746	0.951	1.350	1.387
EURO		-0.638	2.733*	2.659*
UK	48.494**	54.252***		
Germany	40.393**	47.325**		
France	46.632**	53.663***		
Belgium	15.901	18.082*		
Spain	46.340**	52.611***		
Italy	46.046**	53.315***		
Ireland	22.794**	27.893**		
Portugal	40.798**	43.646**		
Austria	31.684**	36.980**		
Finland	39.274**	46.848**		
Netherlands	23.078*	27.584**		
Greece	36.833*	40.668**		
Denmark	39.211**	41.211**		
Sweden	36.623**	39.222**		
Constant	-50.312	-60.380	-5.401	-5.131

Note: *, **, *** denote significance at 10 per cent, 5 per cent, 1 per cent
Source: Author's calculations

The coefficients on the other explanatory variables from the regressions in Table 6-7 reveal the characteristics the EU15 possess that will increase their attractiveness for banking FDI. The coefficient on $DOMS_j$ is negative and statistically insignificant. This result confirms the fact that cross-border banking expansion in foreign markets does not depend on the degree of domestic banking consolidation. This result is partly due to the measure applied in our study as the indicator of cross-border banking investment and its number. More precisely, the variables *BKIMP* and *IVREC* include also other targets than banking institutions. The role of the host country's economic development is not evident in attracting cross-border banking M&As. Although we found positive coefficient on $LPIBCA_j$, which is significant in regression (8), the other indicator of economic growth ($PIBGRWTH_j$) obtained statistically insignificant coefficients. The inflation rate coefficient is also insignificant thus completing the puzzle of insignificance of the economic environment in attracting the banking FDI inflow via M&As. These results do not correspond with the previous evidence provided in the relevant literature where the economic variables were found as significant determinants. The empirical results of this study are also inconsistent with the hypothesis of "client-following" strategy as motivation for cross-border banking investment. The positive coefficient on $EURO_j$ confirms the importance of the single currency Euro to contribute to the acceleration of cross-border banking expansion in European countries. On the contrary, the effect of the Second Banking Directive is less evident given the negative coefficient on SDB_j which is not statistically significant.

Table 6-7 Determinants of incoming banking investment in terms of number of M&As ($BKIMP_j$ as the dependent variable)

Variable	(5)	(6)	(7)	(8)
DOMS	-0.657	-0.666	-0.425	-0.353
PIBGRWTH	-9.115	-6.924	-1.833	-2.462
LPIBCAP	3.255	3.416	1.541	1.252***
IMPS	4.296			-1.809**
INFL	-10.205	-8.537	-4.215	-3.215
OPEN		0.654	-1.305	
SBD	-0.191	-0.112	-0.007	-0.071
EURO	0.139	0.357	0.626	0.636*
UK	13.163***	10.801***		
Germany	6.955*	4.621		
France	9.971***	7.521**		
Belgium	4.528**	3.499*		
Spain	10.885***	8.497**		
Italy	9.103**	6.631*		
Ireland	5.294**	3.920*		
Portugal	7.493**	5.545		
Austria	4.767*	3.193		
Finland	4.288	2.293		
Netherlands	4.797	2.482		
Greece	6.239	3.959		
Denmark	4.787	2.799		
Sweden	4.889	2.870		
Constant	-20.208**	-17.998*	-3.611	-2.438

Note: *, **, *** denote significance at 10 per cent, 5 per cent, 1 per cent
Source: Author's calculations

Conclusion

Creation of the EMU, relaxation of barriers to operating across geopolitical borders, and development of new technologies and communications has led to an acceleration of banking integration process in Europe. In this context, a sharp increase in M&A activity is the widespread trend seen in the European banking sector.

The analysis of FDI by banking institutions based on cross-border banking M&A data identifies the investing and receiving countries of these investments in Europe. Given the number of banking acquisitions in foreign markets, France, Belgium, Germany, Spain, the Netherlands, Austria, Sweden, Luxembourg and Finland had higher level of outgoing investments than receiving banking investments. The second group of countries dominantly receiving banking FDI includes Ireland, Italy, Portugal, UK, and Denmark. Nevertheless, Italy and the UK became investing countries if the volume of cross-border banking M&As is taken into account. Regarding this measure of banking FDI, Austria, France, Luxembourg and Finland became target countries' of cross-border banking acquisitions.

The regressions carried out to reveal determinants of banking FDI do not allow us to confirm the hypothesis of following clients' behaviour as motivation of cross-border banking M&A activity in the EU15 countries. Our empirical results show that the international activity of non-financial firms has no effect on the cross-border banking investment activity. Moreover, we found that the home economy's growth rate has a positive effect on outgoing banking investment. The regressions of cross-border M&A numbers reveal that the low home country's inflation rate has a positive effect on foreign banking investment.

Regarding the determinants of incoming banking FDI, the results suggest that the host economy's growth rate has no effect on the volume of incoming banking investment. Similarly, the host country's inflation rate seems not to be a significant attraction for cross-border banking activity across the EU. Therefore, the opportunities offered by other European markets appear not to be a determinant factor of pan-European banking consolidation. The low degree of concentration of the banking sector increases the potential for acquisitions by foreign banks. However, the results are not consistent with the hypothesis concerning the limited margins for consolidation within national boundaries as a driving factor of banking expansion on the EU market. The second part of our results is consistent with the hypothesis of customer following behaviour as motivation of cross-border banking movements through M&As. We found that the degree of the host country's openness has a positive effect on the volume of incoming banking M&As.

Finally, the European integration process with the implementation of the Second Banking Directive and the EMU proved to be important factors which contributed substantially to accelerate cross-border banking investment within EU15 countries.

References

Berger, Allen N., Robert DeYoung, Hensa Genay and Gregory F. Udell. 1999. *Globalization of financial institutions: Evidence from cross-border banking performance*. Federal Reserve Bank of Chicago Working Papers Series, No. 99–25. Chicago, IL: Federal Reserve Bank.

Berger, Allen N., Qinglei Dai, Steven Ongema and David C. Smith. 2001. *To what extent will the banking industry be globalized? A study of bank nationality and reach in 20 European nations*. Washington, D.C.: Board Governors of Federal Reserve.

Berger A.N. and D.C. Smith. 2003. Global Integration in the Banking Industry. *Federal Reserve Bulletin,* November: 451–60.

Berger, A.N., C.M. Buch, M. DeLong and R. DeYoung. 2004. Exporting financial institutions management via foreign direct investment mergers and acquisitions. *Journal of International Money and Finance* 23(3):333–66.

Bank for International Settlements. 2001. *Report on Consolidation in the Financial Sector.* Basel: Bank for International Settlement.

Blandon, Josep G. 2000. *Cross-border banking M&A in Europe: An empirical investigation*. Place: Universitat Pompeu Fabra.

Boot A. 2003. Restructuring in the Banking with Implications for Europe. *EIB Papers* 8(1):108–29.

Brealey, R.A. and E.C. Kaplanis. 1996. The determination of foreign banking location. *Journal of International Money and Finance* 15(4):577–97.

Buch C.M. and G.L. DeLong. 2004. Cross-Border Bank Mergers: What Lures the Rare Animal? *Journal of Banking and Finance* 28(9):2077–102.

Buch Claudia M. 2000. *Information or Regulation: What is driving the international Activities of commercial Banks?* Kiel Institute of World Economics working paper N°1011. Kiel: Kiel Institute of World Economics.

Buch Claudia M. 2001. *Distance and International Banking.* Kiel Institute of World Economics working paper N°1043. Kiel: Kiel Institute of World Economics.

Claessens, S., A. Demirguç, Kunt and H. Huizinga. 2001. How does foreign entry affect the domestic banking market? *Journal of Banking and Finance* 25(5):891–911.

DeFelice G. and D. Revoltella. 2003. Towards a multinational bank? European banks' growth strategies. *Banque & Marchés n°62.*

Focarelli D. and A.F. Pozzolo. 2001. The patterns of cross-border bank mergers and shareholdings in OECD countries. *Journal of Banking and Finance* 25 (12):2305–37.

Goldberg, L.G. and A. Saunders. 1981. The determinants of foreign banking activity in the United States. *Journal of Banking and Finance* 5(1): 17–32.

Grosse, R. and L.G. Goldberg. 1991. Foreign bank activity in the United States: An analysis by country of origin. *Journal of Banking and Finance* 15(6):1093–112.

Grubel, H.G. 1977. A theory of multinational banking. *Banca Nazionale del Lavoro Quarterly Review* 123:349–63.

Seth, R., D.E. Nolle and S.K. Mohanty. 1998. Do banks follow their customers abroad? *Financial Markets, Institutions and Instruments* 7(4):1–25.

Vander Vennet, R. 1996. The effect of mergers and acquisitions on the efficiency and profitability of EC credit institutions. *Journal of Banking and Finance* 20(9):1531–58.

Vander Vennet, Rudi. 2002. *Cross-border Mergers in European Banking and Bank Efficiency.* University Gent Working Paper No. 152. Gent: University of Gent.

Wengel, J. 1995. International trade in banking services. *Journal of International Money and Finance* 14(1):47–64.

Williams, B. 1997. Positive theories of multinational banking: eclectic theory versus internalisation theory. *Journal of Economic Surveys* 11(1): 71–101.

Notes

[1] The recent attempts by Banco Bilbao Vizcaya Argentaria and ABN Amro to acquire the Italian banks Banca Nazionale del Lavoro and Banca Antonveneta constitute a good example of such situation.

[2] Compared to other sectors, banks lack substantially behind considering the share of cross-border operations of total M&As (Focarelli and Pozzolo, 2000).

[3] This situation could be influenced by the effect of pan-European banking acquisitions. The operations of cross-border M&As in EU countries include the cross-border banking investments between European countries.

[4] The methodology that we use to calculate the indicators of cross-border banking investment is the following:
(i) For outgoing investments of European banks and credit institutions, we examine the number and the value of cross-border banking M&As, where the acquirer nation is an European country without restrictions on the host country.

(ii) Similarly, we consider the number and the volume of cross-border M&As in each EU15 country for measuring the incoming banking investments and credit institutions in EU countries. In our methodology, we define each European country as a target of these banking investments.

CHAPTER SEVEN

INFORMATION EFFICIENCY IN CENTRAL EUROPEAN EQUITY MARKETS[1]

The aim of the paper is to follow previous research (Hanousek and Filer, 1996; Vošvrda *et al.*, 1998) and to test a weak form of market efficiency of capital markets in the Czech Republic, the Slovak Republic, Hungary, Poland, and the United States. Using standard statistical methods, we seek answers to the following questions: (i) Can we observe any information efficiency in Central European capital markets? (ii) Can we observe an improvement of information efficiency in these markets during the time period analyzed? (iii) What, if any, gap in efficiency exists among Central European capital markets and the U.S. (mature) capital market?

Based on our results we also want to address whether there exists any consolidation within Central European equity markets or any convergence to the U.S. market.

Information Efficiency of the Capital Market

Let us start with few definitions. The efficient capital market hypothesis focuses on ability of a market to absorb new information and for participants to react on it. A capital market is said to be efficient if it fully and correctly reflects all relevant information in determining security prices. In other words, one cannot benefit from information relevant to the stock prices that is not already known to the other market participants.

Formally, the market is said to be efficient with respect to some information set if revealing that information does not affect security prices (Campbell *et al.*, 1997). Moreover, one cannot make economic profits by trading on the basis of that information set. Economists often define three levels of market efficiency, which are distinguished by the degree of information reflected in security prices.

A market would be described as being weak-form efficient if the security price reflects all information contained in the historical record of its past prices. In other words, this form of efficiency implies that relative changes of prices follow a random walk hypothesis and therefore price changes are unforecastable. Strategies used by technical analysts fail in such a market.

Semi-strong efficiency of a market means that the information set includes both the history of prices and all publicly available information. Since publicly known information is incorporated in security prices, buying or selling recommendations from fundamental analysts are useless.

Finally, if market prices reflect all available information (both public and private), a market is said to be strong-efficient. In such a market, there is no special information on which an investor can make abnormal profits. In other words, insider information is valueless and therefore insiders do not post better trading results than other market participants (Filer and Hanousek, 1996).

Formally, we can describe the aforementioned definitions as follows:

$$E_t(P_{t+1} \mid \Phi_t) = P_t, \tag{7.1}$$

where E_t is expected value operator, P_{t+1} denotes price of security at time $t+1$, P_t is price of security at time t, and Φ_t is the set of information available to investors at time t. It follows from equation (7.1) that the best estimate for the future price of security is the current price of security.

Models of Testing Efficiency

Basic models used for testing the weak-form of efficiency, rely on various types of the random walk hypothesis including its generalisation.

Random Walk – Type 1 (RW1)

The simplest version of the random walk hypothesis assumes independent and identically distributed (IID) increments and is given by the following equation:

$$p_t = \mu + p_{t-1} + \varepsilon_t, \varepsilon_t \approx IID, \tag{7.2}$$

where p_t is natural logarithm of price of security at time t, p_{t+1} is natural logarithm of price of security at time $t+1$, μ is the expected price change (drift), and ε_t denotes independently and identically distributed error term.

If we consider normality of ε_t (i.e. with the mean value 0 and variance σ^2), we are talking about a Brownian motion. Such a distributional assumption implies that continuously compounded returns are IID varieties with mean μ and variance σ^2.

Random Walk – Type 2 (RW2)

However, the assumption of identically distributed increments of security prices is not fulfilled in the long-term. A shift in the economic, social, technological, institutional, and regulatory environment affects security prices in the capital markets and therefore changes the parameters of distribution of price increments over the long-term. Hence, we relax the assumption of RW1 to include processes with independent but not identically distributed (IID) increments and refer to it as the Random Walk 2 (RW2). Clearly, RW1 is a special case of RW2. The RW2 also allows modelling of more general price processes in the capital markets. For instance, the models with the time-variation volatility that assumes heteroskedasticity in the time series $\{\varepsilon_t\}$ are the case.

Random Walk – Type 3 (RW3)

An even more general type of the random walk hypothesis is the one that relaxes the independence assumption of RW2 to include processes with dependent but uncorrelated increments. We shall call such a type the Random Walk model (RW3). It is clear that RW3 contains RW1 and RW2 as special cases. For example, the following process satisfies assumptions of RW3 but not of RW1 or RW2 is any process for which:

$$Cov[\varepsilon_t, \varepsilon_{t-k}] = 0, \forall k \neq 0, \tag{7.3}$$

but where

$$\exists k \neq 0, Cov[\varepsilon_t^{\,2}, \varepsilon_{t-k}^{\,2}] \neq 0. \tag{7.4}$$

Such a process has uncorrelated increments, but is clearly not independent since its squared increments are correlated (Campbell *et al.*, 1997).

Methods of Testing Market Efficiency

Break Event Point Test

The break event point test is one of the most used nonparametric tests of the random walk hypothesis, i.e. of the tests being independent on particular distribution of increments. For more details see Campbell (1997).

Runs Test

The variance ratio test (Ayadi and Pyun, 1994; Urrutia, 1995) could be applied to all three types of the random walk hypothesis (if properly modified). The test follows the idea that if a time series of the natural logarithm of prices fulfils the random walk hypothesis, then variance of *q-th* derivations has to increase directly as a degree *q* of derivation increases. The variance ratio is defined as follows:

$$VR(q) = \frac{\sigma^2(q)}{\sigma^2(1)}, \tag{7.5}$$

where $\sigma^2(q)$ is variance of *q-th* derivations divided by *q* and $\sigma^2(1)$ is variance of the first derivations (for more details see Lo and MacKinlay, 1989):

$$\sigma^2(q) = \frac{1}{m}\sum_{t=q}^{nq}(\ln P_t - \ln P_{t-q} - q\hat{\mu})^2, \tag{7.6}$$

$$\sigma^2(1) = \frac{1}{(nq-1)}\sum_{t=1}^{nq}(\ln P_t - \ln P_{t-1} - \hat{\mu})^2. \tag{7.7}$$

whereas

$$m = q(nq - q + 1)(1 - \frac{q}{nq}), \tag{7.8}$$

$$\hat{\mu} = \frac{1}{nq}(\ln P_{nq} - \ln P_0). \tag{7.9}$$

P_0 is the first value and P_{nq} is the last value in time series of prices.

If the random walk hypothesis holds, the variance ratio *VR(q)* shall converge to 1. Then two test statistics *z(q)* and *z'(q)* could be derived independent of the fact if we assume for ε_t from equation (7.2) either homoskedasticity or heteroskedasticity. If we suppose homoskedasticity (constant variance), then it corresponds with RW1. On the other hand, if we assume heteroskedasticity (variable variance), it corresponds with RW2 or RW3.

The formulas of the test statistics *z(q)* a *z'(q)*, which under RW1 shall converge to the standard normal distribution N(0,1), are as follows:

$$z(q) = \frac{VR(q) - 1}{\sqrt{\Phi(q)}} \approx N(0,1), \tag{7.10}$$

where

$$\Phi(q) = \frac{2(2q-1)(q-1)}{3q(nq)}, \tag{7.11}$$

$$z'(q) = \frac{VR(q) - 1}{\sqrt{\Phi'(q)}} \approx N(0,1), \tag{7.12}$$

where

$$\Phi'(q) = \sum_{j=1}^{q-1} [\frac{2(q-j)}{q}]^2 \hat{\delta}(j), \tag{7.13}$$

and

$$\hat{\delta}(j) = \frac{\sum_{t=j+1}^{nq} (\ln P_t - \ln P_{t-1} - \hat{\mu})^2 (\ln P_{t-j} - \ln P_{t-j-1} - \hat{\mu})^2}{\sum_{t=1}^{nq} [(\ln P_t - \ln P_{t-1} - \hat{\mu})^2]^2}. \tag{7.14}$$

Technically, if we reject the null hypothesis for the reason that the variance ratio equals 1 (for every time lag), it is enough for rejection of the random walk hypothesis. Nevertheless, we can consider all time lags together and use only one confidence interval that can influence testing results (Stolin and Ury, 1979). When using the test statistics *z(q)*, one shall recall that it is derived for RW1 and therefore shall be tested if natural logarithms of price increments ε_t are IID. On the other hand, when using the test statistics *z'(q)* one shall test only independence or lack of correlation between the increments.

Results of Testing Market Efficiency

Regarding the scope of the paper and strength of the tests used we present only results of the variance ratio test which has the highest predicative power.

Data Used

When testing market efficiency, we used weekly and monthly data from September 1993 to August 2004 from capital markets in the Czech Republic, Poland, Hungary, Slovakia and the United States. The U.S. market is usually considered highly effecient and a benchmark for other capital markets. We used the market indices as proxies of these markets: PX-50 for the Czech Republic, Warsaw Stock Exchange Index (WIG) for Poland, Budapest Stock Index (BUX) for Hungary, Slovak Share Index for Slovakia (SAX), and Dow-Jones-Industrial-Average (DJIA) for the United States.

Apart from the closing monthly and weekly values of the market indices, end-of-month values recalculated to U.S. dollars were used. This fact can play an important role in the view of foreign investors that want to invest in the capital markets analyzed. The results obtained can enrich the already conducted research on market efficiency (under the assumption of no transaction costs occurred in relation to terms of trade).

Variance Ratio Test

In contrast to the break event point test and the runs test used by some authors (Ayadi and Pyun, 1994; Urrutia, 1995), the variance ratio test considers drift μ in the test statistics. On the other hand, a pitfall of the variance ratio test is its dependence on the parameters of data distribution respectively on data normality (at least in case of testing RW1).

Considering every lag being independent and homoskedasticity of the time series ε_t from formula (7.2), we obtained relatively clear results for the weekly values in the period from September 1993 until August 2004 with the lags of 1, 2, 3 and 6 months (more precisely 4, 8, 13 a 26 weeks). While we reject the null hypothesis in Central European markets, the U.S. market seems to be efficient under the RW1 assumption. Technically, if we reject the hypothesis for the reason that the variance ratio equals 1 (for every time lag), it is enough for rejection of the random walk hypothesis. When considering (i) all lags from the interval from 2 to 26 weeks together and (ii) the unique confidence interval of the maximum value of the test statistics for all time lags, we concluded the same results as mentioned above (we reject the hypothesis in Central European markets, but we do not reject it for the U.S. market). All results of estimation are provided in Table 7-1.

Although we have found some statistical support for the weak-form efficiency in the U.S. market, we shall investigate why RW1 was rejected in Central European markets. One reason could be heteroskedasticity in the time series ε_t as a result of increasing market capitalisation, rise in trading activities, and by a non-systematic interference in Central European markets (e.g. privatisation deals in the form of a direct sale of state-owned companies to an investor). All these factors could lead to variable stock price movements in the capital market per time unit and therefore a variable variance of ε_t (or heteroskedasticity) in time series could occur.

For the reasons outlined above we also study the second test statistic $z'(q)$ which is resistant to heteroskedasticity in data and denoted in Table 7-1 in square brackets. As shown by Table 7-1, we do not reject RW1 in any of the markets analyzed.

Table 7-1 Variance ratio test (weekly data, local currencies, long period)

Lag	Hungary	Poland	CR	SR	USA
q = 4	1.33 (4.76)* [0.40]	1.28 (3.89)* [0.21]	1.62 (7.92)* [0.71]	1.71 (9.13)* [0.77]	0.94 (-0.85) [-0.07]
q = 8	1.57 (5.14)* [0.46]	1.44 (3.95)* [0.23]	2.08 (8.74)* [0.87]	2.11 (8.95)* [0.87]	0.85 (-1.21) [-0.10]
q = 13	1.59 (4.00)* [0.37]	1.70 (4.73)* [0.29]	2.18 (7.18)* [0.77]	2.26 (7.65)* [0.85]	0.80 (-1.29) [-0.11]
q = 26	1.65 (3.05)* [0.30]	2.10 (5.06)* [0.33]	1.82 (3.43)* [0.39]	1.54 (2.25)* [0.29]	0.75 (-1.07) [-0.10]
max z(q=2..26)	(5.30)*	(5.06)*	(8.76)*	(9.13)*	(-1.87)
max z'(q=2..26)	[0.48]	[0.33]	[0.87]	[0.91]	[-0.14]

Note: (z – homoskedasticity assumption)
[z' – resistance against heteroskedasticity]
* denotes that the variance ratio differs significantly from one based upon 5 per cent significance level; therefore, RW1 is rejected

Source: Authors' calculations

If we do similar calculations for weekly returns in local currencies during the shorter period from January 1998 to August 2004, we reject RW1 under homoskedasticity assumption only for the Czech market. If we suppose data heteroskedasticity, we do not reject RW1 in any market. Results are reported in Table 7-2.

Table 7-2 Variance ratio test (weekly data, local currencies, short period)

Lag	Hungary	Poland	CR	SR	USA
q = 4	1.15 (1.51) [0.18]	1.14 (1.35) [0.10]	1.33 (3.32)* [0.38]	1.01 (0.06) [0.01]	0.95 (-0.53) [-0.06]
q = 8	1.31 (1.93) [0.24]	1.22 (1.41) [0.12]	1.47 (2.96)* [0.38]	1.05 (0.32) [0.04]	0.87 (-0.82) [-0.09]
q = 13	1.15 (0.72) [0.10]	1.27 (1.29) [0.11]	1.42 (2.03)* [0.28]	1.12 (0.59) [0.08]	0.77 (-1.10) [-0.13]
q = 26	0.98 (-0.05) [-0.01]	1.24 (0.78) [0.07]	1.43 (1.41) [0.21]	1.26 (0.85) [0.14]	0.67 (-1.07) [-0.13]
max z(q=2..26)	(2.10)	(1.41)	(3.32)	(0.85)	(-1.36)
max z'(q=2..26)	[0.26]	[0.12]	[0.40]	[0.14]	[-0.14]

Note: (z – homoskedasticity assumption)
[z' – resistance against heteroskedasticity]
* denotes that the variance ratio differs significantly from one based upon 5 per cent significance level; therefore, RW1 is rejected

Source: Authors' calculations

Table 7-3 shows results of testing RW1 assuming foreign investments (monthly dollar market returns) in the period from September 1993 to August 2004. When comparing results in Table 7-3 (monthly dollar returns) with the results in Table 7-4 (monthly local currencies returns), we can see a movement in the Polish market. Whereas we reject RW1 in terms of local currencies returns in the Polish market, we do not reject it under heteroskedasticity assumption if talking about dollar returns. The other markets did undergo a significant change. Assuming heteroskedasticity, we do not reject RW1 in any market for both dollar and local currencies returns.

Table 7-3 Variance ratio test (monthly data, USD, long period)

Lag	Hungary	Poland	CR	SR	USA
q = 3	0.93 (-0.51) [-0.13]	1.05 (0.35) [0.06]	1.27 (2.01)* [0.35]	1.43 (3.28)* [0.50]	0.92 (-0.67) [-0.11]
q = 6	0.89 (-0.53) [-0.13]	0.95 (-0.22) [-0.03]	0.96 (-0.16) [-0.03]	0.92 (-0.39) [-0.07]	0.85 (-0.73) [-0.12]
q = 9	0.97 (-0.11) [-0.03]	0.71 (-1.06) [-0.16]	1.00 (0.01) [0.00]	0.93 (-0.26) [-0.05]	0.88 (-0.44) [-0.07]
q = 12	1.07 (0.22) [0.05]	0.64 (-1.10) [-0.17]	1.11 (0.34) [0.06]	1.04 (0.12) [0.03]	0.99 (-0.04) [-0.01]
max z(q=3..12)	(-0.78)	(-1.10)	(2.01)	(3.28)	(-0.76)
max z'(q=3..12)	[-0.19]	[-0.17]	[0.35]	[0.50]	[-0.12]

Note: (z – homoskedasticity assumption)
[z' – resistance against heteroskedasticity]
* denotes that the variance ratio differs significantly from one based upon 5 per cent significance level; therefore, RW1 is rejected

Source: Authors' calculations

However, the main pitfall of the variance ratio test is its sensitivity to normality of the time series ε_t defined in formula (7.2). In practice, this assumption is equivalent to normality of market returns and is to be tested. Table 7-5 shows the results of such testing on U.S. dollar market returns.

Table 7-4 Variance ratio test (monthly data, local currency, long period)

Lag	Hungary	Poland	CR	SR	USA
q = 3	1,06 (0,55) [0,13]	1,23 (1,96) [0,31]	1,36 (2,74)* [0,43]	1,41 (3,18)* [0,48]	0,92 (-0,67) [-0,11]
q = 6	1,14 (0,73) [0,16]	1,54 (2,78)* [0,43]	1,03 (0,16) [0,02]	1,00 (-0,02) [-0,00]	0,85 (-0,73) [-0,12]
q = 9	1,27 (1,10) [0,24]	1,85 (3,41)* [0,54]	1,01 (0,03) [0,01]	0,77 (-0,83) [-0,16]	0,88 (-0,44) [-0,07]
q = 12	1,36 (1,22) [0,27]	2,15 (3,88)* [0,62]	1,10 (0,30) [0,05]	0,79 (-0,65) [-0,14]	0,99 (-0,04) [-0,01]
max z(q=3..12)	(1,22)	(3,88)*	(2,74)	(3,18)	(-0,76)
max z'(q=3..12)	[0,27]	[0,62]	[0,43]	[0,48]	[-0,12]

Note: (z – homoskedasticity assumption)
[z' – resistance against heteroskedasticity]
* denotes that the variance ratio differs significantly from one based upon 5 per cent significance level; therefore, RW1 is rejected

Source: Authors' calculations

It follows from the Student spread results that monthly dollar returns in the period from September 1993 to August 2004 do not satisfy the normality assumption except for the U.S. market. Therefore, it confirms its property of a benchmark for other capital markets. We can see in Table 7-6 an improvement of the vast majority of the test statistics for the shorter period from January 1998 until August 2004. As a result, the tests assuming heteroskedasticity reflect reality more precisely than the other ones. Such tests are not so sensitive to data normality and provide a relatively good statistical evidence for non-rejection of RW2 and RW3. Furthermore, the tests imply, not including the U.S. market, that the Czech, Slovak, Polish, and Hungarian markets also posit the weak-form of market efficiency.

Table 7-5 Data normality test (monthly data, USD, long period)

	Hungary	Poland	CR	SR	USA
Average	0.014	0.009	0.008	0.005	0.008
Standard deviation	0.104	0.125	0.098	0.110	0.044
Skewness	-0.40	-0.34	0.48*	2.85*	-0.75*
Kurtosis	4.92*	2.39*	4.03*	20.18*	1.49*
Max. return	0.432	0.352	0.451	0.765	0.101
Min. return	-0.482	-0.437	-0.344	-0.368	-0.164
Student spread	8.8**	6.3**	8.1**	10.3**	6.0
Number of observations	134	134	131	130	139

Note: returns = $100*\ln(P_t/P_{t-1})$; standard error (S.E.) skewness = $[6/N]^{1/2}$; standard error (S.E.) kurtosis = $[24/N]^{1/2}$; N = number of observations
Student spread = (Max return – Min return)/ relative variance
* it differs significantly from one based upon a 5 per cent level
** if Student spread is greater than six, we reject data normality based upon a 5 per cent significance level

Source: Authors' calculations

Table 7-6 Data normality test (monthly data, USD, short period)

	Hungary	Poland	CR	SR	USA
Average	0.007	0.006	0.011	0.004	0.003
Standard deviation	0.099	0.0909	0.086	0.066	0.050
Skewness	-1.75*	-1.17*	-1.00*	0.23	-0.60*
Kurtosis	6.57*	4.04*	3.23*	0.72	1.03
Max. return	0.205	0.206	0.207	0.219	0.101
Min. return	-0.482	-0.437	-0.344	-0.149	-0.164
Student spread	6.9**	6.5**	6.4**	5.5	5.3
Number of observations	79	79	79	79	79

Note: returns = $100*\ln(P_t/P_{t-1})$; standard error (S.E.) skewness = $[6/N]^{1/2}$; standard error (S.E.) kurtosis = $[24/N]^{1/2}$; N = number of observations
Student spread = (Max return – Min return)/ relative variance
* it differs significantly from one based upon a 5 per cent level
** if Student spread is greater than six, we reject data normality based upon a 5 per cent significance level

Source: Authors' calculations

Results Summary

In this section, we present answers to the three questions defined in the introduction.

1. Can we observe any information efficiency in Central European capital markets?
We could not reject the weak form hypothesis of Central European capital markets (especially if the results concerning heteroskedasticity are taking into account).

2. Can we observe an improvement of information efficiency in these markets during the time analyzed?
Yes, we do not reject RW1 in any market during the shorter of period from January 1998 to August 2004. Compare results in Tables 7-1 and 7-2 or with previous research (Hanousek and Filer, 1996; Vošvrda *et al.*, 1998).

3. What gap exists between Central European capital markets and the U.S. (mature) capital market?
Besides the information efficiency, the distribution characteristics of the market returns in the Central European markets also converge to the U.S. market. Thus, the gap between Central European market and the U.S. market is decreasing.

Conclusion

The calculations and results obtained validate the general understanding that the U.S. market is mature and efficient. We concluded that the U.S. market possesses the weak form of efficiency. On the other hand, we are aware of simplifications we made when using the U.S. market index (DJIA) as a proxy of the market (the same simplification was made for other capital markets as well).

Despite the restrictive assumptions applied to the test (e.g. data normality), we could not unambiguously reject the weak form of efficiency in any researched market. Concerning the results of the relatively robust variance ratio tests, we share the opinion that current stock prices in the analyzed markets reflect the past price movements. Therefore, strategies used by technical analysts are useless and could not help investors to make abnormal returns. The same holds when assuming foreign portfolio investments. In other words, the examined markets efficiently incorporate information about exchange rates movements of the local currencies relative to world currencies (in our case against the U.S. dollar).

When analyzing the shorter period commencing in January 1998, one can see an improvement in the test statistics. For this reason, we claim that stabilisation (or an improvement in market efficiency) of Central European markets has been taking place. The U.S. market still seems to be more efficient compared to the Central European markets, but the gap is getting smaller. The fact behind it could be an implementation of standard bourse rules, IT development, Internet and other conventions that make informational flows quicker and more accurate.

On the other hand, we know that our research is not comprehensive. Other topics need to be addressed to make the analysis more precise. These topics include using more robust tests such as GARCH models, testing the semi-strong form of efficiency in Central European markets, testing efficiency not only on market indices but also on particular stocks, and, finally focusing on intra-day stock trading.

References

Anděl, J. 1985. *Matematická statistika*. Praha: SNTL/ALFA.

Ayadi, O.F. and C.S. Pyun. 1994. An Application of Variance Ratio Test to the Korean Securities Market. *Journal of Banking and Finance* 18(4):643–58.

Campbell, John Y., Andrew W. Lo and Archie C. MacKinlay. 1997. *The Econometrics of Financial Markets*. New Jersey: Princeton University Press.

Diviš, K. and P. Teplý. 2005. Informační efektivnost burzovních trhů ve střední Evropě. *Finance a úvěr – Czech Journal of Economics and Finance* 55(9):471–82.

Fama, E. 1970. Efficient Capital Markets: A Review of Theory and Empirical Work. *Journal of Finance* 25(2):383–417.

Filer, Randall K. and Jan Hanousek. 1996. *The Extent of Efficiency in Central European Equity Markets*. Working Paper no. 104. Prague: CERGE-EI.

Hanousek, Jan and Randall K. Filer. 1996. *Informational Efficiency in Central European Equity Markets: The Effect of Macroeconomic Variables on Stock Prices*. Working Paper no. 108. Prague: CERGE-EI.

Janda, K. 1994. Modelování rizika akciového portfolia. *Finance a úvěr* 44(9):463–72.

Jones, Charles P. 1991. *Investments: Analysis and Management*. New York: John Wiley & Sons.

Levene, H. 1952. On the Power Function of Tests of Randomness Based on Runs Up and Down. *Annals of Mathematical Statistics* 23(3):34–56.

Lo, A.W. and A.C. MacKinlay. 1989. The Size and Power of the Variance Ratio Test in Finite Samples: A Monte Carlo Investigation. *Journal of Econometrics* 40(2):203–38.

Stolin, M.R. and H.K. Ury. 1979. Tables of the Studentized Maximum Modulus Distribution and an Application to Multiple Comparisons among Means. *Technometrics* 21(1):87–93.

Urrutia, J.L. 1995. Tests of Random Walk and Market Efficiency for Latin American Emerging Equity Markets. *The Journal of Financial Research* 3(2):299–309.

Vošvrda, M., J. Filáček and M. Kapička. 1998. The Efficient Market Hypothesis Testing on the Prague Stock Exchange. *Bulletin of the Czech Econometric Society* 5:55–67.

Note

[1] Elaboration of this chapter was supported by grant No. 402/05/2123 Efficiency of Financial Markets and New Basel Capital Accord (NBCA) awarded by The Grant Agency of the Czech Republic.

CHAPTER EIGHT

MONETARY POLICY AND ASSET PRICES: WHAT ROLE FOR CENTRAL BANKS IN NEW EU MEMBER STATES?[1]

The chapter deals with the relationship between monetary policy and asset prices. Besides surveying the general discussion, it attempts to extend it to recent developments in the selected new EU Member States (NMS). After a brief description of the current macroeconomic situation in the NMS, the appropriate reaction of monetary policy to asset price bubbles is dealt with. Moreover, the main pros and cons associated with this reaction are summarised. Afterwards, the risks of asset market bubbles in four NMS are evaluated. Since the capital markets are still underdeveloped and the real estate price boom seems to be a natural reaction to the initial undervaluation, the risks are viewed as rather small. The conclusion is thus that it is crucial for central banks in mature economies as well as in the NMS to conduct their monetary policies as well as their supervisory and regulatory roles in a way that does not promote the build-up of asset market bubbles. In exceptional times, central banks of small open economies must be ready to use monetary policy steps as a kind of insurance against the adverse effects of potential asset market bubbles.

Current Developments in the New EU Member States

The NMS went through a successful stabilisation process. With inflation and pressures for nominal appreciation of domestic currencies low (see Appendix 8-A), their central banks lowered short-term interest rates to historically low levels. Figure 8-1 shows the development of the monetary policy interest rates of the selected NMS, namely the Czech Republic, Hungary, Poland and Slovakia (EU4). There is a significant downward trend in all the rates, with the exception of the Polish rate during 2000 and the Hungarian policy swings during 2003. During the period under review, the lowest rates were always seen in the Czech Republic, which is the only economy with experience of a negative interest rate differential against ECB rates.2

Fig. 8-1 Monetary policy interest rates in the EU4 (in %)

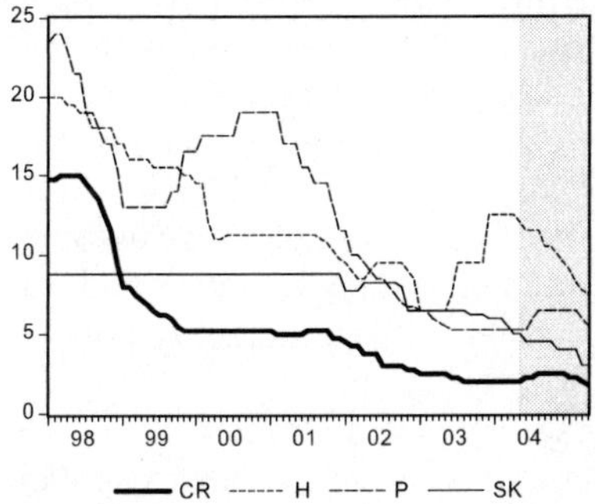

Note: CR=Czech Republic, H=Hungary, P=Poland, SK=Slovakia. The shaded area identifies membership in the EU
Source: Eurostat, EU4 central bank websites

Figure 8-2 presents the development of the average lending rates of the EU4 countries, which also slope down during the last decade, especially in Hungary, Poland and Slovakia. Czech lending rates had already moved to very low levels by 1999. Long-term nominal interest rates also went down sharply, thanks in part to expectations of Euro adoption. In addition, restructured and privatised banks recently began to extend credit to the corporate sector and households again.

Fig. 8-2 Average lending rates in the EU4 (in %)

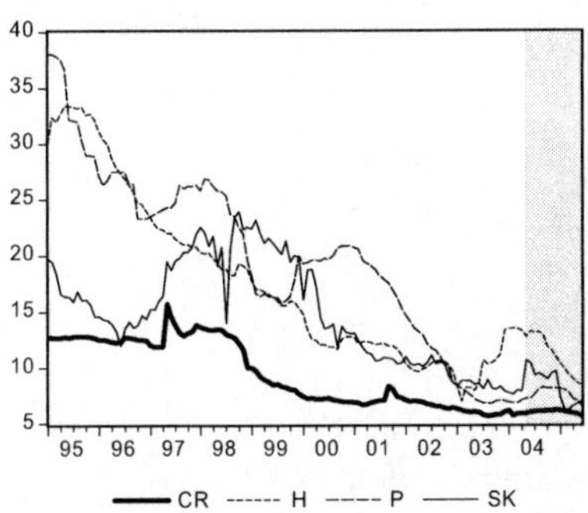

Note: CR=Czech Republic, H=Hungary, P=Poland, SK=Slovakia. The shaded area identifies membership in the EU
Source: IMF-IFS CD-ROM

The combined effect can be seen mainly in a rapid credit expansion in the housing loans segment in the household sector, with yearly increases of between 30 per cent and 50 per cent in most countries (see Figure 8-3). There are fears that the mix of credit boom and optimistic expectations may support investment of a speculative kind and create asset bubbles similar to those experienced by many developed economies in the past. And in the same way, the formation of these bubbles may not be accompanied by visible pressures for consumer price inflation, which is the main focus of central banks. And at the same time, the NMS have become part of the worldwide discussion on the impact of the low interest rate environment, high liquidity and easy availability of credit on asset markets and on the role of monetary policy in supporting and subsequently taming asset price inflation.

The NMS central banks thus now face the same questions as their counterparts in many developed countries: Are current monetary policies supporting the build-up of asset market bubbles? Should central banks incorporate asset prices into their policy decision-making processes and react to asset price inflation with interest rate changes? These particular questions have been the subject of a lively discussion in recent years among central bankers and academics in the U.S. and many other countries. Our intention is to help to extend the discussion to the local scene, even though this may seem premature to at least some observers. For these reasons, we will focus mainly on the aforementioned EU4 economies.

Fig. 8-3 Household credit growth (y-o-y, in %)

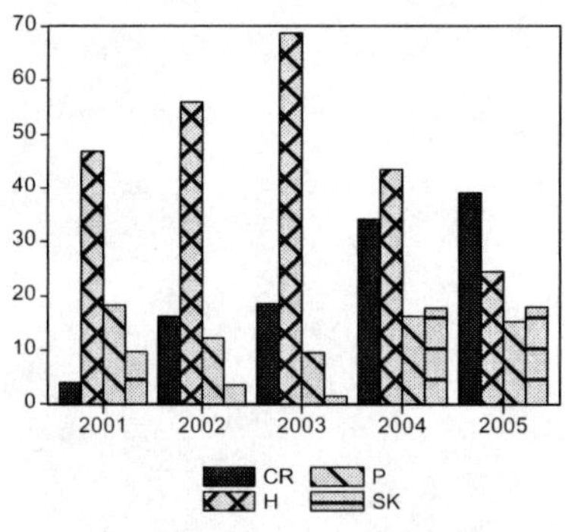

Note: CR=Czech Republic, H=Hungary, P=Poland, SK=Slovakia
Source: Eurostat, IMF-IFS CD-ROM and authors' calculations

How Should Monetary Policy Respond to Asset Prices?

Importance of Asset Prices for Central Banks

Whether monetary policy should actively seek to encourage asset price[3] stability, or even whether it should seek to prevent or at least reduce asset price bubbles, is really one of the key current topics of debate among central bankers. Despite what the media sometimes says, hardly any central banker argues that central banks should completely ignore asset prices and focus only on consumer prices defined in terms of consumer price index (CPI) changes. As stressed by Bollard (2004), for example, economists agree that central banks should take asset prices into account, but they disagree on whether they should respond to asset price drifts.

Central banks automatically take asset price developments into account when setting monetary policy, even if formally they focus on price stability defined solely in terms of prices of consumption. This is primarily because asset price movements impact on CPI inflation and large movements in asset prices can have significant implications for CPI inflation. If prices of real estate, for example, are rising faster than inflation, people try to build more houses. To do so, they demand more building materials, putting pressure on the prices of those materials. In addition to that direct impact, asset price movements also feed into CPI inflation through the "wealth effect". As asset prices rise, people tend to feel wealthier. This can apply to any kind of asset, but in many countries we see this mostly through house prices, due to the high proportion of household wealth associated with housing. The Czech Republic ranks among the countries where housing has a major share in household wealth, and at the same time, the share of net financial assets is relatively low and does not have a clear growth tendency. In countries with developed and broad stock markets, the wealth effect applies also to share prices.

Asset prices also feed through into spending and hence inflation in other ways. For example, asset price increases improve balance sheets, increasing the borrowing capacity of firms and individuals. Increases in net worth tend to increase the willingness of lenders to lend and borrowers to borrow, facilitating a general expansion in spending as well as an expansion in spending on investment in appreciating assets. Most of the time, asset and consumer prices roughly move together and asset prices present no major problem for monetary policy. There are, however, times when asset prices move well out of line with underlying economic fundamentals. Sometimes, asset prices can become disconnected from reasonable expectations of future earnings, resulting in speculative bubbles that cannot be justified by economic fundamentals. Sooner or later, speculative bubbles will burst. But the damage they can do to the economy can be huge. This brings us to the question of whether central banks should try to constrain asset price bubbles.

Three Main Opinions on Asset Price Bubbles

Economists have a variety of opinions on this question. We prefer to divide them into three groups. The first one comprises those who say that a central bank should pay attention to asset market developments, but cannot and should not try to constrain asset price bubbles on their own. Ben Bernanke, a former Fed governor and current Fed chairman, seems to serve as the speaker for this group. We will use his words to define the other two groups and explain his views on the issue. We will then question his views and explain why a more active approach may sometimes be justified.

Bernanke (1999, 2001 or 2002) suggests a very simple rule for central bank policy regarding asset market instability: Use the right tool for the job. Bernanke (2002) says that the Fed has two sets of responsibilities – maximum sustainable employment, stable prices and moderate long-term interest rates on the one hand, and the stability of the financial system on the other. To achieve that, the Fed has two sets of policy tools: policy interest rates and a range of powers with respect to financial institutions. By using the right tool for the job, he means that the Fed will do its best by focusing its monetary policy instruments on achieving its macro goals, while using its regulatory, supervisory and lender-of-last resort powers to help ensure financial stability.

Bernanke agrees that a central bank must monitor financial markets intensively and continuously. To the extent that a stock market boom causes higher spending on consumer goods and investments, it may indicate future inflationary pressures. A policy tightening might therefore be an appropriate reaction. But the goal of the reaction should be to contain the incipient inflation, not the stock market boom. A central bank cannot be an arbiter of security valuation. In other words, it should use monetary policy to target the economy, not the asset markets. He believes that a far better approach is to use micro-level policies to reduce the incidence of bubbles and to protect the financial system against their effects.

To protect the financial system, the central bank should use its regulatory and supervisory powers instead. In particular, it should ensure, together with other financial sector regulators, that financial institutions and markets are well prepared for a large shock to asset prices. To achieve that, commercial banks must be well capitalised and well diversified and they should stress-test their portfolios against a wide range of scenarios. The central bank can also contribute to reducing the probability of boom-and-bust cycles by supporting more transparent accounting and disclosure practices and working to improve the financial literacy and competence of investors. And, if a sudden correction in asset prices does occur, the central bank's first responsibility is to do its part to ensure the integrity of the financial infrastructure – in particular, the payment system and systems for settling trades in securities and other financial instruments. If necessary, the central bank should provide ample liquidity until the immediate crisis has passed.

Bernanke (2002) "sends" the advocates of a more active monetary policy response to asset prices into two broad camps, differing primarily in how aggressive they think the central bank should be in attacking bubbles. The first group favours a "lean-against-the-bubble" strategy. Its representatives agree that a central bank should take account of, and respond to, the implications of asset-price changes for its macro-goal variables. But also, according to this view, a central bank should try to gently steer asset prices away from the presumed bubble path. The theoretical arguments that have been made for the lean-against-the-bubble strategy are not entirely without merit. It seems that it may be worthwhile for a central bank to take out a little "insurance" against the formation of an asset-price bubble and its potentially adverse effects. Bernanke nevertheless believes that leaning against the bubble is unlikely to be productive in practice.

The second group comprises those preferring a more activist approach. Bernanke labels it "aggressive bubble-popping". Aggressive bubble-poppers would like to see a central bank raise interest rates proactively to eliminate potential bubbles. Bernanke views this particular approach as risky and dangerous. He supports this opinion by pointing to Federal Reserve policy in the 1920s. When interest rates peaked in August 1929, the economy was already slowing, though stock prices were still rather high. The Fed tried to prick the stock market bubble, but succeeded only in killing the economy. It seems to us that something similar may also have happened in Japan during the 1990s. The result was the lost decade of the Japanese economy.

We agree that generally there are clear-cut arguments against an activist approach. First, a central bank cannot reliably identify bubbles in asset prices. This seems to be a crucial argument. What we do know is that the monetary policy response to an asset price increase should depend on the source of the increase. And we agree that central banks should not react to asset prices unless they indicate changes in expected inflation. Unfortunately, it is rather difficult to know at any particular point in time whether the increase reflects fundamental improvements or excessively optimistic expectations. It is thus also difficult to know whether the asset price changes indicate improved productivity or higher expected prices. But on some occasions we can be quite sure that a bubble is on the way, because we simply cannot find any fundamentals behind the asset price drift.

Second, even if a central bank can identify bubbles, monetary policy does not possess appropriate tools for effective use against them. A small increase in the policy interest rate can only lead to a correspondingly modest decline in the likelihood or size of a bubble. It is unlikely that a small increase in short-term interest rates, unaccompanied by a significant slowdown of the economy, will induce speculators to modify their equity or real estate investment plans. Interest rates simply have limited power to affect the perceptions that move asset prices in the first place. To materially affect some asset prices, such as housing, interest rates would probably need to move by much more than would be required just to keep CPI inflation comfortably within the target range. Since interest rate changes affect not just house prices, but also the prices of most other assets, goods and services, there would be secondary, unintended consequences, with potentially serious consequences for the economy as a whole.

The third problem is the timing of the central bank's reaction. Once a central bank becomes sure that a bubble has emerged, it will probably be too late to act with interest rate hikes. These may instead conflict with other economic forces that have begun to act. Given the lag that we think applies between an interest rate move and its effect on the real economy, the risk is high that the policy moves would be wrongly timed and only make matters worse. If interest rates are high at the moment a bubble bursts, those high interest rates will still be affecting the economy two years on. This would make the landing harder.

Fourth, pursuing a separate asset price objective could mean having to compromise on the normal inflation objective. Seeking to stabilise rising house prices or an overheated stock market might mean having to force inflation lower than would otherwise be required. It might also mean greater variability in the real economy, interest rates and, potentially, the exchange rate.

Does all this mean that Bernanke is right? We would say that in many ways yes. But we would also say that Bernanke ignores some important aspects. First, he seems to ignore the question of what to do if the bubble is emerging without any signs of inflationary pressures? Inflation measured in terms of consumer prices has not always signalled when imbalances in the economy have been building up. A strong expansion in credit and increasing asset prices have preceded almost all banking crises and the majority of deep recessions in countries around the world over the past one hundred years. In many cases inflation has at the same time been low and stable before the crisis.

A central bank reaction to growth in asset prices is believed to be appropriate only when signals exist that the economy may become overheated. However, the prevailing monetary policy models used to forecast inflation pressures often derive demand pressures (approximated by the output gap) from current inflation pressures. Given that, some signals that inflation pressures may increase in the more distant future may be ignored, especially if monetary policy horizons are too short.

Here we can provide a realistic scenario for a small open economy. It may arise when higher economic growth creates excessively optimistic expectations that lead to nominal appreciation of the domestic currency. In such a situation, very low inflation can prevail even under rapid credit growth and asset price acceleration for rather a long time. When the open inflation pressures finally appear, it may be too late for monetary policy to react. Forecasts of resource utilisation and inflation can also be systematically inaccurate because the models and assessments used do not take account of the independent role that asset prices and debt can play. Also, as a result of structural changes, historical relationships may have changed, thus causing the central bank, for example, to come to incorrect conclusions about the output gap and potential growth. Nevertheless, central banks in increasing numbers compile financial stability analyses that should reveal these particular risks.

If these analyses identify the risk of a bubble emerging, responding is rather challenging. Nonetheless, the risks of the landing from the build-up and bursting of large asset price bubbles warrants taking some risks in an attempt to moderate the problem. There are cases where the asset price misalignment is sufficiently obvious that one can be confident enough to take the risk. Such situations are likely to be rare. And the risks may be considerable. In such a situation, tightening monetary policy may even lead consumer price inflation outside the target range. The central bank may be then blamed for squeezing growth from the economy. Nevertheless, by raising interest rates at an early stage when asset prices are starting to accelerate and before the expansion in credit has become too sharp, the central bank can indeed achieve somewhat lower inflation than is desirable in the short term, but may avoid a subsequent collapse in asset prices that could lead to considerably lower output and inflation in the longer term. And the somewhat tighter monetary policy than otherwise would be able to counter the over-optimistic pricing of financial assets and properties.

Prudential Measures and Regulatory Features as a Solution?

Bernanke also seems to forget that micro-policies are also difficult to apply in reality. He is not the only one. The new issue of the IMF World Economic Outlook (September 2005, p. 13)[4] argues that "in cases where house price inflation remains robust, a combination of moral suasion and if necessary prudential measures could help limit potential risks; over the long term, regulatory features – including those that potentially constrain supply – that may exacerbate price pressures need also to be addressed".

Hilbers *et al.* (2005) provide an extensive list of such measures and features. Among the prudential measures, higher and differentiated capital requirements, tighter loan classification and provisioning rules, dynamic provisioning (accounting for the phase of business cycle in calculating loan-loss provisions), stricter assessment of collateral, or tighter eligibility criteria for certain loans are suggested. Supervisory measures include increasing disclosure requirements, closer inspection and periodic stress testing. Some countries have also applied administrative measures such as bank-by-bank credit limits or mandatory credit rationing. These measures are not generally viewed as the "first best option" for taming excessive credit dynamics. This applies especially to the "prudential measures", which should only be used when normal prudential measures (limits) do not work well and when the new ones can move the system towards the "best practice".[5] All this sounds very well, but the reality is quite frustrating. It is rather difficult to find examples of "prudential measures" or "regulatory features" in use in developed countries. The typical user is a developing or transitional country in major problems, although attempts to apply them sometimes appear in mature economies too.

Can any measures of this kind be recommended to the Czech Republic or other NMS if a housing bubble emerges in the future and, at the same time, no problems with price stability exist? Probably not, and not only because the framework has already been strengthened and there is hardly any room for further tightening. Besides that, the banking sector is preparing for the adoption of the Basel 2 rules. These, together with international accounting rules, make the application of nonstandard measures not so easy.

The possibility of using prudential measures (in terms of anticyclical action) with the intention to address asset price bubbles was convincingly questioned by Bollard (2004). He finds administrative instruments to be blunt, harming newcomers to the market, distorting resource allocation and potentially depriving the private sector of sound investment opportunities. Prudential measures are unlikely to be very effective in addressing asset price cycles, either. The implementation of policy changes would take time, after which there would be potentially long and variable lags in the impact on asset prices. The use of such tools for macroeconomic purposes conflicts with the objective for which such tools were originally designed – i.e. financial stability. Indeed, the use of prudential regulation to moderate asset price cycles might backfire in some circumstances, creating perverse incentives for banks to bias their lending towards riskier ends of the lending spectrum, which in turn could reduce the stability of the financial system.

Asset Markets and Risk of Bubbles in the NMS

The restructuring and strengthening of financial sectors in the NMS has significantly increased access to external financing. This is facilitating the development of investment in various asset markets (the stock market, housing markets, the bond market). Despite remarkable progress, some of these markets are generally still thin and underdeveloped relative to mature economies. Nevertheless, this does not mean that the risks are relatively small. It may rather imply that it is more difficult to analyse these markets and detect potential imbalances. The difficulties are enhanced by incomplete data on the development of the asset markets in the NMS.

From the point of view of international investors, the foreign exchange and stock markets are the most interesting in the countries we are focusing on. Domestic investors usually predominate in real estate markets, with the exception of some major cities. Naturally, fast growth of domestic credit should have the potential to initiate bubbles in these particular markets. Unfortunately, the lack of reliable data on these markets in the NMS prevents us from providing comparisons and deriving conclusions. Besides looking at the EU4 economies, we will comment separately on the Czech asset market events. This is a natural reflection of specific knowledge and lower uncertainty regarding the data.

Despite rapid growth in lending to the private sector, the prudential indicators do not indicate a sizable increase in financial vulnerabilities in the banking systems of the EU4 countries and the NMS in general. Banks are well capitalised, they make hefty profits and the share of nonperforming loans in their portfolios is declining. However, these are normally lagging indicators of banking problems. We must therefore pay attention to the potential risks of the rapid credit expansion. The implications of the rapid growth in lending to the private sector are very often discussed with the other EU4 central banks. We usually agree that the risks are relatively low or even nonexistent. The reason is quite simple – the low base phenomenon.

Foreign Exchange Markets

There is one asset price that is subject to direct reaction of the monetary policy of many central banks – the exchange rate. This reaction is given by the direct impact of the exchange rate on inflation. There might be disputes about whether or not foreign exchange is an asset, as well as whether or not monetary policy interest rates should react to exchange rate swings. In practice, however, the exchange rate is such an important variable that central banks, especially in small open economies, can hardly ignore it. Many central banks which apply a floating regime therefore adjust their interest rates or intervene when facing significant exchange rate changes.

The currencies of the EU4 countries became popular assets with international investors soon after the initial period of transition. The exchange rates of these currencies have been rather volatile at times, and some of the swings can be viewed as bubbles. Figure 8-4 shows the year-over-year changes in the EU4 currencies, demonstrating a relatively high correlation of appreciation and depreciation waves.

Fig. 8-4 Changes in EU4 currencies (y-o-y, in %)

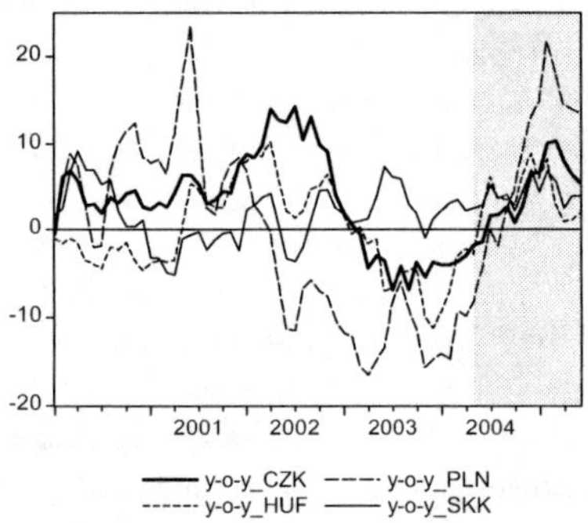

Note: The shaded area identifies membership in the EU.
Source: Eurostat, IMF-IFS CD-ROM and authors' calculations

In the Czech Republic, a bubble-like situation was observed in 2002, when the Czech National Bank (CNB) viewed the sharp appreciation of the koruna as unjustified by the fundamentals, labelled it a bubble and responded by interventions as well as interest rate cuts. The CNB explained its stance by the supposition that the appreciation was being caused by ill-perceived expectations of massive capital inflows due to privatisation sales. The CNB thus tried to spread the correct information among market participants and, besides providing verbal information, had to ensure that the information content was credible. The fact is that the koruna eventually started to depreciate and is still rather weaker compared to its peak in July 2002 (the left-hand side of figures in the appendix). The right-hand side of this figure then shows what we can expect from a floating exchange rate regime: year-over-year appreciations by 10-15 per cent, followed by similar depreciation. PLN seems to be even more volatile than CZK: 20 per cent up in 2001, then 15 per cent down in 2003 and 20 per cent up again in 2005. HUF also behaves like this, although the focus of the authorities on the exchange rate limits the fluctuations.

Stock Markets

Probably the first asset market bubble registered during the recent history of the Czech economy followed the voucher privatisation process in 1993–95. During this period, more than 60 per cent of the population obtained shares in hundreds of firms and privatisation funds. Despite the initial optimistic expectations, the bubble soon burst, since most of the shares lost value rapidly. The bust is captured, albeit only partially, by the decline in the official CNB-120 and PX-50 stock market indices[6] (see Figure 8-5).

Fig. 8-5 Stock market indices in the Czech Republic (in points)[7]

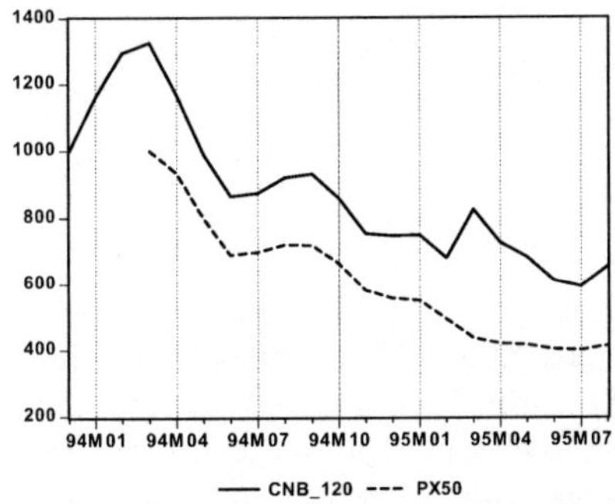

Source: CNB website and authors' calculations

The allocation of shares among the population certainly had a kind of wealth effect, although it was probably not that strong. Hanousek and Tůma (2002) conclude that consumers behaved according to the permanent income hypothesis and demonstrate that only a minor part of the newly created assets actually led to an immediate increase in household consumption. The strong growth in domestic demand in the period was thus driven primarily by the corporate credit boom brought about by the loose financial constraint of the new banking sector. It was no surprise that the stock price bust was followed by a real economy bust later on (Frait, 2000). Monetary policy could not react much, because its objective at that time was to keep the exchange rate fixed.

How about the current stock markets in the EU4 countries? Recent sharp increases in stock exchange indices have already opened a debate on potential overvaluation due to purchases by foreign investors searching for higher yields. Figure 8-6 displays an almost ten-year history of stock exchange indices in the EU4 economies. The movements between the Czech, Hungarian and Polish capital markets have been particularly similar.

Especially from the second half of 2003 onwards, we observe clear strong growth in all the indices.

Fig. 8-6 Stock market indices in the EU4 (1995Q1=100)

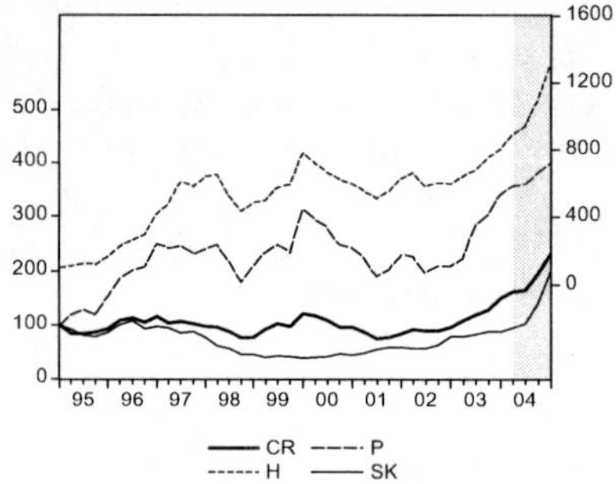

Note: CR=Czech Republic, H=Hungary, P=Poland, SK=Slovakia
Source: Eurostat and authors' calculations

It is not our ambition to add to this particular debate. Instead, we have tried to find out to what extent the cycles in the EU4 stock exchanges have been associated with the corresponding business cycles. With this in mind, we calculate output gaps and stock exchange gaps by detrending the original series using the Band–Pass filter. The final outcomes are presented in Figure 8-7, which also confirms that the development of the Czech, Hungarian and Polish capital markets is in accordance with the development of real GDP. Such a relationship did not apply for any significant period in the Slovak case.

Fig. 8-7 Stock market indices in the EU4 (1995Q1=100)

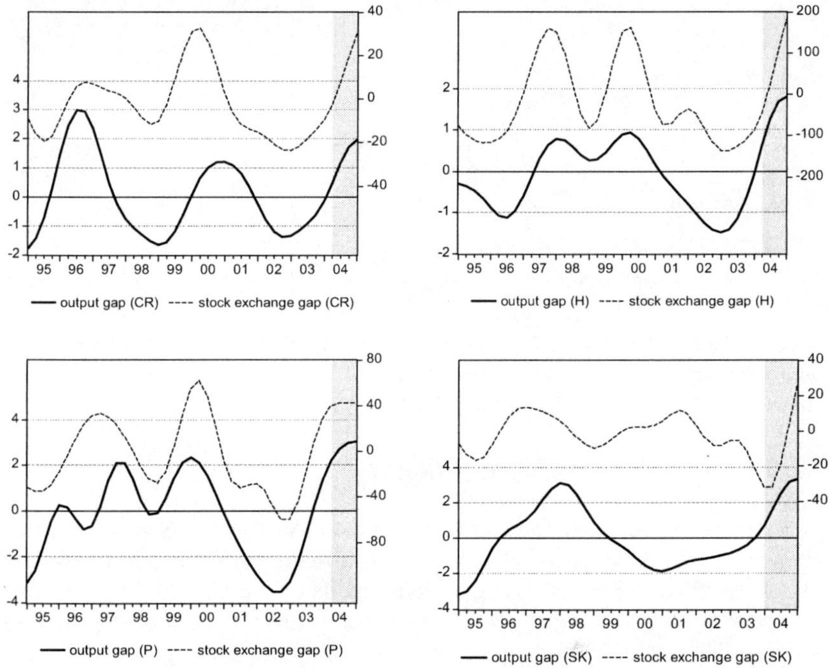

Note: stock exchange gap on rhs; CR=Czech Republic, H=Hungary, P=Poland, SK=Slovakia. The shaded area identifies membership in the EU. Source: Eurostat, IMF-IFS CD-ROM and authors' calculations.

The results suggest that stock prices generally reflect economic activity. Positive output gaps would in this case indicate future inflation pressures; the associated positive gap in stock prices would then provide no new piece of information. The reality is rather different. Standard monetary policy models base their estimations of the actual output gap more on the current state of inflation pressures than on the data on economic activity. Monetary policy models in many countries therefore do not incorporate stock market data. The eventual inclusion of the stock market depends on the country and the structure of the model used. However, the features of the stock markets in the EU4 countries (such as limited issuance of quoted equity and a low level of market capitalisation) mean that their information content is of rather limited importance. Figure 8-8 confirms that the highest market capitalisation is in the Czech Republic (since the second half of 2002) and that in all the EU4 countries the levels are increasing (strongly in the Czech Republic, Hungary and Poland, and slowly in Slovakia).

Fig. 8-8 Market capitalisation in the EU4 (% of GDP)

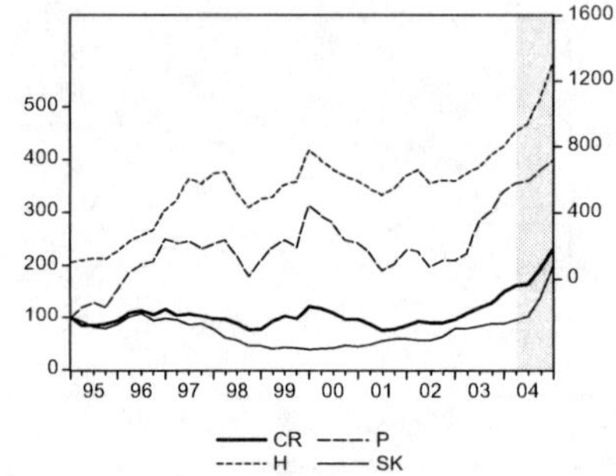

Note: CR=Czech Republic, H=Hungary, P=Poland, SK=Slovakia. The shaded area identifies membership in the EU.
Source: Eurostat and authors' calculations.

Housing Market

The growth rates of the mortgage markets in the NMS in recent years seem tremendous. However, the share of mortgages in GDP is still negligible compared to countries such as the Netherlands or the United Kingdom. This is captured well by Figure 8-9, which plots growth in mortgage lending between 1998 and 2004 against the stock of mortgages as a percentage of GDP. All the EU4 countries are where they should be as catching-up economies.

Fig. 8-9 Mortgage market growth in the EU

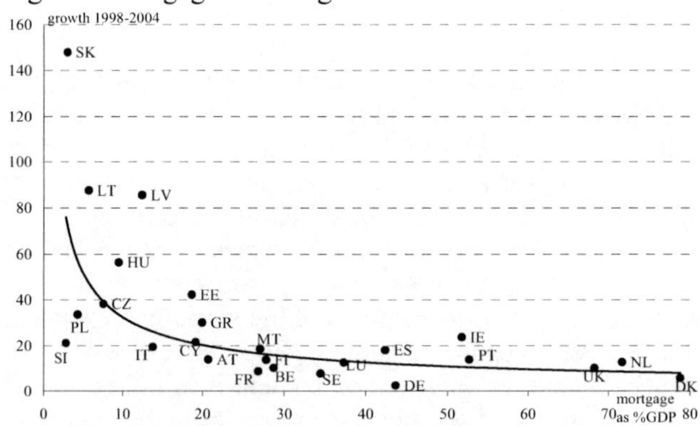

Source: ECB, CNB internal calculations

Housing loans are also the fastest growing component of credit in the EU4 countries. How much should central banks be concerned with a potential house price bubble? It is difficult to say generally because we do not have comparable data series at our disposal. As far as the Czech Republic is concerned, the available data presented in Figure 8-10 can hardly be interpreted as a risk of a bubble. Despite remarkable dynamics in land prices, real estate prices seem to have been flat in the last two years. The price increases to date must be viewed mostly as movements towards more realistic values.

Fig. 8-10 Real estate and land prices in the Czech Republic and Prague (1999Q1=100)

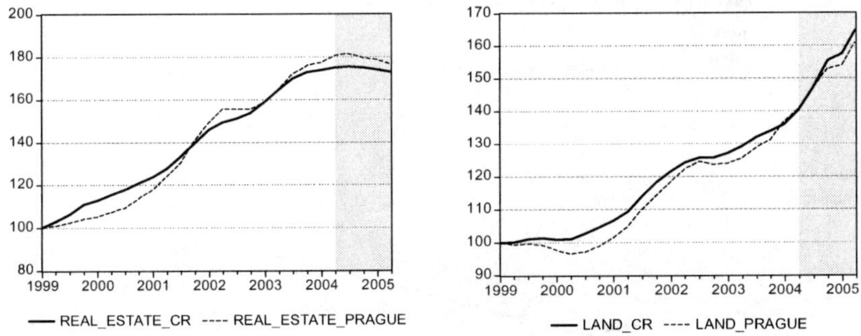

Source: Czech Statistical Office, CNB internal calculations

Global Liquidity, Housing Loans and Real Estate Prices

In the last few years, low nominal and real interest rates plus high global liquidity have been reflected in many countries by relatively high growth in credit and money supply. At the same time, many countries have experienced a real estate price boom. There is an interesting discussion among economists about whether money supply dynamics are causing real estate prices to rise or whether increased money creation is only a natural consequence of increased money demand due to the wealth effect of real estate price developments. This particular discussion is important for assessing the inflationary potential of the current money supply dynamics. If it is a consequence of the above-defined wealth effect, the inflation risk may be low, since once the real estate price growth slows down, demand for money will slow down too. Money supply growth rates would then tend to fall to much lower figures.

Of course, money supply growth may be adding to the real estate price expansion. In many countries, the credit growth is apparently associated with the extension of housing loans. We can see numerous countries with real estate price growth of more than 10 per cent annually in recent years (France, Greece, Ireland, Italy, Spain, United Kingdom, South Africa, New Zealand, United States, and Australia). According to the Economist (which compiles representative indices of real estate prices), relative to income, real estate prices peaked historically in 2004 in the U.S., Australia, United Kingdom, France, Ireland, Netherlands, New Zealand, and Spain. In some countries, structural changes in financial markets seem to be behind this. In some countries of the Euro area, a fall in nominal interest rates to the German level acted as a booster. We plot credit growth and real estate prices in Figure 8-11. We can see a relatively strong correlation, but we cannot assign a causal relation to it.

Fig. 8-11 Credit growth and real estate prices

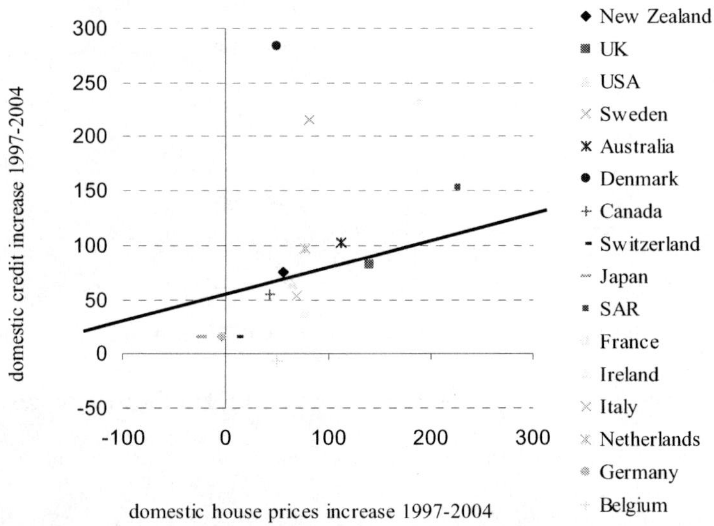

Note: DOMESTIC_CREDIT=65.96+0.088*HOUSE_PRICES
Source: ECB, CNB internal calculations

Real estate market trends should be of concern to central banks in countries where real estate prices have a strong impact on consumer spending. This applies primarily to economies where mortgages with floating interest rates prevail and with widespread "mortgage equity withdrawal" (borrowing that is secured by housing stock but not invested in it). And these are the same countries that are prone to real estate market bubbles associated with periods of low real interest rates and strong credit expansion.

A dominant view among central bankers is one that does not associate actual growth in real assets with inflation, because it does not influence the value of money expressed in goods and services. The reason is simple – future inflation should already be embodied in real asset prices. These can be expressed as the discounted value of future incomes from holding the assets. The discount factor for real asset valuation can be approximated by the real interest rate. If central banks base their decisions on estimated future inflation, they in some way stabilise the real interest rate. Prices of real assets then do not constitute a new piece of information. The application of this particular logic to real estate prices is nevertheless questionable. A number of activities linked to real estate influence the value of money in terms of goods and services. Changes in real estate prices then have a direct impact on domestic demand via the wealth effect or via the ability to borrow against collateral. Real estate price change can thus, under some circumstances, be viewed to some extent as new information for policymakers. As far as the EU4 countries are concerned, the current credit dynamics do not seem to pose risks to asset markets and financial sectors. For their monetary policies, "benign neglect" thus still makes sense.

Conclusion

Central banks have tremendous difficulties in identifying and taming asset price bubbles. Neither monetary policy instruments nor supervisory and regulatory measures can be of much help when a bubble occurs. It is therefore crucial for a central bank to conduct its monetary policy as well as its supervisory and regulatory roles in a way that does not promote the build-up of asset market bubbles. Monetary policy must therefore be maximally forward-looking. Central banks should not be thinking only in terms of the next two years, as is the standard for monetary policy models. Given the potentially long-term nature of asset price misalignments, analyses of financial stability supporting monetary policy-making must look at longer horizons while applying a risk management approach to financial market developments. In exceptional times, central banks of small open economies must be ready to use monetary policy steps as a kind of insurance against the adverse effects of potential asset market bubbles. The reaction to other sorts of bubbles should depend on the particular conditions in the given time. As far as the EU4 countries are concerned, the current credit dynamics do not seem to pose risks to asset markets and financial sectors. For their monetary policies, "benign neglect" thus still makes sense.

References

Bernanke, B. and M. Gertler. 1999. Monetary Policy and Asset Price Volatility. *Federal Reserve Bank of Kansas City Economic Review*. Fourth Quarter: 17–51.

Bernanke, B. and M. Gertler. 2001. Should Central Banks Respond to Movements in Asset Prices? *American Economic Review* 91(2):253–7.

Bernanke, Ben. 2002. *Asset-Price "Bubbles" and Monetary Policy*. Remarks before the New York Chapter of the National Association for Business Economics, New York, October 15, 2002. [online] Access from: < http://www.federalreserve.gov/boarddocs/speeches/2002/20021015/default.htm >

Bollard, Alan. 2004. *Asset Prices and Monetary Policy*. An Address to the Canterbury Employers' Chamber of Commerce, Christchurch, 30 January 2004 [online] Access from: < http://www.bis.org/review/r040206f.pdf. >

Christiano, L.J. and T.J. Fitzgerald. 2003. The Band Pass Filter. *International Economic Review*, 44(2):435–65.

Frait, Jan. 2000. Economic Transition in the Czech Republic: A Real Success? In *The Euro-Asian World: A Period of Transition*, ed Yelena Kaluyzhnova and Dov Lynch, 116–40. London: Macmillan Press, New York: St. Martin Press.

Hanousek, J. and Z. Tůma. 2002. A test of the permanent income hypothesis on Czech voucher privatization. *Economics of Transition* 10(2):235–54.

Hilbers, Paul, Inci Otker–Robe, Ceyla Pazarbasioglu and Gudrun Johnsen. 2005. *Assessing and Managing Rapid Credit Growth and the Role of Supervisory and Prudential Policies*. International Monetary Fund Working Paper No. WP/151/05. Washington, D.C.: International Monetary Fund.

Srejber, Eva. 2004. *What Role Do Asset Prices and Credit Play in Monetary Policy?* Remarks for Adam Smith Seminar, Thun, Switzerland, 30 June 2004. [online] Access from: <http://www.bis.org/review/r040713h.pdf>

Notes

[1] Authors note that everything contained in this paper represents their own views and not necessarily those of the Czech National Bank. However, all errors and omissions remain entirely the fault of the authors. The research behind this paper is supported by the Czech Science Foundation within a project no. GAČR 402/05/2758 "Integration of the financial sector of the new EU member countries into the EMU".

[2] The Czech National Bank set its monetary policy rate (the 2-week repo rate) below the European (ECB) level in three periods: 26 July 2002–6 December 2002, 31

January 2003–7 March 2003, and 29 April 2005–27 October 2005. The negative interest rate differential was always 0.25 p.p., except for the period 1 November 2002– 6 December 2002 (0.5 p.p.).

[3] By asset price we mean the price of something bought to generate income or to sell later on for a profit. Examples are physical assets such as real estate or collectables, and financial assets such as shares, bonds, foreign exchange and other financial instruments.

[4] The recommendations seem to build on the recent IMF Working Paper by Hilbers *et al.* (2005).

[5] This sort of measure was used in the Czech Republic at the end of 1990s. The supervisory authority required banks to build up provisions to cover loss loans collateralised by real estate to 100 per cent of their value over three years. The reason behind the measure was the evidence that during the 1990s banks were lending against rather overvalued real estate.

[6] There were two waves of voucher privatisation. The shares from the first one started to be listed in June and July 1993 (622 plus 333 titles) and those from the second one in March 1995 (674 titles). The CNB-120 index was published from the end of 1993 until 31 December 1999. Publishing of the PX-50 began in April 1994 and over time has changed in composition completely. The index is thus rather an imprecise description of the voucher shares' performance. Many shares in individual firms and privatisation funds that were not included in the index lost value completely and were removed from trading.

[7] CNB-120 = The Czech National Bank monitored trends in the share price movements of 120 issues traded on the Prague Stock Exchange. The component companies were chosen to reflect the economy as a whole and thus all industries (1 March 1995 = 1000 points); The PX50 consists of the most attractive domestic stocks traded on the Prague Stock Exchange in terms of turnover and market capitalisation (5 April 1994 = 1000 points).

Appendix 8-A

Inflation and nominal exchange rates in the Czech Republic

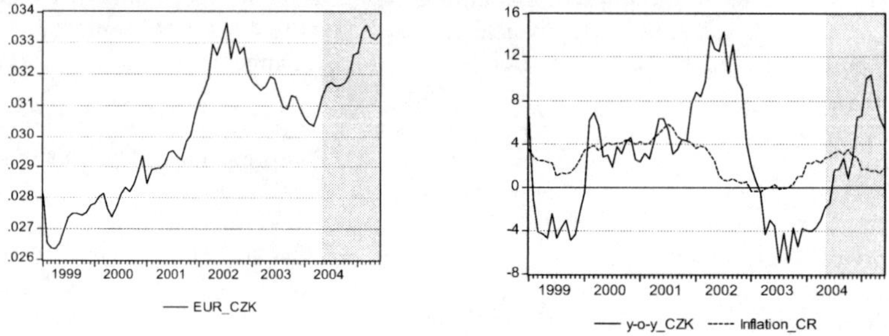

Note: rhs: (+) appreciation, (-) depreciation. The shaded area identifies membership in the EU.
Source: Eurostat, IMF-IFS CD-ROM and authors' calculations

Inflation and nominal exchange rates in Hungary

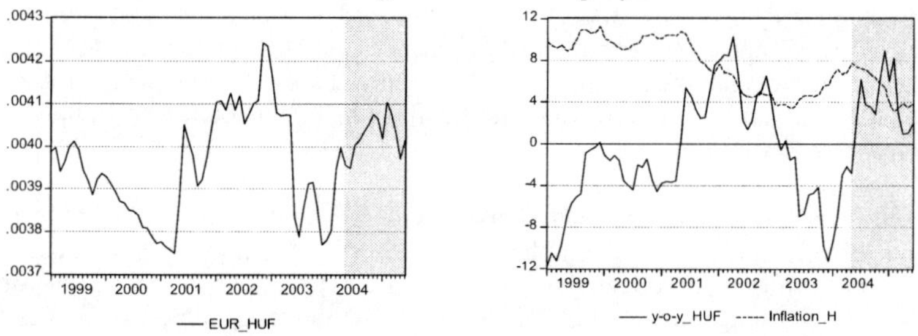

Note: rhs: (+) appreciation, (-) depreciation. The shaded area identifies membership in the EU.
Source: Eurostat, IMF-IFS CD-ROM and authors' calculations

Inflation and nominal exchange rates in Poland

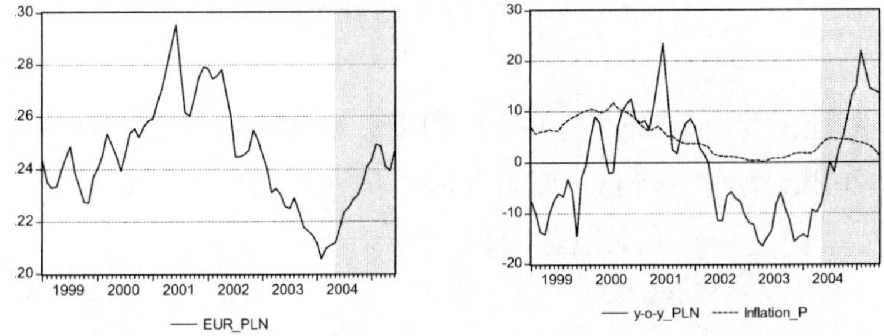

Note: rhs: (+) appreciation, (-) depreciation. The shaded area identifies membership in the EU.
Source: Eurostat, IMF-IFS CD-ROM and authors' calculations

Inflation and nominal exchange rates in Slovakia

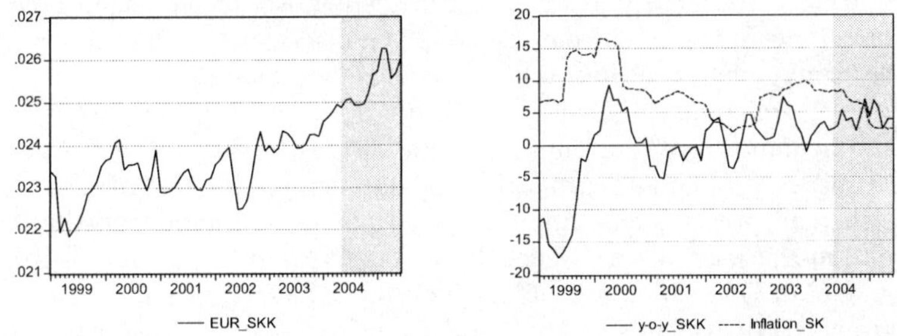

Note: rhs: (+) appreciation, (-) depreciation. The shaded area identifies membership in the EU.
Source: Eurostat, IMF-IFS CD-ROM and authors' calculations

CHAPTER NINE

CURRENCY SUBSTITUTION IN A TRANSITIONAL ECONOMY WITH AN APPLICATION TO THE CZECH REPUBLIC

Currency substitution is a very important concept in the history of economic thought and one of the most ambiguous concepts in economics. A closer look at the way currency substitution has been defined in the vast literature brings little clarity. There we can distinguish several main areas, problems and incentives of current research. We discuss the idea of a locally (regionally) and globally substituting currency and a substituted currency (the currency being substituted). Further, we deal with these issues by discussing transition phenomena of currency substitution (especially in the Czech Republic) and the problem of euroisation (by unilateral or bilateral decision).

This chapter presents an empirical analysis of currency substitution phenomena in the case of the Czech Republic. We introduce the portfolio balance model of Branson and Henderson (1985) which creates the basis for our multi-perspective analysis. This model consists of four equations, two representing the demand for domestic and foreign currency and two describing the demand for domestic and foreign bonds. We modify this model for local Czech conditions and discuss the building of the estimated equations, substituting the variables suggested by theory with their factual equivalents or approximations. Finally, based on our estimates we discuss some of the implications stemming from economic theory and from the experience of other transitional countries.

Currency Substitution in Small Open Transition Economies

In most transition economies, the initial conditions and the process of transformation have been similar, i.e. for more than ten years there have been simultaneous periods of internal and external liberalisation and a process alignment with the more developed countries. Internal liberalisation has been brought about by price liberalisation in a higher inflation environment, restructuring of industries, adoption of new tax systems, etc. External liberalisation has been caused by trade liberalisation and, in particular, by external convertibility of national currencies and liberalisation of capital accounts. Generally it can be concluded that the launch of the reform process was coupled with greater economic uncertainty1 (and in some countries by political instability) and the absence of developed financial markets.

Macroeconomic Policy and Currency Substitution

The implications of currency substitution for macroeconomic policy differ between developed and developing countries and, in two respects, in particular. First are the effects of currency substitution on the efficiency of stabilisation programmes, and second are the effects of currency substitution on the authority revenues received from inflation.

One of the problems of developing countries is the credibility of their stabilisation programmes. The relevant question in this context is: Does dollarisation (euroisation or other -isation) help to stabilise an economy and increase the credibility of its policies? Credibility can increase when foreign currency circulation eliminates the authorities' incentives to manipulate the domestic currency. In the past, many stabilisation programmes have involved fixing nominal exchange rates or establishing crawling pegs. These arrangements have ensured the progressive appreciation of real exchange rates. The other issue relating to stabilisation programmes is the discussion between fixed and floating exchange regimes. Results of currency substitution models and other empirical observations indicate that the presence of a currency substitution exchange rate implies higher volatility, with potentially distribution effects on the economy. These findings lead to the defence of fixed exchange rates (or exchange rate regimes with narrower fluctuation bands) during a "stabilising" period, when currency substitution plays a significant role in the economy.

Inflationary financing of a government deficit poses another relevant question relating to these issues. It can be intuitively said that the higher the substitutability of the domestic currency with foreign currency, the more difficult it is for the government to finance its deficit by printing money. On the one hand, holding foreign currency balances makes it possible to get seigniorage, so that, the demand for foreign currency may act as an inflationary tax. The resulting revenue will be (in the presence of currency substitution) lower for each level of this tax.

Currency substitution also suggests a recommendation for the optimal rate of inflation. The transaction models of currency substitution imply that the marginal rate of transformation (represented by a relative price, i.e. the real exchange rate) between two goods (domestic and foreign) is different from the marginal rate of substitution for these two goods, owing to the costs of liquidity. These liquidity costs are influenced by the rates of inflation in both countries. This model then defines an optimal relative rate of inflation, existing when the marginal rate of transformation is equal to the marginal rate of substitution. If the foreign rate of inflation is known, then the domestic rate of inflation should be set in such a way as to minimise misrepresentation of the aforementioned relative prices.

Quantification of the Degree of Currency Substitution

It is useful to look at how we can quantify or measure the degree of currency substitution. Sarajevs (2000) concludes that, ideally, the measure of currency substitution is the value of foreign currency notes circulating in the economy (as a means of payment and a store of value) and all checking accounts and short-term deposits in foreign currency held by residents in domestic banks and abroad. Available data is lacking not only for transition economies, but also for industrial countries. Therefore, most studies generally calculate currency substitution either as (i) the ratio of foreign currency deposits to M2 (broad domestic monetary aggregates), or as (ii) the ratio of foreign currency deposits to broad monetary aggregates, including foreign currency. The next part will show that these two measures of currency substitution have moved together in the case of the Czech Republic.

Which factors can explain currency substitution in the Czech Republic? A number of competing explanations come to mind: (i) The Czech Republic, with its lack of restrictions on capital flows, is a safe place for foreign exchange dealers from many countries. (ii) A lag occurs as financial markets and economic agents adapt to an economic environment with large foreign exchange flows (as individuals and banks get used to dealing with high levels of currency substitution, there are extra costs associated with turning the situation back). (iii) A sharp increase in the openness of the Czech economy increased foreign exchange balances during the transformation.

Another interesting question is: For whom is currency substitution most relevant? In the presence of inflation, poor people suffer more from inflationary taxation than do others. The poor cannot afford to use financial market instruments (including foreign currency) to avoid the inflation tax. Currency substitution can also make it more difficult for the government to renege on its economic stabilisation programme and fall back on the use of the inflation tax.

Substituting and Substituted Currencies

In this subsection we distinguish a locally (regionally) and globally substituting currency from a substituted one (the currency being substituted). The reason for our terminology is as follows. We think that a local and global dimension of currency substitution can generally be found. While the global currencies are definitely US dollar (USD), Euro (EUR), Swiss frank (CHF) and Japanese yen (JPY), other currencies act more locally than globally. Prior the Euro implementation, the group of the world currencies also consisted of the German mark (DEM). The vast majority of the four global currencies is held by citizens of nations outside the borders of the issuing states. Doyle (2000) presents the relevant research in this area – an estimation of worldwide currency substitution. Using a currency demand equation implied by cointegrating vectors for Canada, the Netherlands and Austria, he estimates for 1996 that only a surprising 30 per cent of USD was held outside the United States, although as much as 69 per cent of DEM was held outside Germany. It must be remembered that foreign holdings of these three main currencies (USD, DEM, CHF) have significantly increased international currency substitution in the world, which roughly tripled between 1986 and 1996.

Of course, several other currencies might qualify to fulfil this role, most notably for historical reasons (the colonisation period). There is at least one candidate: the British pound (GBP).[2] The best candidate countries for "poundisation" include either relatively successful or developed economies such as those of Australia, New Zealand, Canada, South Africa, the Asian tigers (Hong Kong, Singapore and Malaysia) and parts of Middle Eastern territories. So, we see that worldwide currency substitution is not solely an American or Eurozone phenomenon.

Generally, we can specify the reasons for currency substitution, i.e. the reasons why a currency is being substituted: (i) Macroeconomic instability with a sizeable rate of inflation, exchange rate instability and volatility, and a less optimistic country rating. (ii) The existence of a large illegal or underground economy (especially when this sector produces tradable and export goods such as drugs). Examples are to be found in Europe's former socialist bloc. (iii) A history of financial crisis and risk-averse behaviour by economic agents trying to eliminate this potential risk. (iv) The lack of higher-denomination bank notes issued by the central bank.

The largest increase in currency substitution occurred in the last decade, suggesting that the main reasons for this were the collapse of the former socialist bloc in Europe and the tendency toward dollarisation, especially in South America.

The Czech Koruna – A Substituting Currency or Substituted Currency?

We see local substituting currencies as being those which are mostly used in a local environment within a specific economic region. It can be shown that the Czech koruna (CZK) is not only a substituted currency, but has also for several years been the substituting currency for some post-socialist countries. The reasons for this collateral role of the Czech koruna as a substituting currency include the following: (i) Since its inception in 1993, the Czech koruna has remained very stable and not too volatile against the two main currency pairs, i.e. USD and DEM/EUR; (ii) The Czech koruna has not had an inflation rate higher than other transition countries (Figure 9-1); (iii) The Czech koruna has quite a good general reputation abroad; (iv) The Czech koruna became externally convertible quite soon after 1993; (v) The Czech economy has absorbed a fairly significant amount of post-socialist workers, for whom it is better to hold earned money in Czech koruna (rather than exchanging it for world-wide substituting currencies); (vi) The Czech National Bank issues bank notes with a relatively high nominal denomination of CZK 5000. Conversion from the highest GBP, FRF or USD denominations yields a smaller amount of money than reflected in our highest note. The EUR notes have two higher denominations compared to Czech notes and recalculated to CZK: the EUR 200 and EUR 500 notes.

Fig. 9-1 Inflation rates in transition economies (1994–2001, in %)

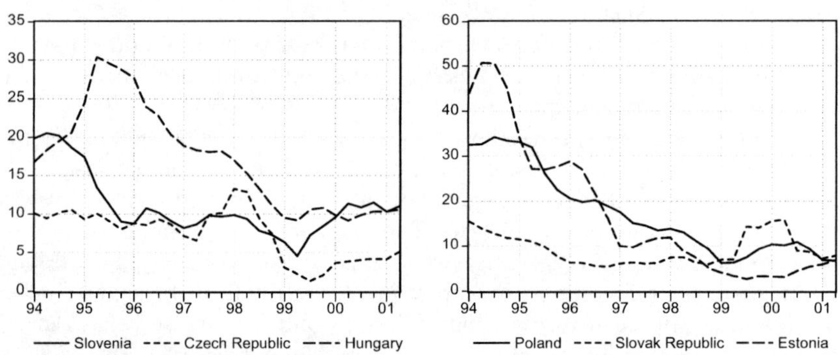

Source: Authors' calculations based on CNB database (http://www.cnb.cz) and IMF-IFS statistics

Currency Substitution, Euroisation and Enlargement Process

The other relevant topic relating to the currency substitution issue (especially from the macroeconomic point of view) is the problem of euroisation in non-eurozone countries, which has become very topical in many transition countries at the end of 2001. Generally, we can distinguish the euroisation process as being based on either a unilateral decision or a bilateral one.

The former (unilateral) decision involves adoption of the Euro without the official agreement and permission of the EU/EMU authorities before a candidate country officially joins the Eurozone.

An accession country may generally see various advantages to adopting the Euro, namely: (i) the stability of its exchange rate to the Eurozone area is increased (incentives for international investment). (ii) the risk of speculative attacks on the domestic currency is virtually eliminated. (iii) the general necessity of holding foreign reserves is lessened (thanks to lower exchange risk). (iv) lower interest rates and lower inflation. (v) lower transaction costs which are larger for small open economies. (vi) re-establishing the domestic currency and re-creating an independent central bank remain theoretically possible (only for unilateral euroisation).

The general disadvantages (risk and costs) might include: (i) the higher probability of runs on commercial banks in the absence of a "national" central bank acting as a lender of last resort and risk of boom bust cycles, as interest rates become very low and the central bank looses this lender of last resort function. (ii) the general or probable lack of foreign reserves. (iii) the low official euroisation of most first-wave accession countries. (iv) as the independence of monetary and exchange rate policy is lost, these could overburden other policies, especially fiscal policy (plus the possibility of political feuding because monetary policy is much less independent of other countries). (v) non-compatibility of monetary policy instruments with the ECB (though not problematic for those countries in the first wave of accession). (vi) the record of dollarised economies has shown that dollarised nations had a lower rate of economic growth than others. (vii) loss of seignorage income. The European authorities have made clear that unilateral euroisation is not a legally and economically sound option for accession countries on their way to the EU and Eurozone.

The latter (bilateral) decision represents the stage of integration into the Eurozone after accession to the EU and after fulfilment of all necessary conditions. The candidate states: (i) will join the EU, (ii) then they will participate in ERM2 (exchange rate mechanism) for at least two years, (iii) have to fulfil the other four nominal convergence criteria (Maastricht criteria) and (iv) in a last step, they will introduce the Euro as their national currency. This will include a non-trivial process of determination of the Euro locking rates for the currencies of transition countries.

The main reason for adopting the Euro as late as possible is the modification of the structure of real appreciation accompanying the real convergence process. This process will only be possible through higher inflation and no longer through appreciation (nominal and real) of the exchange rate. This has important implications for macroeconomic policy in the accession (catching-up) countries.

Empirical Analysis of Currency Substitution in the Czech Republic

Our analysis of currency substitution in the Czech Republic is based on a portfolio model developed by Branson and Henderson (1985), which we further modify to match the conditions in the Czech economy. This portfolio approach enables us to focus on currency substitution phenomenon from several perspectives. It incorporates money demand for both domestic and foreign currencies, and capital mobility, i.e. demand for both domestic and foreign bonds. We consider this approach very useful, since it comprises several independent views on currency substitution analysis, examining the robustness of estimates not only from the perspective of the applied estimation techniques but also from that of different markets (relationships).

We follow Branson and Henderson (1985), without explicit solution of the optimisation problem, and assume that the domestic demand (i.e. that of domestic residents) for assets depends on their relative returns, satisfying the usual wealth constraints:

$$M = M(\overset{-}{i}, \overset{-}{(i^* + e^{ex})}, \overset{-}{e^{ex}}, \overset{+}{PY}, \overset{+}{P^c}, \overset{+}{W}), \tag{9.1}$$

$$eM^* = M^*(\overset{-}{i}, \overset{-}{(i^* + e^{ex})}, \overset{+}{e^{ex}}, \overset{+}{PY}, \overset{+}{P^c}, \overset{+}{W}), \tag{9.2}$$

$$B = B(\overset{+}{i}, \overset{-}{(i^* + e^{ex})}, \overset{-}{e^{ex}}, \overset{-}{PY}, \overset{-}{P^c}, \overset{+}{W}), \tag{9.3}$$

$$eB^* = B^*(\overset{-}{i}, \overset{+}{(i^* + e^{ex})}, \overset{-}{e^{ex}}, \overset{-}{PY}, \overset{-}{P^c}, \overset{+}{W}). \tag{9.4}$$

The first argument in equations (9.1) to (9.4), i, is the return on holding bonds denominated in domestic currency relative to the return on domestic money (that is minus the rate of domestic inflation). It is assumed that all four assets are substitutes in the portfolio. Hence, an increase in i raises the demand for domestic bonds but lowers the demand for their substitutes in the portfolio. The nominal return on bonds denominated in foreign currency is i^*. Expressed in domestic currency, this return becomes i^*+e^{ex}, with e^{ex} the expected change in the exchange rate. It affects the demand for foreign securities positively and that for other assets negatively. Once again, this second argument is in fact a real return differential, where the return on domestic money is minus the rate of inflation. Similarly, the third argument, e^{ex}, is the return on foreign money, converted into the domestic currency.

The fourth argument, PY, represents the home currency value of domestic output and affects demand for all assets positively. P^c is the price of the domestic consumer's consumption bundle expressed in the home currency. An increase in P^c increases the demand for both moneys and lowers the demand for bonds denominated in domestic and foreign currency. The positive effect on domestic wealth W, the last argument, reflects the assumption that all assets are "normal assets".

We modify this portfolio approach to the local conditions of the Czech Republic. Specifically, we take account of the institutional features of the Czech economy, which arise from both historical and recent developments in this country. When we go through the portfolio balance approach, the first equation represents the traditional domestic money demand equation which has been estimated in slightly modified form and analysed by several authors with respect to the Czech economy (Melecký, 2001 and Arlt *et al.*, 2001). The modification (or difference) lies in the fact that the Czech Republic's broad monetary aggregate (M2) includes foreign deposits. Therefore we will concentrate, as regards equation (9.1), on M2 adjusted for foreign deposits.

Equation (9.2) in our case describes domestic demand for foreign currency, i.e. foreign currency in circulation and foreign deposits in the Czech economy. However, monitoring foreign currency in circulation is very difficult and is left for future research. We consider only the demand for foreign deposits. These are probably held in the Czech Republic mostly for their store-of-value purpose (although we would not omit the influence of foreign trade), as the Czech economy is not considerably dollarised (or euroised) and therefore foreign currency is not commonly used as a medium of exchange or unit of account.

The first problem arises when we look at residents' demand for domestic bonds. In the Czech Republic, as a consequence of historical developments, financial intermediation goes largely through the banking sector and the capital markets are generally either inaccessible or illiquid and inefficient. More specifically, owing to the prevalent credit system, the Czech bond market is underdeveloped, so we are left with government bonds and Treasury Bills only. However, these constitute a rather exclusive market that is accessible only to selected large financial institutions. A similar situation exists on the stock market. Furthermore, when considering the demand for credits we face the problem of credit rationing. This has been present in the Czech Republic for, at least, half of our sample period. The above considerations lead us to exclude equation (9.3) from the portfolio approach.

Although an analysis of the demand for foreign bonds, or foreign portfolio assets generally, may be associated with some inconsistency in data series, we attempt to estimate the function capturing the demand for foreign portfolio assets in the case of the Czech Republic as proposed by equation (9.4). In addition, the constraints, or rather controls, on capital movement imposed by the Czech National Bank at the beginning of our sample may influence the results, in the sense of increasing the importance of all foreign variables in determining portfolio investment abroad in our case. We take in to account this aspect while estimating the demand for foreign assets.

Description of the Data Series Used

We use quarterly data spanning the period from the first quarter of 1994 to the second quarter of 2001. Where a particular variable is of discrete form we use a quarterly average calculated as the simple arithmetic average of the monthly end-of-period values for the three months in the current quarter and the last month of the previous quarter. We use seasonally adjusted data only in the case of the scale variable, which is the only one showing a marked seasonal pattern. (Data source: CNB database, i.e.: http://www.cnb.cz.)

Dependent variables

We first attempt to model the *M2cz* variable, representing deposits in the domestic banking system denominated in the Czech currency. This variable is calculated as the difference between the M2 monetary aggregate and deposits in the domestic banking system denominated in foreign currencies. We further subtract Czech currency in circulation, since we cannot include foreign currencies in circulation in our analysis owing to a lack of data series. Figure 9-2 depicts the development of the M2 and *M2cz* series.

Fig. 9-2 M2cz and M2 series

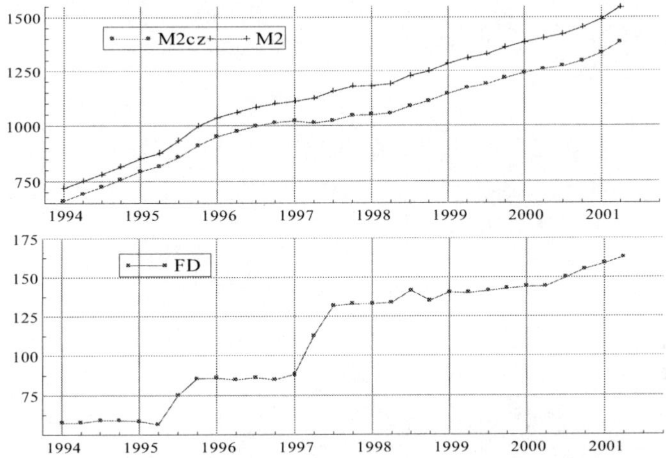

Source: Authors' calculations based on CNB database (http://www.cnb.cz)

The next modelled variable is the ratio of foreign to domestic currency deposits (FD/M2cz); we name this variable the *FD/DD ratio*. The modelled variable is similar to those proposed by Feige *et al.* (2000) in the case of Croatia; and by Mongardini and Mueller (1999) in the case of the Kyrgyz Republic for analogous purposes. We use this ratio to precisely pursue the effect of changing relative prices of assets under consideration on domestic residents' behaviour. We thus differentiate between increases in foreign deposits resulting from an overall increase in wealth and the move from domestic deposits to foreign deposits induced by changes in relative returns. Figure 9-3 shows a rapid increase in the *FD/DD ratio* during the period of currency crisis that seems to be persistent. This may point to dollarisation of the Czech economy from the store of value perspective.

The last dependent variable, that we attempt to explain, is the ratio of cumulative portfolio investment abroad to domestic deposits – we name this variable the *PI/DD ratio*. We use this variable to properly evaluate the effect of changing relative prices of foreign assets and deposits in the domestic currency on wealth allocation. Further, we again attempt to eliminate the effect of rising wealth using *DD* as a denominator. We can see in Figure 9-3 that domestic agents have only recently extended the use of foreign assets for wealth allocation purposes. However, this extension appears to be highly significant.

Fig. 9-3 FD/DD ratio (in %) and cumulative PI/DD ratio (in %)

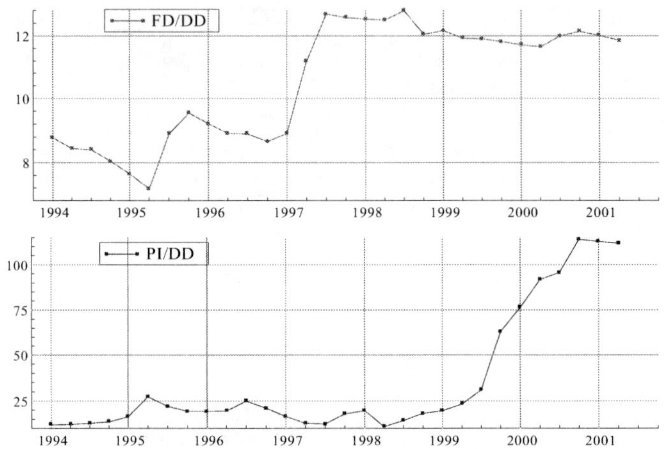

Source: Authors' calculations based on CNB database (http://www.cnb.cz)

Explanatory variables

We use the consumer price index (CPI) as an approximation of the variable P^c in equations (9.1) to (9.4). This index should precisely describe consumption basket price development in the Czech Republic and thus correctly deflate nominal variables from the perspective of the domestic agent. Furthermore, we approximate the variable *PY* in equations (9.1) to (9.4) using domestic absorption (*AE*), which would measure the amount of transactions in the Czech economy and possibly an accumulation of wealth. We employ this variable, as it is more significant for such purposes according to Sommer (1997) and Melecký (2001). Instead of the return on domestic bonds we use the interest rate on credits, since this seems to be the most significant measure of the opportunity cost of holding money and represents an alternative vehicle for wealth creation. For the purpose of measuring return on foreign money we employ two bilateral exchange rates – CZK/USD and CZK/DEM – since they have experienced a somewhat different historical development. This could result in a rather different relative significance of the two variables. We use current and one-period-lagged values of the exchange rate to approximate exchange rate expectations, since we assume that most agents form their expectations adaptively and the rest base their forecast on the random walk process. This approach is, in our opinion, reasonable since the structure of the economy changes quite considerable during transition. Thus, we do not use purchasing power parity or uncovered interest rate parity to approximate "rational" expectations of changes in the exchange rate. Finally, we consider the return on both USD- and DEM-denominated assets to explicitly consider their relative importance in equations (9.1) to (9.4). We calculate this return as the sum of the interest rate and the log of the particular exchange rate, i.e. $i+e$ (see also Govannini and Turleboom, 1992). Figure 9-4 describes the development of our core explanatory variables.

Some readers may notice a certain inconsistency between the introduced model and the explanatory variables used. Namely, although the model implies a use of first differences of nominal exchange rates, we use levels of that variable for three particular reasons. First, cointegration techniques comprise or deal with those first differences either implicitly, as in the case of Johansen procedure, or explicitly, as in the case of DOLS. Second, given the I(1) order of integration of nominal exchange rates (see Table 9-1) we would have to find two cointegration vectors when including the change in the exchange rate instead of its levels, as we do. In another words, since the first difference of nominal exchange rate is stationary itself we have to find two cointegration vectors to be able to justify the existence of stationary linear combination of the remaining I(1) variables.

Third, except for these rather technical reasons, there is another one related to the institutional features and historical development of the Czech Republic's external conditions. Given the identity that express the expected change in exchange rate as a result of interaction of capital flows and trade balance (see e.g. Goldberg, 2000) we can accept the following assumption in the Czech republic's case. Given the fact that we have interest rate differential that drives the capital (portfolio) flows already incorporated in the model, it remains to consider the effect of overvaluation of the real exchange rate. The factors responsible for the fluctuation in the real exchange rate have been different between the first and second half of our sample period. In the first half the fluctuation and thus overvaluation of the real exchange rate was nearly exclusively determined by movements in the domestic price level, given the fixed exchange rate regime prevailing at that time. In the second half, these fluctuations have been the result of both price level and nominal exchange rate movements. And concerning the very end of our sample, the real exchange rate movement has been driven mainly by the nominal exchange rate as the Czech Republic adopted the convergence criteria for EU accession and the consequent adoption of Euro. Since we have the domestic price level already included in our model, inclusion of the nominal exchange rate would complete our set of explanatory variables, given our small sample of observations.

Fig. 9-4 Explanatory variables

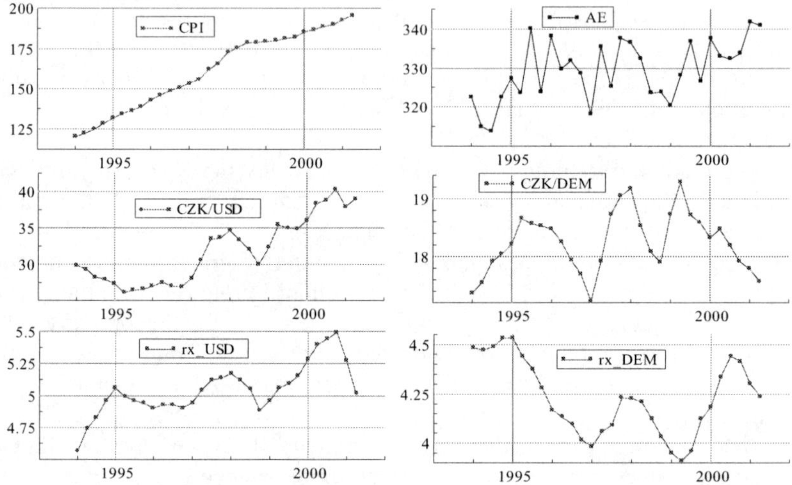

Source: Authors' calculations based on CNB database (http://www.cnb.cz)

Conventionally, we first explore the stationary properties of analysed time series, as they are expected to be integrated of order I(1). Results of applied ADF- and PP-tests are summarised in Table 9-1.

Since the dependent variables are integrated of order I(1), as are most of the explanatory variables, we need to use cointegration analysis to prevent spurious regression phenomenon. For this purpose we use the Johansen technique (see Johansen and Juselius, 1990); the ARDL procedure developed by Pesaran (see Pesaran *et al.*, 1996); the dynamic OLS estimation, DOLS (see e.g Stock and Watson, 1993); and the ADL technique (see e.g. Arlt *et al.*, 2001).

Table 9-1 Unit root tests

Variable	Unit Root Tests		Likely Degree of Integration
	ADF	PP	
m_cz	3.07 (c,t,3)	2.67 (c,t) !!	Rather I(2)
d(m_cz)	1.98 (c,3)	2.18 (c)	
d2(m_cz)	2.56 (2)**	5.45 ***	
fd/dd	1.22 (c,2)	1.96 (c,t) !	I(1)
d(fd/dd)	4.41 (c,t,4)***	3.84 ***	
pi/dd	1.39 (c,t,1)	1.24 (c,t) !	I(1)
d(pi/dd)	3.81 (c,1)***	4.31 ***	
Cpi	1.71 (c,3)	2.34 (c) !	I(1) or I(2)
d(cpi)	3.07 (c,t,2)	4.07 (c,t)**	
d2(cpi)	3.27 (4)***	9.7 *** !	
Ae	3.53 (c,t,3)*	4.63 (c,t) ***	I(0) or I(1)
d(ae)	3.62 (c,4)**	10.60 ***	
Lr	2.40 (c,t,3)	1.39 (c,t) !!	I(1) or I(2)
d(lr)	1.55 (c,2)	3.19 (c)**	
d2(lr)	5.89 (1)***	7.48 *** !	
czk/usd	3.34 (c,t,1)*	2.69 (c,t) !	I(1)
d(czk/usd)	3.63 (c,1)**	3.69 ***	
czk/dem	3.74 (c,1)***	2.56 (c) !	I(0) or I(1)
d(czk/dem)	3.59 (3)***	3.53 ***	
rx_usd	4.02 (c,t,3)**	2.71 (c)* !	I(0) or I(1)
d(rx_usd)	3.07 (3)***	2.49 **	
rx_dem	2.79 (c,4)*	1.88 (c) !!	Rather I(1)
d(rx_dem)	4.99 (c,t,4)***	2.68 ***	

Note: *, ** and *** indicate rejection of the null hypothesis of unit root existence. Numbers in brackets indicate the number of lags included in the ADF test and letters c and t indicate that constant and trend are involved in the particular test. ! indicates violation of the assumption of no serial correlation of residuals.
Source: Authors' calculations

Empirical Analysis of Currency Substitution in the Czech Republic from the Demand for Money Perspective

We analyse the potential presence of currency substitution in the Czech Republic using the demand for money approach. More specifically, we use equation (9.1), which describes demand for deposits denominated in Czech korunas. If currency substitution is one of the important techniques of portfolio allocation, then the opportunity costs of holding Czech deposits with respect to deposits in foreign currency and/or foreign assets are to be significant determinants of the demand for Czech deposits.

The procedure for the empirical analysis of currency substitution in the Czech Republic is divided into three stages.[3] First, we explore the existence of currency substitution concerning the effect of exchange rates. In this stage the particular currencies are assumed to compete as a store of value in the domestic banking system. Second, we examine the potential existence of the extensive part of nominal exchange rate elasticity, since the first case considers only the intensive part (see below). Finally, we extend this analysis to include the determinants relating to capital mobility.

Analysing the demand for deposits denominated in Czech korunas we estimate equation (9.5) of the following form:

$$m_{cz} = \beta_0 + \beta_1 cpi + \beta_2 ae + \beta_3 lr + \beta_4 e^{usd} + \beta_5 e^{dem} + \beta_6 e^{neer} + \xi, \qquad (9.5)$$

where m_{cz} is the M2 monetary aggregate adjusted for deposits in foreign currencies (DFC), i.e. (M2-DFC); *cpi* is the consumer price index, measuring price level development; *ae* is domestic absorption (GDP-NX), measuring the amount of transactions in the Czech economy; *lr* is the lending interest rate, representing domestic interest rates on alternative assets; and *e* is, respectively, the CZK/USD and CZK/DEM nominal exchange rates and the nominal effective exchange rate. We thus explicitly test the significance of the alternative approximation of the Czech koruna performance relative to foreign currencies, i.e. the opportunity cost of holding Czech currency.

In the second stage, we consider the possible extensive part of the exchange rate's elasticity, including in the estimated equation two so-called "ratchet" variables that consist of peak values of the CZK/USD and CZK/DEM exchange rates. Following Mulligan and Sala–I–Martin (1996), we assume that when the actual value of the exchange rate hits the peak value during the analysed period, additional agents always decide to adopt financial technology to help them convert the domestic currency into foreign currency. They do so since they are facing the very level of opportunity costs that they consider too high to accept, given current wealth allocation, and that makes them react in this respect (see also Feige *et al.*, 2000 and Mongardini and Mueller, 1999).

We proceed to the third stage by adding variables that should represent the impact of capital mobility, i.e. the return on foreign assets. We consider returns on U.S. Treasury Bills and German Treasury Bills expressed in Czech korunas, as perceived from the position of Czech residents. The final estimation results using the Johansen's procedure are as follows[4]:

$$m_{cz} = 1.08cpi + 2.52ae - 0.012lr - 0.34e^{usd}_{t-1} - 0.62e^{dem}_{t-1} \tag{9.6}$$
$$(0.06)^{***}\ (0.24)^{***}\ (0.002)^{***}\ (0.07)^{***}\ (0.19)^{**}$$

Summarising our three-stage estimation, we can conclude that the estimating methods applied indicate the presence of currency substitution in the Czech Republic. The important variables accounting for this phenomenon are lagged value of the CZK/USD exchange rate and the lagged value of the CZK/DEM exchange rate. These two bilateral exchange rates seem to be superior to the nominal effective exchange rate. This conclusion may reflect the fact that in certain periods the values of CZK/USD and CZK/DEM evolve in opposite directions, making the NEER less significant (CZK/USD and CZK/DEM are the main components of the NEER).

We find no support for the existence of an extensive part of exchange rate elasticity when using either the Johansen or the other estimation techniques. We can thus conclude that currency substitution performs only through the "intensive" part of exchange rate elasticity.

An inspection of the estimation results gives no support for the existence of significant effect of returns on foreign assets, i.e. capital mobility, on the demand for CZK from the perspective of domestic residents. We can thus conclude that substitution of currency within the domestic banking system (its intensive part) is the only relevant pattern for Czech resident behaviour. Furthermore, in this respect money holdings in Czech currency were substituted by holdings denominated in both DEM and USD.

Finally, all the domestic determinants are highly significant. The coefficient on the *cpi* variable supports linear homogeneity of deposits in Czech currency with respect to the price level. The high coefficient on the ae variable then points to the wealth accumulation effect. In another words, deposits are perceived to be a luxury good, i.e. as agents reach higher income levels they start to save by holding more of their funds as deposits. In terms of the poorest part of population, it implies that after attaining a certain level of income the impecunious agents not only consume but also start to save.

Empirical Analysis of Currency Substitution in the Czech Republic from the Perspective of Demand for Foreign Deposits

In this part, by estimating equation (9.2) we inspect the presence of currency substitution estimating the domestic demand for foreign deposits. We do not consider the pure stock of foreign deposits in the domestic banking system but rather model the ratio of such stock to domestic deposits.

Using the same set of explanatory variables as in the previous case, we estimate (9.7) of the following form:

$$fd / dd = \beta_1 cpi + \beta_2 ae + \beta_3 lr + \beta_4 e^{usd} + \beta_5 e^{dem} + \beta_6 rx^{usd} + \\ + \beta_7 rx^{dem} + \xi, \tag{9.7}$$

where *fd/dd* is the ratio of foreign currency to domestic currency deposit stocks and the explanatory variables are the same as for the money demand. The results of our estimates of equation (9.7) using the Johansen technique are as follows:

$$\underset{\phantom{(0.19)^{***}}}{fd / dd} = \underset{(0.19)^{***}}{1.03cpi} + \underset{(0.01)^{***}}{0.04lr} + \underset{(0.22)^{***}}{0.74e^{usd}} \tag{9.8}$$

Given our results, we conclude that agents are concerned with the real value of the *fd/dd* ratio. Thus we can justifiably assume price homogeneity in the case of *fd/dd* ratio demand. The overall insignificance of the scale variable most probably suggests that foreign deposits are held solely for store-of-value purposes. The estimates of the *lr* effect on the *fd/dd* ratio seem to be robust and significant, though it has the opposite sign than was originally expected.

To explain the *lr* effect we recall that *lr* stands for the interest rate on credits. In the case of the Czech Republic this means the cost of financing, assuming that financial intermediation goes mostly through the banking system. So if *lr* increases, agents probably look for an alternative source of financing. In the absence of effective domestic capital markets, this involves borrowing on foreign or international financial markets, resulting in an increase in foreign deposits in the domestic country when the funds are raised. The mechanism described here is relevant for Czech corporations, as these made intensive use of international sources of financing between 1990 and 1997.

When we move to the estimates of the returns on foreign currency, there is general support for the existence of a significant effect on the *fd/dd* ratio only from the CZK/USD exchange rate. The higher significance of the CZK/USD exchange rate probably results from the higher volatility of this rate, which has made domestic agents more aware of the opportunity cost of holding domestic currency.

From the perspective of capital mobility or (more precisely, in our case) of portfolio investment abroad, there is generally no support for returns on foreign assets having any effects on foreign currency deposits in the Czech Republic. This inference may result from some capital movement constraints at the beginning of our sample and/or lower incentives from domestic residents to invest abroad caused by a lack of information concerning the international market and only slow adoption of the technology necessary for international investment.

Finally, we also include some additional ratchet variables to inspect various potential aspects of currency substitution. First, we employ the maximum level of the *fd/dd* ratio in the history of the estimated sample to inspect the possible dollarisation of the Czech economy. This variable is significant only in the equation estimated by ARDL, leading us to conclude that it is generally not important. Moreover, we again incorporate the historical peak values of the CZK/USD exchange rate to examine the possible presence of an extensive part of its elasticity. Again there is no support for this variable across the estimation techniques used. In the last step, we include historical peak values of inflation to inspect the effect of the creditworthiness of the Czech currency relative to foreign currency. Again, we find no support for such an effect on the *fd/dd* ratio.

Empirical Analysis of Currency Substitution in the Czech Republic from the Perspective of Demand for Foreign Assets

This part is concerned with an examination of portfolio capital movement and its determinants. As a framework, we use equation (9.4) in the portfolio model presented above. We approximate domestic demand for foreign bonds using cumulative gross outflow of portfolio investment. Again, instead of using the pure cumulative value of domestic portfolio investment abroad, we model its ratio to deposits in the domestic currency.

We apply various cointegration techniques to equation (9.9) in log-linear form:

$$pi/dd = \beta_1 cpi + \beta_2 ae + \beta_3 lr + \beta_4 e^{usd} + \beta_5 e^{dem} + \beta_6 rx^{usd} + \\ + \beta_7 rx^{dem} + \xi, \tag{9.9}$$

where *pi/dd* is the ratio of cumulative domestic portfolio investment abroad to deposits in the domestic currency and the set of explanatory variables is defined similarly as in the two previous cases.

The estimation results using the Johansen technique are presented below:

$$\underset{}{pi/dd} = \underset{(0.38)^{**}}{1.14 rx_{t-1}^{usd}} + \underset{(0.30)^{**}}{0.71 rx^{dem}} - \underset{(0.04)^{***}}{0.28 lr} - \underset{(0.70)^{*}}{1.17 e^{usd}} \tag{9.10}$$

The insignificance of coefficients on *cpi* and *ae* show that both the real value of foreign assets holdings and the alternative use of such funds for transaction purposes are not important in the determination of portfolio investment abroad. Such a conclusion may reflect the possible lower liquidity of such assets stemming from exchange rate risks and transaction cost. So we may suspect that once Czech residents invest their funds in foreign assets for store-of-value purposes, such funds are no longer used for prospective direct extension of medium-of-exchange stock. We find a highly significant, negative coefficient on the *lr* variable entering the decision-making process related to the demand for foreign assets.

Moreover, we can infer that there is significant influence of the return on foreign deposits held in the domestic banking system on the holdings of foreign assets, which would offer domestic agents higher liquidity and lower risks, assuming they are better informed about the domestic macroeconomic situation. However, this effect is not significant at the 5 per cent level. Finally, the significance of the returns on foreign assets is what we are most interested in regarding the determination of capital mobility. According to the estimation techniques applied, the approximations of the returns on both USD- and DEM-denominated assets are highly significant. The effect of the return on USD-denominated assets seems to have its peak at around one lag and that of DEM-denominated assets at around the current value. In the Czech Republic's case, domestic agents perceive investment abroad as one possible alternative of wealth allocation. We suppose that this pattern will promote itself even more in the close future.

Summary of the Results and their Implications

We can conclude from our analysis that both currency substitution (i.e. substitution of deposits in the domestic currency by deposits in foreign currency) and capital mobility effects (i.e. altering of deposits in the domestic banking system by holding foreign assets) are elements of Czech agents' behaviour concerning wealth allocation. When we consider the existence of currency substitution in the broad sense relating to the Czech Republic, we have to take into account several implications suggested by theory and/or experience from other transitional countries.

It is widely believed that allowing a foreign currency to coexist with the domestic one provides an opportunity for greater domestic intermediation, promotes financial sophistication by increasing the number of available assets, and increases credibility by raising the cost of poor monetary discipline. Moreover, the rapid development of foreign-currency denominated operations in the domestic banking system affects the stability of monetary aggregates, the dynamics of exchange rates and the government's revenues from seigniorage. Specifically, the higher the money demand elasticity of substitution between moneys, the larger is the shift from foreign to domestic currency as a result of a fall in expected relative inflation and, thus, the greater is the fall in the nominal exchange rate. Currency substitution also reduces monetary independence, which may then endanger the ability of central bankers to implement stabilisation programmes.

In other words, monetary and fiscal policies, the choice of exchange rate regime and interventions in foreign exchange markets are often undertaken in economies that experience "unofficial" or "de facto" dollarisation, i.e. where individuals and firms choose to use a foreign currency as a substitute for some of the monetary services of the domestic currency. Feige *et al.* (2000) suggest that under such circumstances the effective money supply may be much larger than the domestic money supply and may be subject to endogenous behavioural responses reflecting currency substitution on the part of the public. Similarly, the greater the extent and variability of dollarisation, the weaker is the central bank's knowledge of and control over the effective money supply. Such scenarios are, however, of lesser importance in the case of the Czech Republic. On the other hand, unofficial dollarisation will tend to dampen government efforts to employ inflationary finance to impose implicit taxes on domestic monetary assets. And again somewhat similarly, growing unofficial dollarisation reduces the ability of the monetary authority to earn seigniorage from its own currency issue. Unofficial dollarisation also reflects citizens' perceptions of the stability of the domestic monetary regime, the credibility of monetary policies and the perceived stability of the domestic banking system.

Conclusion

In this chapter we have discussed the possible presence of currency substitution and its resulting potential implications in a transitional country. First, we have analysed the performance of currency substitution in small open transition economies, stating the initial conditions and the process of transformation as similar for the countries considered. The first decade of the transformation process has been associated with simultaneous periods of internal and external liberalisation and alignment with developed countries. We have concluded that the launch of reforms was coupled with greater economic uncertainty, resulting in high and volatile exchange rates and inflation, large budget and current account deficits and inducing the use of foreign money for monetary purposes. In this context we have proposed several explanations concerning the factors determining currency substitution in the Czech Republic's case. These are associated with a relative lack of restrictions on capital flow, early adoption of necessary financial techniques and a sharp increase in openness. Moreover, we have discussed perspectives of substituting and substituted currencies in the global and local context. We propose four reasons for currency substitution: macroeconomic instability, the existence of a large illegal or underground economy, the former occurrence of financial crisis, and a lack of higher-denomination bank notes issued by the central bank. We have shown that the Czech koruna is not only a substituted currency, but has also for several years been the substituting currency for some post-socialist countries. A set of arguments for (and against) unilateral and bilateral euroisation has also been included here.

The last part has been dedicated to an empirical analysis of the currency substitution phenomenon in the case of the Czech Republic during the period 1994–2001. We have based our analysis on a multi-perspective portfolio approach. However, we have first modified, or rather reduced, the system, excluding the equation describing the demand for domestic bonds or alternative assets since the capital market is somewhat underdeveloped or, in the case of bonds, generally inaccessible in the Czech Republic. We have thus been left with three equations to describe the demand for domestic and foreign currency and for foreign assets. In this respect we have modelled the demand for domestic currency in circulation plus deposits denominated in domestic currency; the ratio of deposits denominated in foreign currency in the domestic banking system to deposits denominated in the domestic currency; and the ratio of domestic portfolio investment abroad to domestic currency deposits. We have used a set of explanatory variables which approximate those suggested by theory, namely: the consumer price index, domestic absorption, the CZK/USD and CZK/DEM exchange rates, and the returns on U.S. and German Treasury Bills expressed in Czech currency. We have detected the presence of currency substitution in the domestic banking system and capital mobility. Exploring the full implication of these for the stability of monetary aggregates and demand for money, the revenues from seigniorage and the changing dynamics of exchange rates is left for further research.

References

Aarle, van Ban and Nina Budina. 1995. *Currency Substitution in Eastern Europe. Tilburg University.* Center for Economic Research Discussion Paper Series no. 2. Tilburg: Tilburg University.

Arlt, Josef, Milan Guba, Štěpán Radkovský, Milan Sojka and Vladimír Stiller. 2001. *Vliv vybraných faktorů na vývoj poptávky po penězích v letech 1994–2000.* Výzkumná práce č. 34. Prague: Czech National Bank.

Arrau, Patricio, Jose De Gregorio, Carmen Reinhart and Peter Wickham. 1991. *The Demand for Money in Developing Countries: Assessing the Role of Financial Innovation.* International Monetary Fund Working Paper No. 91/45. Washington, D.C.: International Monetary Fund.

Branson, William H. and Dale W. Henderson. 1985. The Specification and Influence of Assets Markets. In *Handbook of International Economics*, ed Ronald W. Jones and Peter B. Kenen, 749–806. Amsterdam: North-Holland.

Bufman, G. and L. Leiderman. 1992. Simulating an Optimizing Model of Currency Substitution. *Revista de Analisis Economico* 7(1):109–24.

Calvo, G.A. and C.A. Végh. 1992. A Model of Exchange Rate Determination Under Currency Substitution and Rational Expectations. *Journal of Political Economy* 85(3):177–85.

Canzoneri, M.B. and B.T. Diba. 1992. The Inflation Discipline of Currency Substitution. *European Economic Review* 36(4):827–45.

Doyle, Brian M. 2000. *„Here, Dollars, Dollars…" – Estimating Currency Demand and Worldwide Currency Substitution.* International Finance Discussion Papers no.657. Washington, D.C.: Board of Governors of the Federal Reserve System.

Feige, Edgar L., Michael Faulend, Velimir Šonje and Vedrand Šošić. 2000. Currency Substitution, Unofficial Dollarization and Estimates of Foreign Currency Held Abroad: The Case of Croatia. In *Financial Policies in Emerging Markets*, ed Mario Blejer and Marko Škreb. Cambridge, MA: MIT Press.

Giovannini, Alberto and Bart Turtelboom. 1992. *Currency Substitution.* National Bureau of Economic Research Working Paper Series, no. 4232. Cambridge: National Bureau of Economic Research.

Goldberg, M. 2000. On empirical Exchange Rate Models: What Does a Rejection of the Asymmetry Restriction on Short-Run Interest Rates Mean? *Journal of International Money and Finance* 19(5):673–88.

Hanousek, J., J. Kubín and Z. Tůma. 1995. Poptávka po penězích a ražebné v období transformace. *Finance a úvěr* 45(7):352–74.

Hanousek, J. and Z. Tůma. 1995. Poptávka po penězích v české ekonomice. *Finance a úvěr* 45(5):249–67.

Johansen, S. and K. Juselius. 1990. Maximum Likelihood Estimation and Inference on Cointegration – With Applications to Demand for Money. *Oxford Bulletin of Economics and Statistics* 52(2):169–210.

Klacek, Jan and Kateřina Šmídková. 1995. *The Demand-for-Money Function: the Case of the Czech Economy.* Výzkumná práce č. 41. Prague: Czech National Bank.

McKinnon, Ronald I. 1985. Two Concepts of International Currency Substitution. In *The Economics of the Caribbean Basin*, ed Michael D. Connolly and John McDermott, 101–13. New York: Praeger.

McNelis, P.D. and C. Asilis. 1992. A Dynamic Simulation Analysis of Currency Substitution in an Optimizing Framework with Transaction Costs. *Revista de Analisis Economico* 7(1):139–52.

Melecký, Martin. 2001. *Stabilita dlouhodobé poptávky po široce definovaných penězích v otevřené ekonomice: případ ČR 1994–2000.* Výzkumná práce č. 38. Prague: Czech National Bank.

Mishkin, Frederick S. 2001. *Financial Policy and the Prevention of Financial Crises in Emerging Market Countries*. NBER Working Paper Series No. 8087. Cambridge: National Bureau of Economic Research.

Mongardini, Joannes and Johannes Mueller. 1999. *Ratchet Effects in Currency Substitution: An Application to the Kyrgyz Republic*. IMF Working Paper no. 99/102. Washington, D.C.: International Monetary Fund.

Mulligan, Casey B. and Xavier Sala–I–Martin. 1996. *Adoption of Financial Technologies: Implications for Money Demand and Monetary Policy.* NBER Working Paper Series no. 5504. Cambridge: National Bureau of Economic Research.

Pesaran, Hashem M., Yongcheol Shin and Richard J. Smith. 1996. *Testing for the Existence of a Long-Run Relationship.* DAE Working Paper no. 9622. Cambridge: University of Cambridge.

Roubini, N. and V. Grilli. 1996. Liquidity Models in Open Economies: Theory and Empirical Evidence. *European Economic Review* 40(3–5): 847–59.

Sarajevs, Vadims. 2000. *Econometric Analysis of Currency Substitution: A Case of Latvia.* Bank of Finland Discussion Papers, Institute for Economies in Transition no. 4/2000. Helsinki: Bank of Finland.

Sommer, M. 1997. Vazba mezi peněžní zásobou, agregátní nabídkou a nominálním domácím produktem ČR v letech 1992–1996. *Bankovnictví* 33(16):12–13.

Stock, J.H. and M.W. Watson. 1993. A Simple Estimator of Cointegrating Vectors in Higher Order Integrated Systems. *Econometrica* 64(4):783–820.

Sturzenegger, F. 1992. Currency Substitution and the Regressivity of Inflationary taxation. *Revista de Analisis Economico* 7(1):177–92.

————. Understanding the Welfare Implications of Currency Substitution. *Journal of Economic Dynamic and Control* 21(2–3):391–416.

Notes

[1] This implies a high and volatile nominal exchange rate and inflation, large budget and current account deficits, and the establishment of new national currencies (in the countries of the former Soviet Union, the new countries of the former Yugoslavia, the Czech Republic and Slovakia).

[2] The French franc (FRF) was other suitable currency for "-isation", i.e. "francisation", before the euro was introduced. It could have been applied on French former colonies in Africa, which used the Central African franc. This currency was for long time pegged to the French franc.

[3] We choose this approach since we want to consider a wide range of possible foreign variables that might be important determinants of currency substitution and we have only a small number of observations.

[4] See Appendix 9-A for the final estimation results using ARDL, DOLS and ADL.

Appendix 9-A

Final estimates of the demand for deposits denominated in Czech currency

Variable	Estimation methods			
	JOH(1)	ARDL	DOLS	ADL
m_{cz}(-1)	-----	-----	-----	0.80 (0.05)***
cpi	1.08 (0.058)***	2.19 (0.56)***	2.11 (0.11)***	1.30 (0.02)***
ae	2.52 (0.24)***	1.55 (0.60)***	0	0
ae(-1)	-----	-----	-----	0.35 (0.03)***
lr	-0.012 (0.002)**	-0.034 (0.008)***	-0.023 (0.003)***	-0.02 (0.001)***
czk/usd	0	-0.80 (0.24)***	-0.44 (0.08)***	0
czk/usd(-1)	-0.34 (0.07)***	0	-----	-0.40 (0.03)**
czk/dem	0	0	-0.71 (0.17)***	0
czk/dem(-1)	-0.62 (0.19)**	-1.10 (0.65)**	-----	0
neer	0	-1.20 (0.56)**	0	0
rx_usd	0	0	0	0
rx_usd(-1)	0	0	-----	0
rx_dem	0	0	-0.15 (0.04)***	0
rx_dem(-1)	0	0	-----	0
constant	unrestricted	unrestricted	-----	0

Note: *, **, *** indicate significance at 10 per cent, 5 per cent and 1 per cent probability levels respectively. 0 denotes an acceptance of zero-restriction on the particular coefficient and ----- indicates that the given variable was not included in the estimated equation. In the case of multi-equation estimation methods (JOH, ARDL) the variables *mcz*, *cpi* and *ae* were assumed to be endogenous.

Source: Authors' calculations

The only dissimilarities compared to the Johansen estimates reported in the main text are the significance of nominal effective exchange rate in the

ARDL estimates and the significance of CZK/DEM exchange rate and return on German assets in the DOLS estimates. Nevertheless, the results presented in the main text are consistent with the results from the other estimation methods.

Appendix 9-B

Estimates of equation (9.7) using various techniques

Variable	Estimation methods			
	JOH(1)	ARDL	DOLS	ADL
fd/dd(-1)	-----	0	-----	0.31 (0.15)**
cpi	1.03 (0.19)***	1.13 (0.14)***	1.48 (0.13)***	1.03 (0.19)***
ae	0	0	-2.05 (0.41)***	0
lr	0.04 (0.008)***	0.04 (0.006)***	0	0.04 (0.007)***
e_usd	0.74 (0.22)***	0.76 (0.14)***	0	0.74 (0.18)**
e_dem	0	0	2.24 (0.83)**	0
rx_usd(-1)	0	-0.18 (0.074)**	0	0
rx_dem	0	0	0	0
constant	unrestricted	-5.56 (0.52)***	0	-3.01 (0.73)***

Note: *, **, *** indicate significance at 10 per cent, 5 per cent and 1 per cent probability levels respectively. 0 denotes an acceptance of zero-restriction on the particular coefficient and ----- indicates that the given variable was not included in the estimated equation. In the case of multi-equation estimation methods (JOH, ARDL) only the *fd*/dd variable was assumed to be endogenous.
Source: Authors' calculations

We can account for the significant negative coefficient on the *ae* variable in the DOLS estimated equation with following explanation. The increase in transaction amounts in the domestic economy is an impulse for the transfer of foreign deposits into domestic currency sight deposits for transaction (medium-of-exchange) purposes, although this hypothesis has no support from the other estimates.

Although the CZK/DEM exchange rate estimation seems to approximate the own rate of return on FD in the case of the DOLS estimation, this variable is not significant when the other estimation methods are used. We can however conclude that returns on foreign currency significantly affect the demand of domestic agents for foreign-currency-denominated deposits.

Appendix 9-C

Estimates of equation (9.9) using various techniques

Variable	Estimation methods			
	JOH(1)	ARDL	DOLS	ADL
pi/dd	-----	0.40 (0.12)***	-----	0.40 (0.12)***
cpi	0	0	2.36 (0.77)***	0
ae	0	0	0	0
lr	-0.28 (0.04)***	-0.27 (0.03)***	-0.41 (0.06)***	-0.27 (0.03)***
e_usd	-1.17 (0.70)*	-0.90 (0.53)*	-2.35 (1.26)*	-0.90 (0.33)*
e_dem	0	0	0	0
rx_usd(-1)	1.14 (0.38)**	1.21 (0.34)***	-----	1.20 (0.26)***
rx_dem	0.71 (0.30)**	0.78 (0.27)***	0.77 (0.28)***	0.78 (0.17)***
constant	unrestricted	0	0	0

Note: *, **, *** indicate significance at 10 per cent, 5 per cent and 1 per cent probability levels respectively. 0 denotes an acceptance of zero-restriction on the particular coefficient and ----- indicates that the given variable was not included in the estimated equation. In the case of multi-equation estimation methods (JOH, ARDL) only the *pi/dd* variable was assumed to be endogenous.
Source: Authors' calculations

The results in the table presented above supports findings from the main text. The only additional finding is the significant positive coefficient on the *ae* variable in the DOLS estimated equation. As expected, this variable approximates the positive effect of increasing wealth on the demand for foreign assets.

CHAPTER TEN

EXCHANGE RATE DYNAMICS IN SELECTED NEW EU MEMBER STATES

All Central and Eastern European countries (CEECs) face a trade off between exchange rate stability and flexibility. The recent literature on optimum currency area (OCA) criteria in the CEECs surveyed by Fidrmuc and Korhonen (2006) shows that these countries increasingly constitute an optimum currency area with the EMU. Similarly, Fidrmuc and Senaj (2006) estimate several probit models of the adoption of fixed exchange rates in a broad set of 167 developed and developing countries between 1995 and 1999, which imply surprisingly high probabilities of de jure and de facto fixed exchange rate regimes in the CEECs (see Table 10-1). In addition, Horváth (2005) finds that the CEECs fulfill OCA criteria at approximately the same level as the Euro area countries before they adopted Euro.

By contrast, the developments especially in Central Europe[1] showed a process of increasing exchange rate flexibility during the previous decade, which was reversed only recently by the first accessions to the Exchange Rate Mechanism II (ERM II).[2] In particular the conditions of acceding economies, relatively flexible exchange rate regime has appeared to be more appropriate to deal with the high capital flows, productivity improvements and the increasing appreciation of exchange rates also in the nominal terms (see Égert and Lommatzsch, 2004). At the same time, the exchange rate peg was replaced by monetary policies putting more emphasis on inflation stabilisation. Actually, nearly all countries of our sample have adopted different types of inflation targeting.[3] Still, several CEECs have used interventions at the foreign exchange market (see Holub, 2004 or Égert and Komárek, 2005). On the one hand, these actions were largely motivated by inflation and competitiveness pressures, which depend in small and open economies heavily on exchange rates. On the other hand, this development corresponds also to the fear of floating phenomenon analyzed by Calvo and Reinhart (2002).

These arguments mean that some CEECs are likely to pursue a de facto exchange rate policy of implicit target zones around time-varying equilibrium exchange rates, which is similar to the proposal of target zone around a fundamental equilibrium exchange rate proposed by Williamson (1985) and

Edison *et al.* (1987). Similarly like in Krugman's (1991) exchange rate target zone model, the volatility of exchange rate at the borders of target zones should be smaller than in the area close to the central parity if the regime is fully credible. In the opposite case, we should observe that exchange rate volatility increases with the distance from the equilibrium exchange rates. Furthermore, expectations may be formed differently in the appreciation and depreciation parts of the target zones, which may cause significant asymmetric effects. Finally, countries following pure inflation targeting policy are likely to show no significant differences in exchange rate volatility with respect to the equilibrium exchange rates.

The estimation of this pattern of exchange rate behaviour necessitates the estimation of the equilibrium exchange rates and models of exchange rate volatility by generalized autoregressive conditional heteroskedasticity (GARCH) models. We perform this estimation in two steps. First, we estimate the monetary equilibrium exchange rates for quarterly data. Second, we use these estimated in the subsequent GARCH estimations.

Table 10-1 Estimated probabilities of intermediate and fixed exchange rate regimes (1995–1999, in %)

Country	**De jure classification**		**De facto classification**	
	Intermediate regimes	Fixed exchange rate regimes	Intermediate regimes	Fixed exchange rate regimes
Czech Republic	30.7	50.7	20	62
Poland	32.5	43.9	23	44
Slovakia	29.1	54.2	19	64
Comparable countries				
Austria	32.1	45.6	22	50
Ireland	28.5	56.6	17	69
Portugal	32.7	43.2	21	56
Spain	33.4	38.8	23	44
Sweden	32.9	41.4	21	57

Source: Fidrmuc and Senaj (2006), authors' calculations

The chapter is structured as follows. The next section reviews the literature on the exchange rate target zones. Section three presents the estimates of the equilibrium exchange rates and the estimations of GARCH models are carried out in section four. Section five discusses the developments in the Czech Republic. Finally, section six concludes.

Krugman Target Zone Model

We briefly describe the main features of Krugman (1991) model of target zones and related empirical applications. For comprehensive survey of this literature, we refer a reader to Kempa and Nelles (1999).

The fixed exchange rate regime with a non-zero fluctuation band is often called a target zone. The motivation for maintaining target zone is typically that some flexibility in exchange rate fluctuations is allowed, while the bands in principle assure an elimination of the eventually excessive fluctuations common under free float exchange rate regime.

Krugman (1991) provides a seminal contribution to an analysis of exchange rate dynamics under target zones. Previous approaches to exchange rate modelling in the target zone assumed that exchange rate behaves as the free float inside the band and as the fixed exchange rate regime at the edge of the band. In consequence, fluctuation band has no influence on exchange rate behaviour inside the band, which Krugman labels as naive view. Krugman (1991) stresses the role of exchange rate expectations and argues that existence of credible fluctuation band influences the exchange rate behaviour not only at the edge of the band, but also inside the band. The basic setup of his model is as follows.

Krugman consider a log-linear monetary model in continuous time (note that we discuss monetary model in the section three). Exchange rate, s, at time t depends on fundamentals, f, represented by money supply, m, velocity, v, and expected change of the exchange rate, $E(ds)/dt$.

$$s_t = f_t + \gamma E(ds)/dt \tag{10.1}$$

where

$$f_t = v_t + m_t .$$

The velocity of money, v, is assumed to be exogenous and driven by continuous-time random walk, $dv = \sigma dz$. Furthermore, m is controlled by the central bank.

Next, Krugman (1991) assumes that fluctuation band is completely credible, i.e. the bands will never be breached. Thus, the value of exchange rate, s, lies always between $\underline{s} < s < \bar{s}$, where $\underline{s}$ and $\bar{s}$ are lower and upper edges of exchange rate band. In addition, no intra-marginal interventions are assumed; the central bank thus intervenes only when the exchange rate hits the band. For convenience, m is set to zero.

Under these assumptions, s is affected by v and $E(ds)/dt$. In case of free float, $E(ds)/dt = 0$, the expected change of exchange rate is zero. However, in target zone, when exchange rate is close to the edge of the band, the foreign exchange market participants expect that central bank will intervene in order to keep the exchange rate inside the band. As a result, the expected change of exchange rate is non-zero, but either positive or negative depending whether the exchange rate reaches weaker or stronger side of the fluctuation band. In this case, the relationship between s and v is no longer linear. As a result, exchange rate is mean-reverting (this is typically labeled as honeymoon effect in target zone literature). Besides, exchange rate becomes completely insensitive to fundamentals at the edges of the band (which is known as smooth pasting). Using stochastic calculus, the general solution of the model (10.1) is as follows:

$$s_t = f_t + A\exp(\mu f_t) + B\exp(-\mu f_t), \tag{10.2}$$

where

$$\mu = \sqrt{2/\lambda\sigma_f^2} \text{ and } \sigma_f^2 = (\sigma_m + \sigma_v)^2 .$$

σ_f, σ_m and σ_v denote the standard deviation of the fundamentals, money supply and velocity, respectively. λ is the elasticity of real money supply to interest rates. A and B are constants.

Krugman target zone model has also interesting empirically testable implications. Since v follows random walk (note that this results in variance of v depending positively on time), the distribution of s inside the band is U-shaped. Next, as the exchange rate approaches the edge of the band, it is less sensitive to fundamentals and thus less volatile. Put differently, the more the exchange rate deviates from its central parity, the less volatile it is expected to be.

There have been several papers examining the Krugman model empirically. Engle and Gau (1997) examine whether the position of spot exchange rate within the band is associated to its volatility using the data from several EU countries participating in the European Monetary System in 1986–93. They find rather mixed support for the Krugman model, namely only in few countries the negative relationship between the deviation of the exchange rate from its central parity and the exchange rate volatility is detected. Crespo–Cuaresma *et al.* (2005a) study exchange rate dynamics in a majority of EU members over different sample periods. Primarily, they test for the so-called effective band within the officially announced band. The motivation is that central banks typically do not wait until the exchange rate hits the official band, but rather start intervening already within the band. Exchange rate volatility in selected CEECs is also analyzed by Kočenda and Valachy (2005).

Monetary Equilibrium Exchange Rate Models

Following Crespo–Cuaresma *et al.* (2005b and 2005c), we estimate an extended version of the monetary exchange rate model for selected countries. Our approach relaxes the purchasing power parity condition, which is assumed to hold only for tradable products (see Clements and Frenkel, 1980). This implies that the Balassa–Samuelson effect may play a role in the analyzed countries, as noted, for example, by Égert and Lommatzsch (2004).

The monetary model of the exchange rate has become something of a workhorse in the exchange rate literature. An estimable reduced form is usually generated from an ad hoc framework comprising money demand functions in the home and foreign country. The monetary model is usually presented as a two-country, two-money, two-bond (where the bonds are assumed to be perfect substitutes) model. Money demand relationships are given by standard Cagan-style log-linear relationships:

$$m_{jt} - p_{jt} = \beta y_{jt} - \varphi i_{jt}, \qquad (10.3)$$

$$m_t^* - p_t^* = \beta y_t^* - \varphi i_t^*, \qquad (10.3')$$

where m denotes money demand, p denotes the price level, y is output, and finally i is the interest rate. The CEECs are denoted by the subscript j, while the asterisk denotes a foreign country (Euro area). All variables (apart from the interest rate) have been transformed into natural logarithms.

As far as we are looking at the period, when all CEECs have already fully liberalized capital flows, we assume that the uncovered interest parity (UIP) holds,

$$i_{jt} - i_t^* = \mathrm{E}_t\left(s_{jt+1}\right) - s_{jt}, \qquad (10.4)$$

where $\mathrm{E}_t\left(s_{jt+1}\right)$ refers to the conditional expectation operator using all information available in period t. Using the UIP condition and assuming rational expectations (see Groen 1998, 2002), we obtain the relative price levels between the countries as

$$p_{jt} - p_t^* = m_{jt} - m_t^* - \beta(y_{jt} - y_t^*). \qquad (10.5)$$

Furthermore, we reflect that the purchasing power parity (PPP) assumption is clearly not tenable given the extant empirical evidence especially for the CEECs. One important explanation for the persistence in real exchange rates is the existence of real factors, such as the Balassa–Samuelson effect, which drive the nominal exchange rate away from its PPP-defined level. Since such real effects are likely to be at least as important for the current group of accession countries, we incorporate a Balassa–Samuelson effect into the monetary equation. Following Clements and Frenkel (1980), we assume that overall prices in the home and foreign country are a weighted average of the price of traded and nontraded prices,

$$p_{jt} = \alpha p_{jt}^{T} + (1-\alpha) p_{jt}^{NT}, \qquad (10.6)$$

$$p_t^{*} = \alpha p_t^{T*} + (1-\alpha) p_t^{NT*}, \qquad (10.6')$$

where p now represents overall prices, incorporating both traded and nontraded components, p^T represents the price of traded goods, p^{NT} is the price of nontraded goods and α denotes the weight (for simplicity we assume the same weights in both countries). We consider the definition of the real exchange rate, defined with respect to overall prices (measured by CPI):

$$q_{jt} = s_{jt} - p_{jt} + p_t^{*}, \qquad (10.7)$$

where q is the real exchange rate. We define a similar relationship for the tradedable sector and assume the international equalisation of tradable prices,

$$q_{it}^{T} = s_{it} - p_{it}^{T} + p_t^{T*} = 0. \qquad (10.8)$$

Using (10.6), (10.7) and (10.8), the following expression may be obtained for the real exchange rate:

$$q_{jt} = q_{jt}^{T} - (1-\alpha)\left[\left(p_{jt}^{NT} - p_{jt}^{T}\right) - \left(p_t^{NT*} - p_t^{T*}\right)\right] \qquad (10.9)$$

Using expression (10.9) in (10.5), we may obtain the following equation:

$$\begin{aligned} s_{jt} &= m_{jt} - m_t^{*} - \beta_1 (y_{jt} - y_t^{*}) - \\ &- (1-\alpha)\left[\left(p_{jt}^{NT} - p_{jt}^{T}\right) - \left(p_t^{NT*} - p_t^{T*}\right)\right], \end{aligned} \qquad (10.10)$$

where the nominal exchange rate is predicted to appreciate as the relative price of nontraded to traded goods rises. Finally, several empirical applications identify tradable prices with producer prices. Using the definition of consumer prices in (10.6) and (10.6') for home and foreign country respectively, we note that the last term can be expressed as differential of the overall and producer prices:

$$s_{jt} = m_{jt} - m_t^* - \beta(y_{jt} - y_t^*) - \left[\left(p_{jt} - p_{jt}^T\right) - \left(p_t^* - p_t^{T*}\right)\right] \quad (10.10')$$

We estimate the monetary model jointly for a panel of all four involved countries since the individual time series are relatively short (from 1994:9 to 2004:9) including fixed and time effects, μ and θ, respectively. Therefore, we assume that the income elasticity, β_1, is equal across countries. In turn, we allow the coefficients on money demand and the relative price term differ from unity as implied in the model. Thus, the final empirical specification becomes:

$$\begin{aligned} s_{it} &= \mu_i + \theta_t + \lambda\left(m_{it} - m_t^*\right) - \beta(y_{it} - y_t^*) - \\ &- \rho\left[\left(p_{it} - p_{it}^T\right) - \left(p_t^* - p_t^{T*}\right)\right] + \varepsilon_{it}, \end{aligned} \quad (10.11)$$

where ε is the error term.

Because all involved variables are non-stationary, Kao (1999) and Kao and Chiang (2000) recommend dynamic OLS (DOLS) and DOLS with time effects (DOLST), which can be found in Table 10-2. All coefficients are close to values generally reported in the literature. Most importantly, money elasticity and relative price elasticities are both very close to unity (0.8 and 1.1 respectively). The panel cointegration test (panel ADF test) confirmed that the specifications provide a true cointegrating relationship. Therefore, we continue our empirical analysis with the ARCH analysis of exchange rate volatility. Although there are not many differences between the specifications, we use DOLS for the further analysis.

Table 10-2 Panel estimation of the monetary model (1994:9–2004:9)

Parameter	DOLS	DOLS-T
λ	0.831*** (85.462)	0.833*** (52.196)
β	0.791*** (21.095)	0.974*** (16.161)
ρ	1.145*** (16.089)	0.873*** (6.589)
No. of observations	504	504
Panel ADF test	-17.397***	-35.353***

Note: t-statistics are in parenthesis. *** denotes significance at the 1 per cent level. The intercept, fixed and time effects are not reported.
Source: Authors' calculations

Autoregressive Conditional Heteroskedasticity (ARCH) Models

Generalized ARCH Models

The GARCH models are generally applied for estimations of the conditional volatility of high-frequency (daily) exchange rate changes (see Baillie and Bollerslev, 1989). Following Engle and Gau (1997), we test one of the implications of Krugman (1991) model of target zones. Krugman shows that the conditional volatility of exchange rate decreases as exchange rate approaches the edge of the target band. As a result, we estimate whether the deviation of the exchange rate from its equilibrium decreases the conditional volatility. Our baseline specification is a GARCH(1,1) model,

$$\Delta s_{jt}^{D} = \mu_j + \xi_{jt}, \tag{10.12}$$

$$\sigma_{jt}^{2} = \gamma_{j1} + \gamma_{j2}\xi_{jt-1}^{2} + \gamma_{j3}\sigma_{jt-1}^{2} + \delta_j \left| s_{jt-1}^{D} - s_{jt-1}^{F} \right| + \omega_{jt}, \tag{10.13}$$

where s^D and s^F denotes the spot daily exchange rate of currency to Euro and the equilibrium exchange rate[4] estimated in the previous section, respectively. We do not include any explanatory variables except for constant to equation (10.1), because daily exchange rates are expected to be influenced largely by news and other random events (see Bask and Fidrmuc, 2005, for the discussion of high-frequency exchange rate movements in the CEECs). The constant term in equation (10.12), μ, shows the average rate of appreciation or depreciation. The error term, ξ, of the mean equation (10.12) is assumed to have a conditional variance, σ^2, specified by (10.13).

The conditional variance equation includes in addition to the ARCH term, ξ_{t-1}, and GARCH term, σ_{t-1}^2, also the distance between spot and equilibrium exchange rates, which is the major variable of our interest. Krugman's (1991) model implies that δ is negative, i.e. the conditional volatility decreases as exchange rate moves towards the edge of the band, as long as the announced or implicit target zones are fully credible. The opposite is true for target zones subject to speculative attacks. Finally, we expect no relationship between the conditional variance and the equilibrium exchange rates if no target zones are specified.

Our dataset in this part contains daily exchange rates of Czech, Polish, Romanian, and Slovak currencies to Euro between September 1994 and September 2004. Although we have longer time periods, we use only a more recent period. On the one hand, the starting point of our analysis is determined by the creation of the Euro. Thus, we avoid observations characterized by possibly non-standard volatility due to the change-over in the Euro area countries. On the other hand, all CEECs introduced free floating policies supported by a kind of inflation targeting regime in this period. These countries also did not experience any severe currency crisis during the analyzed time. As Hungary and Slovenia experienced policy changes related to the introduction of the floating exchange rates in the former case and the participation in the ERM II in the latter one, we exclude these countries from our analysis.

Table 10-3 reports the estimations of (10.12) and (10.13) for the Czech Republic, Poland, Slovakia, and Romania between January 1, 1999, and October 1, 2004. The results provide several interesting insights. First, we can see that the EU New Member States do not show any significant trend of nominal appreciation or depreciation. In turn, the Romanian currency depreciated significantly during the period, which corresponds to the de facto crawling peg applied by the Bank of Romania (see Crespo-Cuaresma *et al.*, 2005c). Second, we can see that the conditional volatility significantly depends on actual lagged squared error term and lagged conditional variance of the error term. Furthermore, the sum of the ARCH and GARCH term is relatively high, which indicates that the volatility of the shocks in all countries is quite persistent. Nevertheless, the sum of both coefficients is significantly lower than unity in all countries except for Romania.

Table 10-3 Estimates of the effect of spot position in the band on conditional volatility

	Czech Republic	**Poland**	**Slovakia**	**Romania**
μ	0.000 (-0.944)	0.000 (-0.224)	0.000 (-1.373)	0.001*** (4.844)
γ_1	0.000*** (6.903)	0.000*** (4.348)	0.000*** (8.396)	0.000 (1.289)
γ_2	0.104*** (7.064)	0.081*** (6.905)	0.178*** (12.291)	0.066*** (11.613)
γ_3	0.779*** (27.667)	0.846*** (39.285)	0.705*** (29.930)	0.935*** (155.565)
δ	1.410*** (4.616)	0.470*** (3.593)	-0.746*** (-5.712)	-0.057 (-0.779)
$\gamma_2 + \gamma_3$	0.883 [0.000]	0.927 [0.000]	0.883 [0.000]	1.001 [0.693]
Period	1.1.1999– 1.10.2004	1.1.1999– 1.10.2004	1.1.1999– 1.10.2004	1.1.1999– 1.10.2004
N	1501	1501	1501	1501

Note: We report z-stats in parenthesis and p-values of the Wald test that $\gamma_2 + \gamma_3 = 1$ in brackets. ***, **, and * denote significance at 1 per cent, 5 per cent, and 10 per cent, respectively. For clarity of the discussion in the text, the coefficient δ is multiplied by 10^5.
Source: Authors' calculations

Finally, we find that the deviation of the spot exchange rate from its equilibrium level is significant for the new member states, but insignificant (negative) for Romania. However, we find a positive negative coefficient only for Slovakia, while the volatility in the Czech Republic and Poland increases significantly with the distance from the equilibrium levels. This implies that the implicit target bands have been more credible in Slovakia than in the Czech Republic and Poland. This would also correspond to the institutional design of monetary policy in Slovakia, which put more emphasis on the exchange rate developments (see Zeman, 2004, and Ivaničová and Chocholatá, 2006) than the conduct of monetary policy in the early inflation targeting countries of the region. Nevertheless, we have to keep in mind that all coefficients are very small, although the Czech Republic shows the highest impact (in absolute value) of exchange rate deviations from the equilibrium.

Threshold ARCH Models

We can often see that the volatility of financial variables is different along positive and negative trends (see Engle and Ng, 1993). The downwards movements of share prices are usually associated with higher volatility of financial data. In this regard, Zakoian (1990) and Glosten *et al.* (1998) proposed the Threshold ARCH models to analyze asymmetric volatility.

Central banks may be also likely to fight against the currency depreciation more intensively than against currency appreciation. The ERM II has even some inherited certain asymmetric components as countries are allowed to appreciate the central parity, but its depreciation causes a violation of the exchange rate criterion (see de Grauwe and Schnabel, 2005). Thus, the exchange rate target zones may be more credible if exchange rate is approaching the depreciation limit (that is, the upper bound according to our definition of exchange rates) of the target band. In turn, a central bank may define its objective in relation to the national competitiveness. Several transition countries have been often concerned by the excessive exchange rate appreciation and some even aimed to stabilize its real exchange rate (see Coricelli *et al.*, 2006). This may be especially important for the EU New Member States with the strong appreciation trends due to the Balassa–Samuelson effect. Crespo–Cuaresma *et al.* (2005a) find important asymmetric volatility effects both in EU15 countries as well as in the CEECs.

Correspondingly, we extend the standard TARCH model as we take into account also the position of the spot exchange rate in relation to its equilibrium value. Our estimation specification is as follows,

$$\Delta s_{jt}^{D} = \mu_j + \xi_{jt}, \tag{10.14}$$

$$\begin{aligned}\sigma_{jt}^{2} &= \gamma_{j1} + \gamma_{j2}\xi_{jt-1}^{2} + \gamma_{j3}\sigma_{jt-1}^{2} + \gamma_{j4}D_{jt-1}^{arch}\xi_{jt-1}^{2} + \\ &+ \delta_{j1}\left|s_{jt-1}^{D} - s_{jt-1}^{F}\right| + \delta_{j2}D_{jt-1}^{s}\left|s_{jt-1}^{D} - s_{jt-1}^{F}\right| + \omega_{jt},\end{aligned} \tag{10.15}$$

where D^{arch} is a dummy variable which equals 1 if the residual from the mean equation, ξ, is negative and zero otherwise. Similarly, D^{s} is a dummy variable equal to 1 if the spot exchange rate is lower than the equilibrium value, that is, if the exchange rate is in the appreciation part of the target zone.

In general, we can see that the asymmetric effects are important in all new member states, while the arch and garch terms remain highly significant in all countries. Table 10-4 shows that the asymmetric arch terms, γ_4, are negative and significant in Poland and Slovakia. This indicates that the financial markets are paying more attention to the appreciation trends, which has stabilizing effects on the exchange rate. Furthermore, we can see that the persistence of exchange rate shocks is higher during the depreciation periods in Poland (and no longer significantly different from unity) and Slovakia than otherwise. This also corresponds to the generally observed stylized facts that financial markets behave more turbulently during crisis times than during bully periods.

Table 10-4 Asymmetric estimates of the effect of spot position in the band on conditional volatility (TARCH models)

	Czech Republic	**Poland**	**Slovakia**	**Romania**
μ	-0.000 (-1.041)	0.000 (0.448)	-0.000 (-0.949)	0.001*** (4.673)
γ_1	0.000*** (7.291)	0.000*** (4.553)	0.000*** (6.990)	0.000*** (0.917)
γ_2	0.093*** (4.744)	0.111*** (6.104)	0.211*** (10.608)	0.066*** (11.128)
γ_3	0.760*** (24.927)	0.876*** (45.167)	0.697*** (24.695)	0.933*** (108.259)
γ_4	0.029 (1.260)	-0.129*** (-5.507)	-0.084*** (-3.204)	0.004 (0.257)
δ_1	2.550*** (3.595)	-0.071 (-0.410)	-0.715*** (-4.737)	0.008 (-4.737)
δ_2	-0.859* (-1.746)	1.210*** (5.188)	0.896* (1.772)	-0.049 (-0.310)
$\gamma_2 + \gamma_3$	0.852 [0.000]	0.987 [0.375]	0.908 [0.000]	0.999 [0.907]
$\gamma_2 + \gamma_3 + \gamma_4$	0.881 [0.000]	0.858 [0.000]	0.824 [0.000]	1.003 [0.756]
Period	1.1.1999– 1.10.2004	1.1.1999– 1.10.2004	1.1.1999– 1.10.2004	1.1.1999– 1.10.2004
N	1500	1500	1500	1500

Note: We report z-stats in parenthesis and p-values of the Wald test that $\gamma_2 + \gamma_3 = 1$ and $\gamma_2 + \gamma_3 + \gamma_4 = 1$ in brackets. ***, **, and * denote significance at 1 per cent, 5 per cent, and 10 per cent, respectively. For clarity of the discussion in the text, coefficients δ are multiplied by 10^5.
Source: Authors' calculations

Finally, we can see that also the credibility of target zone is different depending on the current position of the spot exchange rate in relation to its fundamental value. First, the sign of the credibility term becomes also negative (but insignificant) in Poland. Second, we find also significant asymmetric effects in Poland and marginally significant in the Czech

Republic and Slovakia. In Poland and in Slovakia, we can see negative sing of δ_1 (standing for credible target zones) and positive value of δ_2 (increasing the volatility if the spot exchange rate is on the appreciation side of the target zone).[5] This implies that the depreciation parts of the target zones are relatively more credible than the appreciation parts in both countries. Surprisingly, we observe exactly the opposite case for the Czech Republic, while Romania shows no statistically significant behavior of exchange rate volatility with respect to the equilibrium exchange rate.

Conclusion

In this paper we analyze high frequency exchange rate dynamics in the selected EU new member states in 1999–2004. Our sample consists of four inflation targeting countries: the Czech Republic, Poland, Slovakia and Romania that maintain flexible exchange rate policies. Based on the standard monetary model extended for Balassa–Samuelson effect, we first estimate the equilibrium exchange rates in these countries using panel data cointegration techniques.

Next, we examine the exchange rate volatility in connection to the estimated equilibrium exchange rate. Here, we follow the target zone model by Krugman (1991), which shows, that exchange rate volatility should decrease, if the exchange rate is close to the edge of (credible) fluctuation band. We estimate GARCH (1,1) model of daily exchange rate volatility in the sample countries and find that the volatility is quite persistent. In addition, the exchange rate is more volatile the further it is from its equilibrium in the Czech Republic and Poland. On the other hand, Slovak currency volatility decreases with the distance from the equilibrium value of exchange rate. This suggests greater credibility of implicit fluctuation bands for Slovak currency in comparison to the remaining sample countries and that Slovak monetary policy authority puts more emphasis on exchange rate developments.

Our TARCH results point to systematic asymmetries in the exchange rate volatility in the EU New Member States. The volatility of exchange rate is especially pronounced in Poland and Slovakia, when exchange rate appreciates heavily from its equilibrium. The opposite is visible for the Czech Republic. Czech currency is found to be much more stable, when it is overvalued. Interestingly, Romania shows no systematic pattern in the exchange rate volatility, when the currency is misaligned.

References

Baillie, R.T. and T. Bollerslev. 1989. The Message in Daily Exchange Rates: A Conditional-Variance Tale. *Journal of Business and Economic Statistics* 7(3):297–305.

Bask, Mikael and Jarko Fidrmuc. 2005. *Fundamentals and Technical Trading: Behavior of Exchange Rates in the CEECs*. Mimeo.

Calvo, G. and C. Reinhart. 2002. Fear of Floating. *Quarterly Journal of Economics* 117(2):379–408.

Clements, K.W. and J.A. Frenkel. 1980. Exchange Rates, Money, and Relative Prices: The Dollar-Pound in the 1920s. *Journal of International Economics* 10(2):249–62.

Coricelli, F. Jazbec, B. and I. Masten. 2006. Exchange Rate Pass-through in EMU Acceding Countries: Empirical Analysis and Policy Implications. *Journal of Banking and Finance*. Forthcoming.

Crespo–Cuaresma, Jesus, Balász Égert and Ronald MacDonald. 2005a. *Non-Linear Exchange Rate Dynamics in Target Zones: A Bumpy Road towards a Honeymoon.* The William Davidson Institute Working Paper, No. 771. Ann Arbor: The William Davidson Institute.

Crespo–Cuaresma, J., Fidrmuc, J. and R. MacDonald. 2005b. The Monetary Approach to Exchange Rates in the CEECs. *Economics of Transition* 13(2):395–416.

Crespo–Cuaresma, J., Fidrmuc, J. and M. A. Silgoner. 2005c. On the Road: The Path of Bulgaria, Croatia and Romania to the EU and the Euro. *Europe-Asia Studies* 57(6):843–58.

De Grauwe, P. and G. Schnabl. 2005. Nominal Versus Real Convergence – EMU Entry Scenarios for the NewMember States. *Kyklos* 58(4):537–55.

Edison, H.J., Miller, M.H. and J. Williamson. 1987. On Evaluating and Extending the Target Zone Proposal. *Journal of Policy Modeling* 9(1):199–227.

Égert, Balász and Kirsten Lommatzsch. 2004. *Equilibrium Exchange Rates in Transition: The Tradable Price-based Real Appreciation and Estimation Uncertainty.* The Williams Davidson Institute Working Paper, No. 676. Ann Arbor: The William Davidson Institute.

Égert, Balász and Luboš Komárek. 2005. *Foreign Exchange Interventions and Interest Rate Policy in the Czech Republic: Hand in Glove?* Czech National Bank Working Paper, No. 7/2005. Prague: Czech National Bank.

Eichengreen, Barry. 1994. *International Monetary Arrangements for the 21st Century.* Washington, D.C.: The Brookings Institution.

Engle, Robert F. and Yin–Feng Gau. 1997. *Conditional Volatility of Exchange Rates under a Target Zone.* University of California at San Diego Working Paper, No. 06/97. San Diego: University of California.

Engle, R.F. and V.K. Ng. 1993. Measuring and Testing the Impact of News on Volatility. *Journal of Finance* 48(5):1749–78.

Fidrmuc, J. and I. Korhonen. 2006. Meta-analysis of the business cycle correlation between the Euro area and the CEECs. *Journal of Comparative Economics*. Forthcoming.

Fidrmuc, J. and M. Senaj. 2006. Exchange Rate Regimes in Slovakia and the New EU Member States. *Finance a úvěr – Czech Journal of Economics and Finance*. 56(1–2):40–57.

Glosten, L.R., R. Jaganathan and D. Runkle. 1993. On the Relation between the Expected Value and the Volatility of the Normal Excess Return on Stocks. *Journal of Finance*. 48(5):1779–801.

Groen, Jan. 1998. *The Monetary Exchange Rate Model as a Long-Run Phenomenon*. Tinbergen Institute Discussion Papers, 98–082/2. Amsterdam: Tinbergen Institute,

Groen, J. 2002. Cointegration and the Monetary Exchange Rate Model Revisited. *Oxford Bulletin of Economics and Statistics* 64(4):361–80.

Holub, Tomáš. 2004. *Foreign Exchange Interventions under Inflation Targeting: The Czech Experience*. Czech National Bank Research and Policy Note, No.1/2004. Prague: Czech National Bank.

Horváth, Roman. 2005. *Exchange Rate Variability, Pressures and Optimum Currency Area Criteria: Implications for the Central and Eastern European Countries*. Czech National Bank Working Paper Series, No.8/2005. Prague: Czech National Bank.

Ivaničová, Z. and M. Chocholatá, 2006. Monetary Policy and Exchange Rate in Slovak Republic between 1999 and 2005. *Slovak Journal of Economics – Ekonomický časopis*. Forthcoming.

Kao, C. 1999. Spurious Regression and Residual-Based Tests for Cointegration in Panel Data. *Journal of Econometrics* 90(1):1–44.

Kao, Chihwa and Min–Hsien Chiang. 2000. On the Estimation and Inference of Cointegrated Regression in Panel Data. In *Advances in Econometrics Volume 15 – Nonstationary Panels, Panel Cointegration, and Dynamic Panels*, ed Badi H. Baltagi, 179–222. Oxford: Elsevier.

Kempa, B. and M. Nelles. 1999. The Theory of Exchange Rate Target Zones. *Journal of Economic Surveys* 13(2):173–210.

Krugman, P. 1991. Target Zone and Exchange Rate Dynamics. *Quarterly Journal of Economics* 56(3):669–82.

Kočenda, Evžen and Juraj Valachy. 2005. *Exchange Rate Volatility Before and After Regime Shift: A New Measure and New Evidence from Transition*. Mimeo.

Williamson, John. 1985. *The Exchange Rate System*. Washington D.C.: Institute for International Economics.

Zeman, J. 2004. Equilibrium Exchange Rate of the Slovak Koruna. *Slovak Journal of Economics – Ekonomický časopis* 52(9):1035–50.

Zakoïan, J.M. 1994. Threshold Heteroskedastic Models. *Journal of Economic Dynamics and Control* 18(5):931–44.

Notes

[1] On the other hand, several smaller transition economies in South East Europe and the Baltic States have adopted currency boards or comparably fixed exchange rate regimes. This development confirms Eichengreen's (1994) bipolar hypothesis that small and open economies have to decide between the extreme points of exchange rate flexibility.

[2] Estonia, Lithuania and Slovenia joined the ERM II in 2004, while Cyprus, Malta, Latvia and Slovakia followed in 2005. Furthermore, Slovenia is already expected to fulfil the Maastricht criteria meaning that it will be able to introduce the Euro by January 2007.

[3] Czech Republic and Poland adopted inflation targeting in 1998, Romania and Slovakia followed in 2005.

[4] We use the values of estimated equilibrium exchange rate for each day of particular months. Alternative procedures (e.g. values smoothed over some periods) yield largely the same results.

[5] Note that, by definition, the opposite is true for the depreciation side of the target zone.

CONTRIBUTORS

Asma Ben Salem is a Ph.D. Student in Economics at the University of Lyon 2, France, with an emphasis on banking consolidation and diversification strategies in Europe, attached to GATE (Groupe d'Analyse et de Théorie Economie). She worked as a research fellow at the Economic Research Department in Crédit Agricole for six months. Her research concentrates on international economics, financial institutions and services, international banking and finance and corporate finance.

Karel Diviš is a Ph.D. student at the Institute of Economic Studies of Faculty Social Sciences, Charles University in Prague, Czech Republic. Besides his MA degree in Finance at the same institution, he received a MA degree in Mathematics at Faculty of Mathematics and Physics of Charles University. His research focuses on the performance and efficiency of financial markets.

Cândida Ferreira is Assistant Professor of the Department of Economics at ISEG–UTL (Technical University of Lisbon, Portugal). She teaches courses in monetary economics, finance and macroeconomics. She has a Ph.D. and a Master Degree in Macroeconomics and she has been teaching at ISEG–UTL since 1985. Her research focuses on macroeconomics, monetary economics and political economy. She collaborates in evaluating different Marie Curie Programmes to increase and develop the research activities in the European Union and associate countries.

Jarko Fidrmuc is Professor of European integration and political economy with emphasis on Eastern Europe at the Economics Department of University of Munich, research fellow at the CESifo Munich, Germany, and visiting Associate Professor at the Department of Applied Mathematics and Statistics, Comenius University in Bratislava, Slovakia. After he received his Ph.D. in Economics at the University of Vienna, he was affiliated with the Institute for Advanced Studies in Vienna and the Austrian National Bank (Oesterreichische Nationalbank). His research concentrates on international economics and applied econometrics, especially in fields related to exchange rates, trade, and monetary integration.

Jan Frait is a member of the Board and Chief Executive Director of the Czech National Bank. He is also Professor of Economics at the Technical University of Ostrava, Czech Republic. Currently he serves as a Chief Editor of the Czech Journal of Economics and Finance, a scholarly journal published by the Charles University in Prague. His current research activities focus on monetary policy issues, especially on the links between global financial markets and, exchange rates, and subsequent monetary policy responses in a small open economy.

Roman Horváth is the Head of Monetary Analysis Unit at the Czech National Bank and a Ph.D. candidate in Economics at the Faculty of Social Sciences, Charles University in Prague. He received his M.A. degree in Economics from Central European University in 2004. His papers have been published in several respected refereed journals. His research interest is on policy issues in international economics.

Tamás Isépy is Assistant Professor at Veszprém University, Faculty of International Economics in Hungary and a Ph.D. student at Budapest University of Technology and Economics in Hungary. He teaches courses in international finance and international economics. His research activities focus on the relationship between financial structures and economic growth as well as banking regulation and the effects of the New Basle Accord implementation.

Luboš Komárek is an advisor to the Bank Board Member at the Czech National Bank, associate professor at the Prague School of Economics and vice-president of the Czech Economic Society. He has published in refereed journals such as the "Czech Journal of Economics and Finance", "Eastern European Economics", "Politická ekonomie" and "Economic Systems". His research is mainly oriented to the equilibrium exchange rate, currency substitution, FX interventions, monetary policy transmission mechanisms and estimation of financial integration.

Martin Melecký is an economist at the Monetary Policy and Research departments of the Nederlandsche Bank. He has published in refereed journals as the Czech Journal of Economics and Finance, Eastern European Economics and Politická ekonomie. His research focuses on modelling currency preferences, third-currency effects, exchange rate risk premiums, estimation of the effects of external crises on growth cycles, evaluation of DSGE models, and modelling of uncertainty about central bank preferences and its implications for monetary policy.

Stanislav Polouček is a Professor of Finance and Head of the Department of Finance at Silesian University, School of Business Administration in Karviná, Czech Republic. He has wide teaching experience of regular finance courses in the Czech Republic, Poland and Slovakia and in lectureships in other foreign universities. He is the chairman of the International Programme Committee of a yearly finance and banking conference that takes place at the Silesian University. His research concentrates on banking sector development in developed as well as transition countries, and monetary theory and policy.

Daniel Stavárek is Assistant Professor of International Finance and Banking at Silesian University, School of Business Administration in Karviná, Czech Republic. He received a Ph.D. degree from the Technical University of Ostrava, Czech Republic. He has extensive teaching experience in lectureships at foreign universities. He has published in refereed journals such as "Eastern European Economics", "Czech Journal of Economics and Finance", "Slovak Journal of Economics" and "European Review of Economics and Finance". His research activities focus on financial sector efficiency as well as exchange rates and foreign exchange markets. He is a member of the Regional Executive Board of the Czech Economic Society.

Petr Teplý is a Ph.D. student and junior lecturer at the Institute of Economic Studies of Faculty Social Sciences, Charles University in Prague, Czech Republic. He received his MA degree in Finance at the same institution. In addition, he has studied accounting and controlling at Johannes Kepler University in Linz, Austria, and finance at The University of Otago in Dunedin, New Zealand. His research focuses on efficiency and institutional framework of financial markets.

Janek Uiboupin is a researcher of the Pan-European Institute at Turku School of Economics and Business Administration, Finland. He has received a Ph.D. degree from the University of Tartu, Estonia. He has teaching experience in the field of financial sector and monetary policy. He worked as a visiting researcher at the Bank of Estonia. His research concentrates on cross-border cooperation and regional development, financial sector development and foreign banks entry in Central and Eastern Europe. He is a member of the Estonian Economic Society.

Jaan Vainu is a senior researcher and the Head of the Department of Statistics and Econometrics at Tallinn University of Technology, Estonia. After obtaining his Ph.D. in Statistics from Vilnius University he worked as Associate Professor at the University of Tartu, Head of the Internal Auditing Unit at the Estonian Social Bank, and Professor at the Estonian Public

Service Academy. His research focuses on applied econometrics, statistics and bank performance analysis.

INDEX

D

E

M

N

O

P

R

T

U

V

W